RITA

THE MEN IN HER LIFE:

EDWARD C. JUDSON—Rita's first husband, twenty years her senior, he was willing to sell her to the highest bidder.

HARRY COHN—Rita's boss. The studio executive whose legendary megalomania nearly destroyed her.

ORSON WELLES—This marriage made headlines and made Rita the Movie Mom of the decade. It remains one of the great love stories, untold—until now.

CARY GRANT—Rita adored him—"the bigger the star, the nicer the person."

ALY KHAN—When she married him, she became real-life royalty, but it was her fortune that supported his wild, lavish lifestyle.

DICK HAYMES—Husband number four. Known as Hollywood's "Mr. Evil," he nearly ruined her life.

HOLLYWOOD CREATED THE TERM "LOVE GODDESS" TO DESCRIBE HER....Her beauty, talent, fame and wealth were the American Dream come true. Each of her five marriages was meant to endure forever. But disappointment and disillusionment followed every joy. The love she craved—and so desperately needed—eluded her, then slipped tragically beyond her grasp.

RITA

The Life of Rita Hayworth

JOE MORELLA
EDWARD Z. EPSTEIN

A DELL BOOK

Published by
Dell Publishing Co., Inc.
1 Dag Hammarskjold Plaza
New York, New York 10017

Dell ® TM 681510, Dell Publishing Co., Inc.

ISBN: 0-440-17483-X

Reprinted by arrangement with Delacorte Press

Printed in the United States of America

First Dell printing—November 1984

The authors gratefully acknowledge the many people, integral to the life of Rita Hayworth, who generously shared their recollections, insight, and knowledge of the lady and her times. In some instances, in keeping with their wishes, their names have not been revealed.

Rita

PROLOGUE

As the decade of the eighties dawned, it seemed she had managed, once again, to scrape through the troubles besieging her. She had overcome all obstacles, including her alcoholism. Her facelift had been a success; she looked like her old self again and created a sensation wherever she went. It appeared she was on the threshold of a new life.

Then, in June 1981, the tragic news was revealed:

RITA HAYWORTH 'SENILE'

Though no surprise to her intimates, the news was a shock to the nation. People shook their heads with disbelief and dismay. It was almost as though a member of their own family had been stricken.

Was Hayworth *that* old? Hardly. Rita is seven years younger than President Reagan.

"*Alzheimer's disease . . . early senility . . . complicated by chronic alcoholism . . .*" continued the reports on the woman who had been an American institution for over forty years.

Rita Hayworth—the woman who had *everything*. Beauty. Talent. She had achieved the American dream: fame, wealth. She was the woman whose looks set the standard for her generation. The sex symbol for whom the term *love goddess* was coined. The first Hollywood star to become a real-life princess.

She had even been a successful mother, with two beautiful,

healthy daughters she had raised single-handedly to become self-sufficient women.

But her own life had been one of disappointment.

"I haven't had *everything* from life. I've had too much," she observed.

Myths about her have overwhelmed and supplanted truths:

Her marriage to Orson Welles was a disaster. This lie has been so magnified and embellished over the years that the truth—that theirs was one of the great love stories—has never been revealed.

Prince Aly Khan offered her an undying love and a dazzling life-style of limitless luxury. In truth, he spent *her* money. And how was a woman to cope when her famous, charming husband was a satyr whose appetites extended to every pretty woman in sight?

Edward Judson, her first husband, twenty years her senior, had been willing to sell her to the highest bidder. Her boss, movie mogul Harry Cohn, was a sadist who, in the end, was intent on destroying her. Dick Haymes, her fourth husband, almost ruined her life and career, reinforcing his reputation as "Mr. Evil." James Hill, her last husband, was her attempt to lead a life of quiet respectability, a quest which, unfortunately, eluded her.

From childhood Margarita Cansino had been swept into a life that she ultimately could not endure. Through a grueling apprenticeship leading to international film stardom—through five marriages and divorces—through years of personal and professional strife—Margarita had formed her own defense, passive resistance, and there was power in passivity.

"She is almost the perfect embodiment of that quality of passivity which poets, in more classically minded times, thought of as the essence of the female nature," observed writer Winthrop Sargeant at the height of Rita's success. "Few women have more willingly and deftly submitted to becoming the passive material out of which a myth can be created."

Rita Hayworth's tactics of passive resistance appeared to work for her—but appearances were deceiving.

"She never knew she was 'Rita Hayworth,'" says Phil Silvers, his voice breaking with emotion as he recalls the young woman he knew so well.

Public relations expert Henry C. Rogers, who was instrumental in aiding twenty-year-old Rita to become a star, is of the opinion that she was exploited unmercifully. "I have no doubt that such treatment had an adverse effect on her entire life."

"I ask that whatever you write about Rita, please be gentle and kind—because that's the kind of lady she is," says Glenn Ford, protective, cautious, distrustful—Ford and Rita created screen history together in *Gilda* and three other films.

Rita is described by *all* her closest friends as shy, reserved, and closemouthed. An intensely private individual. Vulnerable and sincere. A most unlikely candidate to cope with the mega-stardom she attained.

Hers is a story that epitomizes Hollywood and the system whereby a Margarita Cansino can be transformed into a Rita Hayworth, then marketed, milked—and victimized by her own celebrity.

Jackson Leighter, former president of the Beckworth Corporation (Rita's production company) and one of her oldest friends, observes about women like Rita who became superstars, "The atmosphere was too rarefied for them."

Others confirm that Rita was a down-to-earth person who was unequipped to cope with the treacherous world of show business. She wasn't vicious, grasping, manipulative, acquisitive—all traits synonymous with people making it to the top rung. Yet she remained on top for a generation. There was always interest in the redhead who had that "something extra." That special quality which transcended the ordinary, captured the imagination, piqued people's curiosity.

Her personal life was certainly more exciting than any role she has ever played. And from the stages of vaudeville to the sound stages of Hollywood to the playgrounds of Europe, there was always a man guiding and influencing Rita Hayworth. Men *created* "Rita Hayworth." Molded her. Used her.

"They fell in love with Gilda—and woke up with me," lamented Margarita Cansino.

Her image epitomized the forties, and she capped the decade in true Cinderella fashion by marrying a prince.

The most important man in Margarita's life, however, was not a prince, or a husband, or a lover. Nonetheless, Margarita Cansino's future had been determined by him before she had even been born.

ONE

Volga Haworth had come from a well-to-do and well-bred family. Her father had begun his successful printing business from practically nothing, but he was a proud man: the Haworth family's roots went back almost to the Pilgrims. Volga's mother was an O'Hara. There were well-known actors on both sides of the family tree. Still, Haworth was horrified when he discovered that his daughter's burning ambition was to have a career on the stage.

As soon as she was able to, Volga ignored the social conventions of the day, the ridicule of her peers, and her father's wrath by running away from home to fulfill her dubious dream.

The stage was a wicked profession indeed in 1916, and there were names for women who sought careers as actresses. Follies girl Marion Davies always chuckled that they were thought of as "f-f-fast." Marion's stutter made it sound even funnier.

Eduardo Cansino first saw Volga Haworth onstage in the Ziegfeld Follies. Twenty-one-year-old Cansino, with his older sister Elisa, was already a star. Ziegfeld himself had invited the Cansinos to the show that night, because he wanted them to join it. Cansino and his sister were one of the most highly sought-after and critically lauded dancing teams of the day; the up-and-coming duo of Fred and Adele Astaire greatly admired their work.

The Cansinos, originally from Seville, Spain, were well-bred: their impressive lineage dated back hundreds of years. Antonio Cansino—called Padre—was known throughout the capitals of

Europe for his terpsichorean talent; he had even performed for royalty. His dancing school, located in Madrid, was world-famous.

"I want to be a bullfighter!" young Eduardo had exclaimed as a boy, when he ran away from home. But the youth returned and finally gave in to his father's desire: "You will become a dancer," Antonio Cansino proclaimed, "like me and your five brothers." The children in strict Spanish families did not defy their elders. They obeyed. And soon Eduardo came to love the profession his father had chosen for him.

Neither Volga nor Eduardo were typical show business types. They weren't from deprived backgrounds, or gutter fighters seeking fame and fortune in the theater. The myth that would arise later, that Rita Hayworth was a poor Mexican girl whose parents were from a "lower caste" of society, is laughable.

"Do you know Eduardo has turned down Mr. Ziegfeld's offer to appear in the Follies?" Volga asked excitedly of her fellow chorines. "Ziegfeld won't meet his salary demands!"

The other girls were suitably impressed. But not half as impressed as Volga. Over the next few weeks she saw Eduardo frequently; her fiery temperament and his stoic façade seemed to confirm the cliché that opposites attract.

He proposed marriage. He had much to offer. Although only a youngster, he was earning fifteen hundred dollars a week, was considered one of the best dancers in the country, and had a fabulous future.

"But *my* wife cannot be an actress," the young man informed his beloved in no uncertain terms. "Wives must have babies and remain home."

Volga was not prepared for this. She had dreams of fulfilling her deep-rooted desire to perform. Since childhood she had envisioned herself as a great star of the stage. But she had been disillusioned by her behind-the-scenes observations of show business. Life as a performer was hardly what she had expected it to be. It had come as quite a shock to her when she learned that one of the girls in the Follies chorus had bedded down more girls than Ziegfeld and playboy Paul Block combined.

But when Volga announced her intention to marry, her father was livid, almost apoplectic.

"My God! *A Spaniard!*" was his incensed reaction, and he swore he would have nothing at all to do with her if she didn't change her mind.

But he could not deter the iron-willed young woman.

On October 17, 1918, eighteen-year-old Volga gave birth to a daughter, who the couple named Margarita.

"When I looked at Margarita—a few minutes after she was born—I was terribly disappointed," reminisced Eduardo. "I had wanted a boy. What could I do with a girl?"

But girl or boy, she was a Cansino and would follow in the family tradition. "My parents were living in a theatrical hotel in New York when I was born," recalled Rita, "which perhaps made me a vaudeville veteran at birth."

Soon they would all be going on the road. Eduardo wanted Volga to look after his business interests as well as the baby. "I am no good at figures and that sort of thing."

Volga complied, but she resented the fact that her own career was obviously never going to materialize. She would never have the opportunity to develop her own talents and would have to be satisfied standing in the reflected glow of Eduardo's. She compensated by dominating the household.

When the situation depressed her, as it sometimes did, and frustration engulfed her, she yelled at Eduardo and threw things across the room. He would calm her down, but then usually leave the house for a rehearsal or a performance.

Volga sometimes had a drink or two to relieve the tension—no harm in that, she reasoned. And she did love being with her baby, who had a quiet disposition, and never screamed or whined. Margarita was like an alabaster doll, with huge eyes that seemed to take in everything.

Soon Volga informed Eduardo that she was pregnant again. Eduardo Junior was born only eighteen months after Margarita. "We cannot live with the children in rooming houses and hotels," announced Eduardo. The Cansinos soon bought a house in Jackson Heights, Queens, a pleasant suburb of Manhattan.

But Volga's moods of depression intensified after the arrival of her third child, another son, Vernon, three years later. Increasingly, she took refuge in the bottle, and ofttimes behaved in a peculiar manner. These were days before psychiatry was commonplace, and signs of alcoholism and mental illness were generally ignored.

At times like these, Volga was tolerated and regarded as "strange" by her husband's close-knit relatives, who could find no visible reasons for her unhappiness. She had a successful young husband, three healthy babies, and ran the business! In addition, Grandpa Haworth had forgiven her and welcomed her, Eduardo, and the grandchildren to his home. What more could a woman ask?

Meanwhile Margarita was developing into a cute, pudgy child. She became acquainted with dancing school when she was four. An uncle, Angel Cansino, taught in one of the studios in the huge Carnegie Hall complex, and over the next few years Margarita attended classes every day.

"I didn't like it much, but I didn't have the courage to tell my father, so I began taking the lessons," Rita recalled as an adult. "Rehearse, rehearse, rehearse. That was my girlhood." But at the time Margarita *seemed* to enjoy dancing, and there was no doubt she was talented.

During the 1920s several of Eduardo's brothers came to America and joined the family's vaudeville act, now known as The Dancing Cansinos. Even Padre—Don Antonio Cansino, Eduardo's revered father—came to America, to visit his grandchildren. Margarita adored him, and he, likewise, her. He made her a pair of castanets and taught her how to play them.

When she was seven years old, Margarita was added to the vaudeville act. Seemingly spontaneously (although she had in fact been carefully rehearsed), the little girl darted out at the end of the act, performed a few steps, and played her castanets. The audience responded enthusiastically.

Then, one fateful night, Margarita boldly improvised during her routine. Her father was furious, and afterward sat her down and made it clear that she was never to do that again. It was unprofessional. She was never to do anything onstage that wasn't meticulously rehearsed and perfected.

It wasn't until years later that the importance of this particular episode surfaced. Unwittingly, Eduardo had suffocated the girl's enthusiasm. Although she never questioned her family's love for her, Margarita realized that their expectations of her professionalism were paramount. From this point on, her intense desire to please them took precedence.

There were never any outward signs of rebellion. Her nature seemed as stoic as her father's. No one suspected that Volga's erratic moods and fiery temper might be lurking in the personality of Margarita. She appeared to be the perfect, raised-in-the-Spanish-tradition child, totally obedient to her father's wishes.

She wanted to make her parents proud of her. Her father encouraged her to be competitive, as did, of course, her mother. She was a Cansino. She was expected to succeed.

Grace Godino, who as a child was a student of Eduardo's and as an adult became a friend of Rita's (as well as her stand-in), tells a revealing story about Margarita and Padre. On one occasion, at a gathering of friends and relatives, a young dancer was performing a difficult series of Spanish steps—fancy, fast "heel work."

Padre boasted, "My granddaughter can do that!" Margarita, standing behind him, whispered, "I can't do that, Grandpa!"

"Yes, you can! You are a Cansino. The honor of the family is at stake." Somehow the young girl managed to perform the routine flawlessly—as the crowd cheered her on.

In 1926 talking pictures were about to debut. Cansino and his sister had been asked to star in the dance segment of the sound-film musical "prologue" that would be coupled with a Warner Bros. feature film, *Don Juan*. (The movie, starring John Barrymore and Mary Astor, was not a "talkie," but it was the first feature film to boast a sound track.) Volga was pleased. "Efrem Zimbalist, Mischa Elman, and the New York Philharmonic will also appear in Eduardo's prologue!" she boasted.

But Eduardo Cansino's days as a performer seemed numbered.

Elisa wanted to retire so she could be with her husband and growing son, and she was determined to leave the business. She was older now. Time for performing and traveling was over. She would settle down. Teach. There were no other women in the Cansino family to replace Elisa. Since Eduardo could not perform alone, he turned his attention to teaching and choreographing.

Eduardo believed the future was in sound films. Within a year the Cansinos were living in Hollywood. Eduardo's services as a choreographer were immediately in demand by the major studios, and the dance studio he opened was an instantaneous success.

Through the late 1920s Eduardo was a very busy man. He worked with top stars, choreographing numbers for their films. A young girl named Betty Grable was a student, as well as dancer Grace Poggi and a dark-haired young actress named Margo. Margarita took lessons right alongside them. Many pals from vaudeville days—including James Cagney—dropped by the studio. Other friends and many of Eduardo's relatives visited the Cansinos in Hollywood.

It was a circuslike existence at home, with friends from vaudeville "dropping by" and often staying for months. On one occasion, remembered Vernon Cansino, "We had sea lions—trained, of course—staying in the house. Our bathroom—the bathtub—belonged to them for two weeks!" In the midst of all the boisterous activity Margarita remained quiet and reserved—but also observant.

Things were going well professionally for the Cansinos, and problems were minimal until October 1929. *Variety*'s famous headline said it all: WALL ST. LAYS AN EGG. Volga had kept a sharp eye on the Cansino family's investments, but all was lost in the disastrous crash. To make matters worse, musical films had fallen out of vogue at the box office, and producers' demands for Eduardo's services dwindled. Business at his dance studio also plummeted.

Although he continued teaching, he had to supplement his income. He began choreographing live "prologues," mini-stage shows which preceded first-run films at major theaters. In the spring of 1931, Eduardo was choreographing a prologue for the

Carthay Circle Theatre in Los Angeles, where an eagerly awaited Irene Dunne vehicle, Fannie Hurst's *Back Street,* was to premiere. Eduardo's nephew Gabriel (Elisa's son) was in the show.

One morning Gabriel phoned, frantic. "Oh my God, Uncle Eduardo!" he said. "My partner has broken her leg!"

When Eduardo informed Volga of what had happened, her face lit up. "Margarita can do it!"

Despite her apprehension, Margarita filled in as her cousin's dancing partner. This was a turning point in her life. Not because critics went into ecstasies at discovering a new star (in fact, Margarita was barely mentioned in the reviews at all). Not because there were any standing ovations from the audience. But because Margarita's performance was a revelation as far as the most important man in her life was concerned. For the first time, her father saw her in a new light.

"Volga!" he excitedly exclaimed to his wife. "Jesus, all of a sudden I wake up. She has a figure. She ain't no baby anymore. We can't wait around here, I think!" With the astute instincts of a pro, Eduardo made a major decision: he would stop wasting his time. He would start a new dance team—this time with his own daughter! Cansino was thirty-six, Margarita going on fourteen, but onstage they would look like brother and sister—or husband and wife.

When Prohibition was repealed, the Hollywood nightclubs reopened with a vengeance. Eduardo tried to book the new act into the top spots, where they would earn top dollar. "But the girl's underage," he was told. "The law doesn't allow kids to work where liquor is sold."

Such rules did not apply across the border, in Mexico, where the "in" getaway spot was Agua Caliente, near Tijuana. The Caliente racetrack was owned by movie mogul Joseph Schenck and several of his cronies, including Barron Long and singer Harry Richman. Agua Caliente featured not only the racetrack but also a fabulous gambling casino and, for those more athletically inclined, a plush golf course. The Hollywood crowd also availed itself of the friendly services of all classes of pimps and prostitutes in neighboring Tijuana. *All* things were to be found in Tijuana, including cut-rate abortionists for those not wealthy or influential enough to have the job done neatly in Los Angeles.

It was in Tijuana, at the flashy Foreign Club Café de Luxe, that the Cansinos obtained their first booking. They were the headliners, and the act went over well. Eduardo's specialty was complicated footwork, while Margarita excelled playing the castanets. One of their dances had Eduardo and Margarita conclude the number so that they were practically kissing on the mouth!

Margarita's breasts had developed amply and both Volga and Eduardo noticed how men backstage—and out front—eyed her lasciviously. And so began a new ritual. "Your father and I are going to do a little gambling, Margarita, before the next show," Volga would announce. "Papa and I want you to rest and stay in the dressing room."

"But—"

"There's all kinds of characters around this place, so we're going to lock the door."

Margarita would then flop on the faded brocade sofa and begin reading the movie magazines that always intrigued her.

Her parents locked the door behind them.

"Margarita was a *very* sheltered girl," confirmed Vernon Cansino, reflecting on his own childhood as well. "But, you must understand, our parents *meant* well. If someone had sat them down and angrily told them, 'You are not doing what is best for your daughter,' they would have been deeply hurt. My father was teaching her a *profession*. She would be able to earn her own *living*. She would have a *trade*. How was that *hurting* their daughter? How would she be better off gallivanting around with indiscriminate young men?"

Many girls, given the choice, would have opted for Margarita's life-style, having an inordinate opportunity to indulge a young girl's penchant for pretty clothes, makeup, and being in the spotlight, but none of this particularly appealed to Margarita. Especially since there was such a strict double standard. It was made clear to her that "dressing up" was for the stage. Offstage, she was expected to remain a pure young girl.

She did as she was told. She pleased her parents. The pattern didn't vary. Unfortunately, Margarita was not developing inner resources that would be essential for her survival in later years.

There was no glamour, no glory, no fun for the young girl during this period, and she began to resent her father bitterly for the suffocating life-style he was imposing on her.

Eduardo accepted an engagement for them aboard one of the luxurious, notorious gambling ships popular during this period. The vessels were always anchored outside the three-mile limit. When illness forced Cansino to miss a few shows, Margarita went on as a soloist, and her performances were none too successful. She hadn't the repertoire—or the expertise—to carry a show alone.

But then came the booking at Agua Caliente, courtesy of Eduardo's former student, Grace Poggi, a close friend of Joseph Schenck's. Eduardo and Margarita were in fine form for the show. The duo became a hot Caliente attraction—father and daughter sometimes performing twenty shows a week. It was grueling work, but during that time Margarita was noticed by many important film people.

"A beautiful Mexican," clucked the sophisticated crowd. She certainly looked Mexican—her brown hair was dyed coal black and worn combed severely back into a bun. Dolores del Rio and Lupe Velez were big stars at this time, and Margarita, still displaying baby fat, looked like their much younger, plumper sister. The Mexican "look" was good for the act.

During this time Margarita appeared as an extra in some films shot in Tijuana and in Hollywood. Ellen Brandt, widow of George Brandt, relates, "My husband George was a kid, along with George Sidney, under contract to Columbia in the thirties to produce low-budget movies. They used to make B pictures, and my husband later told me that he saw this fantastic young broad dancing in Caliente, passing herself off as Mexican. She was very exotic, and George used her in a potboiler called *The Devil's Cross*. Of course later, when she was a big star, everyone assumed he had slept with her. But George said that, unfortunately, it wasn't true."

Margarita and her father both appeared as extras in a Dolores del Rio starrer, *In Caliente*.

The Cansino act was extended again and again, and they played in Caliente for almost a year. It was wonderful exposure. There were always casting agents, producers, directors, and stars in the audience.

"They are interested," noted Volga with glee. "Mr. Laemmle, Mr. Stromberg—I can see they are interested." The dream of Margarita Cansino, movie star, began to form in the minds of Eduardo and Volga. Margarita was only fifteen—a trifle young for such a step—but then again Volga had been only seventeen when she married Eduardo!

But Margarita wasn't whisked off to Hollywood. There was some interest from Warner Bros. casting agent Max Arnow, but the resulting screen test didn't garner her a contract. This was a particularly disappointing development for the Cansinos, because Warner Bros. was where the innovative new musical *42nd Street* had been made, and that film's success revolutionized musicals.

Besides, the Warner lot boasted top behind-the-scenes musical talent, and Eduardo had prayed the studio would recognize Margarita's potential. But while she exuded voluptuousness in person, the teenager photographed pudgy, her hair seemed too severe, her hairline too low—she was hardly in a league with the women who were, at the moment, Hollywood's ideals: Crawford, Garbo, Shearer, Harlow.

Nor did she have the petite perfection of her prototypes, Dolores del Rio, Lupe Velez, and Lili Damita. Margarita was five six, like her mother—very tall for the day.

The black-haired young girl had just danced a difficult *jeta,* a Spanish folk dance, and received enthusiastic applause from the tough, tipsy Caliente audience.

Winfield Sheehan's bright blue eyes carefully studied her. He turned to Joe Schenck. "Can that kid speak English, Joe?"

Schenck smiled. "Speak English? She's as American as Janet Gaynor, for Christ's sakes."

"I want to meet her." Sheehan thought she'd be perfect for Fox's Spanish-language films, but wondered why some other company hadn't already signed her. He turned to one of his dinner guests, Hearst movie columnist Louella Parsons. "What do you think of her, Louella?"

Miss Parsons, a plump, dark-haired woman pushing fifty, was the most powerful movie columnist in the world. She could make or break a career with her pronouncements in print. But she was an expert at noncommittal statements under circumstances such as these. "She's very Spanish," smiled Louella.

Schenck dispatched an aide to summon Margarita to their table. She arrived in a few moments, accompanied, of course, by her father.

Sheehan had met Eduardo several years earlier, when Cansino choreographed some dance numbers for Fox. Sheehan suddenly realized that this girl must be a relative of Cansino's.

Eduardo shook Sheehan's hand. "Señor, how good to see you. Permit me to present my daughter, Margarita."

"You're her *father?*" Sheehan was shocked. "You don't look old enough. Where have you been hiding her?" He turned to Margarita. "You were wonderful, young lady."

Margarita was tongue-tied; she blushed and managed a quiet "Thank you."

Schenck smiled and chewed on his Havana cigar. He hadn't the slightest interest in Margarita Cansino's screen potential or her potential in any other area.

"Who represents you?" asked Sheehan as one of the nightclub photographers appeared and took a group picture of the table. Schenck waved him away. The din in the club made it hard to hear. Margarita's answer was unintelligible.

"What? Speak up, dear, we can't hear you!" said Louella, her voice slightly shrill.

"My wife and I represent her," offered Eduardo, smiling.

"Let's talk where it's quieter," said Sheehan. Louella was looking at Margarita intently, studying her, and the columnist would later write: "When she came to our table she turned out to be painfully shy. She could not look at strangers when she spoke to them and her voice was so low it could hardly be heard. Hardly, it seemed to me, the material of which a great star could be made."

In Eduardo's dressing room, with Margarita seated and silent on the sofa and Volga standing by, Sheehan said to Eduardo, "I'll pay for you and the girl to come to Hollywood so we can test her. What do you say?"

Eduardo and Volga were disappointed. They had expected more of an offer than that. But Cansino had had no other film offers for Margarita. He conferred with Volga, and finally *she* said, "Very well, Mr. Sheehan. We can see you believe in our daughter as we do. We accept."

Margarita said nothing, merely sat and stared at Winfield Sheehan and smiled her warm smile.

On the trip back to Los Angeles, Sheehan told Louella, "I'm bringing her out to the studio."

Louella no longer held back her opinion. "Winnie dear, I think you're making a mistake! She's too heavy, she's not all that pretty, and she's *so* shy! Onstage she catches the eye, but darling, the camera is a different thing altogether!"

Margarita's screen tests—one silent, one sound—turned out well and Sheehan was excited. "She's got something—it's that smile," he noted, as he watched rushes of the tests in the Fox executive screening room, at the studios at Western and Sunset.

The youngster had many assets: high cheekbones, strong jawline, beautiful skin. Margarita's Latin look would be retained by the makeup people, per written instructions from Mr. Sheehan.

Studio personnel had their suspicions about Mr. Sheehan's new protégée. While she had a regal bearing and exuded a definite "hands off" rather than a "let's play" attitude, studio gossips saw her as a pretty Mexican kid the boss had found in Caliente or Tijuana, and they clucked knowingly. When it was discovered she was actually the daughter of the respected Eduardo Cansino—also recently hired to coach dancers at the studio—they changed their story slightly.

The girl was signed to a standard long-term contract, renewable by the studio every six months. The contract had to be signed by her father, since she was still a minor. Sheehan dispatched a memo to all department heads, including the head of publicity: "I believe we have a girl who will be every bit as big at the box office as Dolores del Rio—bigger, because she is younger and can dance. But we shall have to bring her along slowly: train her; build her into an asset that Fox will be able to utilize for many years. And do not call attention to the fact that she is underage."

Sheehan ordered voice lessons, acting lessons, lessons in how to speak, walk, pose. From Margarita's point of view, possibly the best news was that she would be working with other coaches. Not just her father. Out from under Papa's thumb at last.

Volga was beside herself with joy—her baby's big break had come, and it would be clear sailing from now on.

Margarita's ambition was focused: she would become a fine actress as well as dancer. She worked harder than any of the other young girls being groomed. When she left the studio at the end of the day, she continued working on her lessons at home.

She was also taking lessons in swimming, tennis, and horseback riding (although she feared horses) and excelled at all of them. She had gone on a stringent diet, which produced spectacular results. She posed for endless publicity stills in the studio gallery. She was being molded into the product that Hollywood was so adept at creating. Of all the girls given that opportunity, only a tiny percentage would possess that intangible something which translated into the quality so necessary on film: charisma.

The next step was a new identity. "Margarita Cansino is too long a name for marquees," decreed Sheehan. It was shortened to Rita Cansino, and the sixteen-year-old was assigned her first role. It was in the Spencer Tracy–Claire Trevor epic *Dante's Inferno*. Rita performed a dancing sequence with Gary Leon, choreographed by her father. Leon broke his ankle and it was weeks before the sequence could be completed.

The film, photographed by Rudy Maté—who would later film some of Rita's most important pictures—wasn't released until a couple of the girl's subsequent movies hit the market, but when it was, some of the trade papers singled out Rita's dancing for praise.

In the late 1940s, when Spencer Tracy was queried about Rita, he said of *Dante's Inferno,* which was the last picture he made under his old Fox contract, "It was one of the worst pictures made anywhere, anytime. The fact that Rita survived in films after that screen debut is testament enough that she deserves all the recognition she's getting."

These early years at Fox were a hectic time for the young girl, but she exhibited a sense of humor about them. She even played practical jokes on her brothers; for the first time, she seemed to be having some fun.

She was thrilled—despite suffering an attack of nerves—when assigned her first *real* film, that is, one in which, in addition to a dance sequence, she would play a *scene*. And it was opposite a matinee idol, Warner Baxter, Fox's top male box office star. (Fox's leading female player was Janet Gaynor.)

The film was an elaborate production, exotically titled *Under the Pampas Moon*. Rita rehearsed so intensely that she could recite her few lines backward. Told to report for work at nine A.M. she showed up promptly—only to discover she should have arrived at seven for makeup in order to be ready to work at nine.

"Where the hell is Rita Cansino?" demanded the assistant director, and when an ashen-faced Rita meekly stepped forward, she was petrified.

"Get her to makeup, fast."

When she finally came on the set, ready for work, she was too nervous and distraught to remember her few lines. The assistant director screamed at her. Warner Baxter took pity on the young girl: "Just relax, everything will be fine."

In her short scene with Baxter, it is evident that the girl had made a new friend who would not betray her for many years: the camera.

Next came a bit role in Fox's profitable, top-of-the-line Charlie Chan series. Rita, in her ultradark makeup and exotic saris, looked more Arab than the real thing. *Charlie Chan in Egypt* gave her only a couple of moments in front of the camera, but it was experience and she learned from it.

Sheehan had enormous confidence in the girl's potential and announced at a weekly meeting of his producers and production executives that he was thinking of remaking *Ramona*—a big silent hit with Dolores del Rio—in the new Technicolor process. "And I think Rita Cansino will become a star in the role."

There was disagreement over this. Perhaps because Rita Cansino was a girl who didn't court producers on the lot or make herself available for their parties, she wasn't particularly well liked. She was a rare commodity on the Hollywood scene—a *lady*—and the only big shot who seemed interested in exploiting *only* her talent was Mr. Sheehan, who, luckily for Rita, was still head of the studio and the one who counted most.

If the company was to function properly, however, Sheehan needed the goodwill and support of his staff, and a united effort would be far more effective in creating a star than one in which important members of the team were opposing him. To mollify them, Sheehan proposed trying Rita out in a leading role in an A programmer; and he agreed that Rita should make color screen tests for *Ramona* to convince one and all that she had what it took to play the role.

This placed the girl under a lot of pressure. She was, after all, only seventeen. She had recently embarked on a massive self-improvement regimen, and was always overanxious to please. When a scene wasn't going right or she found it difficult to give a director the expression he needed, she became so angry with herself that she burst into tears. She was high-strung beneath the cool-appearing façade. To some on the scene she seemed just a scared little girl following through on what was expected of her by her family.

Rita was assigned a lead in the programmer *Paddy O'Day,* in which popular child star Jane Withers had the title role. Rita was a Russian dancer, and her love interest, the film's "hero," was played by Pinky Tomlin. Tomlin had just become nationally popular, thanks to the hit song "The Object of My Affection," which he'd written and sung and which soon became a standard.

While the film was in production, Rita dated him—at the behest of the studio's publicity department. "Let's get both your names in the papers so the picture will be a big hit." This kind of ploy, teaming up two contract players to generate a "romance" for the fans, was standard practice of the day. Naturally, the seventeen-year-old was still living with her parents, and Eduardo supervised her social life. But he allowed this date because it was business.

Regarding "dates" for publicity purposes, it's important to note that, unlike most of her contemporaries, Rita was never comfortable with this sort of thing, nor would she ever be at ease giving interviews. She was not a gregarious girl, and because of her rigid upbringing she was not prone to revealing her background or feelings under any circumstances. The aura surrounding her later image was highly deceiving in this regard, because on film and in still photographs Rita projected nothing remote—quite the opposite.

Rita and Tomlin "painted the town" to garner press coverage for *Paddy O'Day*. They made the rounds of leading nightspots. As the studio-chauffeured limousine was driving them to the Cocoanut Grove at the Ambassador Hotel, Tomlin turned to Rita and asked, "Do you like the Ambassador?"

"I don't know," she said. "I've never been there."

Tomlin was surprised. Who hadn't been to the famous Cocoanut Grove? "I was twenty-eight at the time, and I thought she was twenty-three or twenty-four. We had a couple of brandy ices at the Grove." They had their picture taken.

Tomlin then suggested that the couple go to the Club Alabam, which was on Central Avenue downtown—which, as Tomlin describes it, "was the Harlem of Los Angeles." Louis Armstrong was playing there. Armstrong and Tomlin were old friends—the trumpeter had given Tomlin his first musical job, on a riverboat in St. Louis. "Louis came over and had a drink with me and Rita," recalled Tomlin.

As the evening progressed, Tomlin realized Rita had become drunk. On the drive home she became ill. She was suddenly petrified about what her father would say.

"Papa will kill me!" she told Tomlin.

Instead of taking her directly home, Tomlin stopped and telephoned his roommate and college chum, Duke Taylor. "What'll I do?"

"Bring her here first," said Taylor.

The two young men lived in an apartment on Hayworth Avenue. While Tomlin made coffee, Taylor found a bathing suit for Rita to wear and took her down to the pool. When she was sufficiently sobered up, Tomlin drove her home, and waited in the car while she scurried into the house.

When she saw him at work the next day, she thanked him for taking care of her. In Tomlin's words, "She didn't realize she'd had so much to drink. And I said, 'Hell, didn't you ever have anything to drink before?' 'Nothing but wine,' she said." Tomlin also noted he hadn't realized how *young* Rita actually was.

"I want to thank you," she said. "You could have taken advantage of me last night."

She and Tomlin became pals and he relates that a few days later she sought his advice. There was a producer who was coming on with the usual line, and she was wondering whether she should believe him. Tomlin advised her to ignore the man's proposition, because she had looks and talent and could make it without the casting couch approach.

While she was making *Paddy O'Day,* she also worked feverishly on learning the script of *Ramona.* There were hours spent on costume fittings and makeup tests. She was very excited by the project, and psychologically it became the most important thing in her life. She was nervous, insecure, and frankly inexperienced insofar as carrying the lead in such an elaborate production. But all was going well. The machinery to turn Rita Cansino into a full-fledged star was ready to click into gear.

Studio politics have been responsible for the ultimate success or failure of many stars, and Rita's life was to be no exception. She now experienced a traumatic event because Darryl Zanuck had engineered a major move in his own career.

Zanuck was one of the all-time Hollywood production geniuses. The thirty-three-year-old cigar-chomping wunderkind had left Warner Bros. as head of production in 1933, after a disagreement with Jack Warner, and formed a partnership with Joe Schenck: Twentieth Century Pictures. Schenck and Zanuck's Twentieth Century company had already produced and distributed twenty pictures through United Artists, but the men were in the market for a studio of their own—and additional capital. With producer William Goetz (L. B. Mayer's son-in-law) as their ally, Schenck and Zanuck took over Fox, which became Twentieth Century-Fox.

Zanuck's first move was to get rid of most of the Fox executives, including Winfield Sheehan. But it didn't happen overnight. In the months during which Sheehan retained his power, Rita made two films. One was *A Message to Garcia,* a Barbara Stanwyck picture, in which Rita played Stanwyck's sister and affected a foreign accent; her scenes were cut from the final print. The other was a potboiler called *Human Cargo*.

Then Sheehan decreed, "We're going ahead with *Ramona*." Rita made color tests with Don Ameche and Gilbert Roland. When Zanuck saw the tests, he said, simply, "No." He had another actress in mind for the role, one who had considerably more experience than Rita.

When Rita was called into producer Sol Wurtzel's office, she was prepared to discuss the usual script changes for *Ramona*. She was absolutely flabbergasted when he told her that the Zanuck regime was now running the show and Rita wouldn't be in the picture.

"Wha—what?" said the girl, color draining from her face.

"I'm sorry. Loretta Young will be doing the part."

The girl left Wurtzel's office in a daze. Tears stung her eyes. Sobs welled up in her chest and then wracked her body as the full impact of the devastating rejection hit her. There was no one to confide her innermost feelings to. She was only seventeen and her life was suddenly falling apart, after so many years of hard work. What a failure she was—all those lessons, people telling her how good she was—how good could she be? They didn't want her.

"It was the worst disappointment of my life," Rita later remembered vividly, her voice trembling. "I cried my eyes out—but it didn't do any good."

A few days later she received a phone call from one of Zanuck's flunkeys. She needn't bother to return to the studio at all—her option had been dropped. "Zanuck just didn't have the time, or so he later said, to meet me face to face and tell me his decision," Rita reflected.

Yet her courage hadn't deserted her. She vowed she'd make them regret their mistake, eat their words. She'd look back on 1935 as the worst year of her life. The opportunity for success had been cruelly snatched from her and it left an indelible scar. Regarding *Ramona* she said, as late as 1972, "I think I can still recite my dialogue from memory."

TWO

The most mysterious man in Rita's life now entered the scene. He has been described as an oil man, a businessman, a wealthy playboy, a gambler, a salesman, an entrepreneur, and an agent for Italian-made automobiles.

He was, in short, a promoter. And possibly, as public relations consultant Henry Rogers describes him, something less seemly. Whatever he was—or wasn't—Edward Judson's past was a mystery. He had conned many in Hollywood into believing he was wealthy and influential.

The myth is that Judson was on the Fox lot trying to hustle Winfield Sheehan when, along with the mogul, he saw Rita's screen tests for *Ramona*. Some stories claim he called Rita directly. Others say he met with Eduardo Cansino. Still others claim he met with Volga Cansino. Judson himself said, "A friend gave me her telephone number, and told me Rita was a stay-at-home, quiet, and studious girl. As un-Hollywood as can be."

Sources indicate that most likely Judson finagled an introduction to Eduardo Cansino, who was also on the lot, and convinced the man that he could do a great deal for Rita's career. Judson did not make much headway until Rita's option was dropped at Fox; then the Cansinos became vulnerable to Judson's blandishments.

Eduardo had never seen his daughter as despondent and depressed as she'd been over the *Ramona* rejection. Cansino met with Judson, who was outgoing, friendly, charming. He had the kind of personality that was necessary to advance a girl's career in the glib-talking world of show business.

Judson explained that he knew many people in the film business and that Cansino's daughter should meet them all. "She should be seen in all the right places, wearing the right clothes . . ."

"And can you do all that?" asked Cansino.

"I'm in a position to do a *lot* of things." He wasn't lying. Judson was an expert in the art of hustling and promoting, two talents that always worked well in Hollywood. All Judson had to determine was whether or not Rita was all that she appeared to be on screen. Was she malleable—would she do as she was told? Or was she a temperamental creature who would be a lot more trouble than she was worth?

Judson was not disappointed. He was surprised at how shy and quiet she was. She seemed to have no "personality" at all, but she definitely exuded a sweetness of disposition that was most unusual. And she was better-looking offscreen, minus the heavy Latin-style makeup. That Mexican "look" was something Judson decided to eliminate right away.

Rita responded immediately to Judson's attitude. Actually, he seemed a godsend. While she expected things to be done *his* way—just like her father—he was *not* her father.

"To be truthful, I was almost embarrassed the first time I took Rita nightclubbing," recalled Judson. "She didn't have the clothes, naturally, to look the part. I said to myself, 'She could be gorgeous if someone took an interest in her.'

"I offered to take her to a gown shop and see that she got smart clothes. But because she had been raised in a strictly religious, old-fashioned home, she was shocked and promptly rejected my offer. I assured her there were no strings attached. I merely wanted to help her.

"The more I thought of what could be done with a girl like Rita, the more intrigued I became with the idea of being a masculine fairy godmother to this little Cinderella."

Naturally, this male fairy godmother was not doing this without thoughts of some remuneration. He deemed Rita an investment that could pay off handsomely. Star-making was the kind of spectacular gamble that appealed to Judson's promoter instincts. The one-in-a-million shot. And he was immediately successful in obtaining freelance jobs for Rita.

Although Judson's contacts at the prestige studios—M-G-M, Warner Bros., and Paramount—were negligible, he did know people like Nat Levine at Republic and Harry Cohn at Columbia, where he got Rita a small part in a film called *Meet Nero Wolfe*. It was a one-shot contract. The film's stars were Edward Arnold and Joan Perry, a beautiful New York model who would eventually become Mrs. Harry Cohn.

While at Columbia, Judson met Helen Hunt, a petite, beautiful, thirty-five-year-old brunette who had joined Columbia in 1928. Miss Hunt had been an apprentice to George Westmore, the father of the famed Westmore brothers, Hollywood's hairdressing-and-makeup "royal family."

When Helen Hunt joined Columbia, it was a poverty row studio, with no permanent staff—makeup artists and hairdressers were hired on a picture-to-picture basis. But as the studio grew and in-house departments were set up, Helen Hunt was put in charge of hairdressing.

Today, Miss Hunt recalls Ed Judson vividly: "He had a great deal of charm. No one knew where he got his money, but he told me that he had done a favor for some man in the South, and that that fellow used to send him a hundred dollars a month." That was not a fortune, but in 1936 it was certainly spending money.

In 1936 and 1937, through Judson's efforts, Rita appeared in four other pictures, westerns with Tom Keene, Tex Ritter, and Robert Livingston. All were independent productions, all forgettable: *Rebellion; Trouble in Texas; Old Louisiana; Hit the Saddle.*

"She was afraid of horses," remembered Keene, "yet she always did what the director told her to do. 'Honey, you tell him you don't want to break your neck,' I told her once when I saw she was really scared. She smiled and thanked me, but she said, 'Oh no, I couldn't do that. He wouldn't hire me again.'"

Ed Judson realized that freelancing wouldn't result in any important kind of career for Rita. She needed a studio behind her. His best chance to get her a long-term contract was through Harry

Cohn, and Judson finally managed to convince Cohn that signing her was only a small investment.

Columbia had no prestigious major stars under contract; almost three quarters of its product were B pictures—serials, an occasional independent release, and series such as *Blondie*. Director Frank Capra was the studio's one great superstar, and Harry Cohn had come to resent him deeply, because Capra was considered by all to be the real talent behind Columbia's success. Cohn had busily wooed other top directors and stars who were available on a freelance basis, and Columbia had enjoyed prestige and acclaim with such recent productions as *Theodora Goes Wild* and *The Awful Truth*.

The signing of Rita Cansino couldn't have been a less significant event. Cohn took no interest at all in the unknown who had already flopped at Fox—except for her name. "Latin types are out. She sounds too Mexican," Cohn argued, even though she had been cast as a Spanish dancer in her first Columbia programmer.

"How about her mother's maiden name?" Judson asked. "Her uncle Vinton has done okay at RKO." Vinton Haworth, Volga's brother, was by this time a successful character actor and radio star. (Vinton was married to Lela Rogers's sister, and was, by marriage, Ginger Rogers's uncle. For decades, Rita Hayworth has been incorrectly identified as Ginger Rogers's cousin.)

"Haworth. If it's pronounced Hayworth," said Cohn, "why the hell isn't it spelled that way?"

They added the *y* and Rita Hayworth was born.

Shortly after Rita was signed, Helen Hunt ran into her, with Judson, in a little restaurant on the corner of Sunset near Gower. Judson called Helen over to their table, and the couple confided, "We're going to be married tonight. We're driving to Vegas. But it's a secret—don't tell Harry."

"I won't," said Helen, who had already been working for Cohn for almost ten years and knew *never* to offer information to her boss.

Up until this point the Cansino family had regarded Judson merely as Rita's agent and business manager—it never occurred to them that he had any designs on their daughter. After all, she was only eighteen. She had revealed absolutely nothing to her parents about marrying Judson. The man was over forty—older than Eduardo!

"Our mother really despised Ed Judson," recalled Vernon Cansino. "She disliked everything about him."

Volga was so upset on learning of the sudden wedding plans that she took to her bed. Eduardo, too, was furious. "If I had thought you would take advantage of Rita, I would never have permitted this," he told Judson angrily. "I thought you were interested in her *career*."

But Rita could not, would not, be deterred, and her decision marked the beginning of a painful estrangement from her family. On May 29, 1937, Margarita Cansino and Edward Judson were married. Judson neglected to inform his young bride of a few details regarding his past, and Rita, not a suspicious girl, wasn't asking any questions.

However, she was in for a few surprises.

Soon after the marriage, Judson, prompted by his dislike of Volga, demanded an accounting from Rita's parents of the girl's earnings while she had been a member of the dancing Cansinos, since "she had more than carried the act." Rita was nonplussed when he insisted that her parents repay her for her performing. Eduardo and Volga were flabbergasted, but with their customary pride they complied.

Starlet Rita Hayworth appeared in a succession of five Columbia pictures in 1937; added to the three she had made for independent producers, that made *eight* films in one year. These were pictures usually made in less than ten days each (a shooting schedule comparable to an episode of a TV series today), and virtually no care at all was taken in any aspect of the productions.

"They slapped a layer of makeup on you," recalled Rita, "sewed up the costume you were wearing—which was still warm from someone else having worn it in some other picture just like the one you were making—and said, 'Here are your lines. Say them. Cut! Print!' "

The titles of the Columbia pictures, like those of the independents, were straight out of penny dreadfuls of the day: *Criminals of the Air; Girls Can Play; The Shadow* (not connected in any way to the hit radio series); *The Game That Kills; Paid to Dance.*

Rita was working harder than she had with her father. As was the custom of the period, she was posing for publicity photographs ad nauseum—"Miss New Year's," "Miss Valentine"—but nothing much was happening as far as public reaction was concerned.

A change in her appearance was in the offing, suggested by Judson and accomplished with the help of Helen Hunt. "Eddie came to me, and said, 'Can we do something about her hairline? What do you know about electrolysis?' I sent him to the woman who was the president of the Electrolysis Association of America. They took photos of Rita, blew them up, and drew lines indicating where the hairline was and where it should be."

Miss Hunt says that Judson paid twenty-five dollars a session for the treatments, out of his own money. Electrolysis was a slow, painful process, and Rita wasn't too happy about it, but she went along with it because she knew it was necessary. Over the years much has been written about the electrolysis, but Helen Hunt says, "The change was important but subtle. Eventually, I told Harry Cohn that Judson was paying out of his own pocket, and Cohn was impressed that Judson was investing his own money. The studio then took over the payments."

Until the treatments were completed, "I used to bleach the front of Rita's hair," recalls Helen Hunt, "so the hairline wouldn't be so prominent—the cameramen were always after me to lighten her hair."

Hunt also recalls that during this period Rita was hard at work studying with the studio drama coach, Ben Snyder. But it would take more than acting lessons and a raised hairline to put her on the map, and Judson knew it. Hollywood was a town bursting with beautiful women, and a gimmick was needed to launch another one. But *what* gimmick?

Bob Taplinger at Warner Bros. had come through for Lana Turner by tagging her "The Sweater Girl." Ann Sheridan was "The Oomph Girl," Lupe Velez was "The Mexican Spitfire," and Clara Bow had been "The 'It' Girl." What Rita needed was a great press agent, reasoned Judson, and he kept an eye out for the right man. Meanwhile, malleable Rita plodded along, working hard, doing as she was told—and waiting for the break to come.

Judson took over every aspect of her life. A person who was

there remembers, "One day I went with them to a seamstress, where Rita was having some skirts made. Judson told Rita where to stand, and she stood there, motionless, for what seemed like hours, as the seamstress took measurements and made alterations. Eddie did all the talking. He chose the fabrics, the colors, and the styles of the skirts. And he haggled over the price. Rita never said a word."

Rita would later admit that she was never allowed to make any decisions. "You're such a child," Judson told her. "I'll take care of things."

Rita had unquestioning faith in her husband, until the shock of discovering she was in fact the *third* Mrs. Judson! She felt betrayed. She gave him the silent treatment. Ed told her she was "behaving like a child," and that the other wives were "from another chapter of my life."

But it was an experience Rita would not forget. Nothing in her background had prepared her for something like this. This man was, after all, her husband, the man she had left her family for. Had Volga been right all along? But it was too late to change anything now.

Although Judson's first wife was an unknown, his second wife was a celebrity. The much-married Hazel Forbes had been a Ziegfeld beauty. She was in *Whoopee!* on Broadway in 1928, when she met Judson, then a salesman for the deluxe Italian-made Isotta-Fraschini automobiles.

Hazel and Judson were married in January 1929, but soon split. Hazel obtained a divorce in December 1929 and returned to the cast of *Whoopee!* Shortly afterward, she married the heir to a toothpaste fortune, who died and left her all his money. She then wed singing star Harry Richman, and later divorced him.

Revelation of Judson's marriage to Hazel Forbes, especially when the popular press kept referring to her as "the toothpaste heiress," added a certain glamour to his past, which he marketed to the hilt in Hollywood.

Helen Hunt remembers, "He said he was a salesman and I guess he was. He was certainly good at convincing people. He used to talk the local jewelers and dress shops into lending gowns and jewelry for Rita to wear when they went nightclubbing. He would take her to the Cocoanut Grove and Ciro's and they would sit in the line of dancing so that people could see this beautiful young woman."

Many a starlet's career had been launched in places like Ciro's, the Grove, and the Trocadero. No one realized that more than Ed Judson. Dressing properly was every bit as important in these ersatz pleasure palaces as it was before the camera. The rules were simple: Catch the eye. Maintain people's attention. Radiate the feeling that you're having incredible *fun*. Get your picture taken.

"It was rather amusing," noted Robert Benchley, "to observe blissfully happy, world-famous lovers suddenly drop their dazzling smiles and scan the room—in opposite directions—once the lens-boys had filled their quota of snapshots!"

Making it in the nightclub circuit was a deadly serious business. "It was hard to really have fun when you had to be 'on' every minute," said Joan Blondell. Knowing the headwaiters and ingratiating yourself with them was as important as knowing the right producers and directors. It was a rat race, with obvious pitfalls. But Judson successfully navigated and guided Rita through it.

"Do I mind all the photographers, the attention?" said Rita Hayworth later on. "I should say not—I just think of the times I had tried to *attract* attention at the Trocadero!"

Unknown to Harry Cohn, Helen Hunt was very helpful to Judson and Rita during this period. "I used to sneak a girl out of the department to go over and do Rita's hair before she went night-clubbing. Sometimes I'd even sneak a car out of the studio to have the girl driven over. Or I'd go myself."

The nightclubbing began to pay off. Rita's name was mentioned in columns, her picture was getting into the papers, even Columbia executives back in New York began to take note of her.

Columbia cast Rita in five pictures in 1938, all of them interesting only in retrospect because Rita was in them. They were all B films, with titles to match: *Who Killed Gail Preston?; There's Always a Woman; Convicted; Juvenile Court; Homicide Bureau.*

"They were all pretty bad," said Rita bluntly many years later. "Did I learn anything from doing them? Yeah, I learned you don't learn much from people who are just interested in getting something done *fast* instead of *right*."

George Cukor was to direct an A picture for Columbia—Katharine Hepburn and Cary Grant in Philip Barry's *Holiday*. Cukor was a man who always did things *right*. At Cohn's behest Cukor tested Rita for the role of Hepburn's younger sister, and the experience was an important one for Rita. She was able to work with Katharine Hepburn, whose professionalism and technical expertise were a revelation to the young Hayworth. "I learned more from her in three days than I had in working for a year in B films," she said.

Hepburn even got along with Harry Cohn—she respected him for hiring her in the face of industry opposition, for this was during the period when she was considered box office poison.

Rita did not get the role in *Holiday*, but she did get some valuable advice from Cukor regarding a top diction coach. Rita took his advice, and the lessons with the coach paid off handsomely in later years.

Cohn was beginning to take notice of Rita Hayworth. Another studio, RKO, had borrowed her—at a profit to Columbia, of course—for *The Renegade Ranger*, a western with George O'Brien, and when she returned to the lot Cohn cast her in *The Lone Wolf Spy Hunt*, with Ida Lupino and Warren William, the first film in which Rita got her own stand-in—a girl named Ellen Duffy—and costumes designed specially for her.

Rita and Judson still made the rounds of nightclubs and she continued to spend hours posing for publicity photos in the gallery. The portrait photographers attempted to make Hayworth resemble Hedy Lamarr, the current glamour sensation. In Hollywood, imitation was always the keynote. Originality seeped through in spite of the system, not because of it. Rita was merely one of dozens—including top stars!—whose resemblance to Lamarr was exaggerated (or manufactured, if it didn't exist at all) in the hope of cashing in on another star's success.

In late 1938 talk at Columbia centered around Howard Hawks's upcoming production, *Only Angels Have Wings*. A story with an aviation background, it was going to be an AA production, with Cary Grant, Jean Arthur, Thomas Mitchell, and silent picture great Richard Barthelmess in a comeback try.

There have been many fanciful stories on how Rita gained

Hawks's attention. In one version he spotted her in a nightclub, in another he saw one of her B films. What really happened is far less dramatic and much more businesslike.

George Chasin, a handsome young agent with the Small Agency, which represented Rita at the time, today recalls, "I sat for days outside Howard Hawks's office, then decided to sit during the lunch hour by the door through which Mr. Hawks would have to exit for lunch. When he finally came out for lunch, I walked with him along the corridor to be able to talk with him and asked that he test Rita for the picture. I had never met Mr. Hawks before that time. He stated that Linda Winters (who was a client of Mr. Hawks's brother) was already assigned to the film. However, he did agree to make a test, and Rita finally wound up in the role." (Chasin recalls that Hayworth left the Small Agency shortly after that to go to the Edington-Vincent Agency.)

Only Angels Have Wings was one of those films that created a buzz in the industry during production—expectations were high. With Rita in this film, Judson had something to be excited about. Howard Hawks was "class"—a consummate director, a man with prestige—and he was one of the most sought-after talents in Hollywood. With Hawks at the helm, Rita Hayworth would be in a picture that would *have* to garner major attention. Judson began calculating how he could make the most of this opportunity to further his wife's career.

Rita was definitely out of her league, experience-wise, with the impressive *Angels* cast. Cary Grant was helpful to her, and she appreciated it, but Rita was just plain scared.

Hawks, a master at working with actors, conferred with Grant about helping Rita to react properly, and during the course of the film the two men improvised several scenes which brought forth the proper responses from her. Cameraman Joe Walker did the rest, photographing the seductively costumed twenty-year-old girl to perfection.

Despite her nervousness on the set, onscreen she radiated a mature, knowing sexual allure. This was ironic considering Rita's strict upbringing and her equally stifling marriage to Ed Judson. This "sex" quality was simply within her and registered on film; at one point, after a take in which she had to give Cary Grant a long, come-hither look, Hawks asked her what she had been thinking. "He was looking at me in a strange way," Rita answered.

Hawks said, many years later, "I don't really think she knew how intensely sexy she seemed to others. I've run into that with other women—Lauren Bacall, for example. These girls were very, very young and very inexperienced when they became stars. I'm not sure Rita *ever* really knew what it was all about. I never worked with her again, unfortunately—but I never did another picture that had a leading-lady role that her quality would have been right for."

Cary Grant, many years later, said he regretted that he and Rita didn't work together again. He said he would have wanted it to be in a musical: "We might have ended up as the Fred Astaire and Ginger Rogers of Columbia."

Rita adored Cary Grant—like Katharine Hepburn, he had been kind, responsive, and helpful. "That was quite a lesson to me. The bigger the star, the nicer the person. Well, not always," she laughed, "but in those cases I was very, very lucky."

There are rumors that Jean Arthur, always an introvert off-camera, was not friendly toward Rita during *Angels*. Helen Hunt reveals how these unfounded rumors started: "They were taking still photos in the gallery—that was standard practice then, after a film was completed. The photographer wanted a shot of Rita and Jean, and Jean said, 'I'm not going to stand next to her.' 'Why?' I asked. 'What's the matter?' 'That beautiful girl and *me*?' And she turned and walked out of the gallery."

Angels and *The Lone Wolf Spy Hunt* were not the only pictures Rita made that year (1939). She had also appeared in a Columbia programmer called *Special Inspector*. Her contract was up for renewal. She was earning $250 a week, and the renewal option, if exercised, would bring her up to $300. Cohn tried one of his usual tactics. He demurred, then let it be known he *might* pick up her option—but only if she'd forfeit the raise.

George Chasin and Morris Small came up with an alternative: apply the fifty dollar raise to dramatic lessons. Rita was then studying with Grace Fogeler. Cohn agreed, as all awaited release of *Only Angels Have Wings*.

Judson knew this was the time for the big push. He had met

twenty-five-year-old press agent Henry C. Rogers and his wife, Roz, at a poker game. Delve into the hows and whys of any movie star's success and you will—in *every* instance—find an equally talented and astute press agent behind the scenes. The man or woman who determines how to present the star so that the press —and the public—will be intrigued.

"Every man can look back and pinpoint the turning point in his life when fate stepped in and set him on the path which determined his future," notes Rogers, speaking of his fateful encounter with Judson.

Rogers was impressed at how *fiercely* ambitious Judson was for his wife. He remembers that Rita was ambitious, too, "but Eddie did all the talking. Judson proposed that I become Rita's press agent, for a fee of five percent of her income on a three-year deal. She was making around three hundred dollars a week and my cut would be fifteen dollars a week."

How to make the press and public aware, in a big way, of Rita Hayworth? The idea grew out of a discussion Judson and Rogers had about Rita's clothes. Rogers went to the West Coast editor of *Look* magazine, who had never heard of Rita Hayworth. But when Rogers told him that Rita spent her whole salary—$15,000 a year, an enormous amount to the average American, on clothes, the editor was hooked.

Then Rogers produced his ace card: Rita's wardrobe had won an important fashion award from Jackson Carberry, president of the Fashion Coutouriers Association of America.

"Everything I told Gene Herrick was a lie," Rogers now reveals. "The telegram was written by me and sent to Rita at the studio. There was no such person as Jackson Carberry. There was no such fashion group. I had made it all up."

Judson and Rogers had to come up with Rita's spectacular wardrobe when a top *Look* photographer, Earl Theisen, was assigned to do the story. They did, borrowing from shops, designers, and department stores all over town. Theisen shot innumerable photos. And one was used as a *Look* cover.

Now there was more than ample attention when Rita and Judson made the nightclub rounds. Interestingly, Henry Rogers observes that while Rita was certainly a beautiful girl, she didn't, in his opinion, have the kind of magic in person that, for example, Lana Turner did. Or Joan Crawford. "Those women lit up the room with their personalities." Rita was, incredible as it may seem, somewhat bland, according to Rogers. A fact hard to digest when looking at her unique face in photographs taken in the night-spots at that time.

"My wife said, 'Why are you bothering representing this girl? She just doesn't have it,'" says Rogers. "But then we went to a screening of *Only Angels Have Wings*. When Rita appeared on the screen, Roz turned to me and said, 'My God, you were right. She's got it. She's going to be a big star.'"

Rogers confirms what many through the years have declared. That Rita waited until she was in front of the camera before turning on any of her magic. In person she seemed lethargic—"Unquestioning. I guess that's the best word to describe her. She just did whatever Judson told her to."

One afternoon when Rita was late for a photo session at the couple's home, Judson cracked jokes and kept the press amused until Rita finally came out of the bedroom, beautifully groomed. She walked directly over to Judson and, in the manner of a daughter seeking advice and approval from a father, asked, "Is this okay?"

He looked her over carefully and gestured toward a brooch fastened at the neckline of her dress. "Pin that over there," he said, pointing to her shoulder. She complied immediately. "Now you look just right." He motioned to the photographers. "Okay, boys. We're ready."

Henry Rogers recalls that even at this early date Rita had the ability to simply "tune out." She would stare into space and seem to be in a world of her own. "I can't say I ever got to *know* her, but I got to know Eddie Judson pretty well."

The publicity stunt that landed Rita on the cover of *Look* was a great success, but Rogers notes, "I would not do it today. All our standards are different. The standards of journalism are different, as are the standards of press-agentry."

The *Look* cover, and Rita's success in *Only Angels Have Wings,* made her one of Columbia's leading contract players. Suddenly Rita Hayworth was getting fan mail. Rogers was busy keeping her name in the columns and fan magazines, and Judson kept after Harry Cohn to give Rita better roles in better pictures.

Cohn was mulling over how to proceed with Rita professionally. Personally, however, he knew how to proceed. It was standard operating practice for Cohn to make a play for every woman who worked for him. Cohn was often crude but always very direct.

"There were no exceptions," recalls Helen Hunt. "He even made a play for me. A group of us from the studio were once in New York on a business trip. It was Cohn's birthday, and he called my room. 'Whaddya doin' tonight?'

" 'Are you asking *me* what I'm doing?'

" 'You gotta come to my party.' Cohn then gave me the usual line. I later checked with some of the other girls and found he had used the same line on them. Later that night he called me to his room. He was in bed, naked.

" 'I think you and I should have an affair.'

" 'You've got the wrong person,' I said. 'I won't do it. Is there anything else you want?'

" 'No,' he said.

"I left. It was as quick as that."

Helen Hunt's theory is that Cohn felt he *had* to try it with everyone at the studio. "*Of course* he tried it with Rita," she declares. "But he got nowhere."

Others have confirmed Cohn's early obsession with Rita Hayworth. Cohn was still married to his first wife, Rose, but they had been separated for years. He wanted children. She couldn't have any, but she would not allow him to divorce her. He was currently involved with the beautiful Joan Perry. But he had his eye on others, not the least of which was Rita Hayworth.

"I was giving a New Year's Eve party," recalls Helen Hunt, "and I invited Rita and Eddie, of course. Since Cohn knew everything that was happening at the studio, he knew about the party and he implied that he was going to come too. 'I wanna see your new house,' he said. He was going to the theater that night and said he'd be by later. Then, about eleven o'clock, he called. 'I'm not coming. I'm not gonna chase Rita.' "

Like Howard Hawks, Cohn was one of those men who assumed that women whose careers he furthered would be grateful enough to take the initiative. And there is every reason to believe that where Rita was concerned, Ed Judson led both Hawks and Cohn on.

As 1940 dawned, Rita was twenty-one and at last regarded as one of *the* exciting new girls on the screen. Hawks had advised Cohn to see how the public reacted to Hayworth in *Angels* before deciding on her next picture. When it was obvious Rita had struck a chord, Cohn really didn't know what to do with her. The studio was geared to producing pictures, not stars.

Cohn cast Rita in a musical called *Music in My Heart,* in which her leading man was handsome crooner Tony Martin. The package was a notch above the type of programmer Columbia had used her in previously, but after *Only Angels Have Wings* it was hardly a powerhouse showcase.

Hayworth was featured in a showy femme fatale role in *Blondie on a Budget.* Showcasing upcoming stars in studio series was standard procedure in the thirties and forties. Over at M-G-M the Andy Hardy pictures would be the training ground for the studio's biggest stars.

It was evident Columbia knew they had *something* in Rita. The question was what to do with her. Then other studios made overtures to borrow her. Cohn was thrilled when M-G-M asked to use her in *Susan and God.*

Rita was scared. "Who wouldn't have been?" she said. "Going to M-G-M—the studio that had made Garbo and Gable!" She was also practical about the assignment. "I used to dream of being given a part where I could really act. But since that was never written into the scripts, I finally began to hope that they would give me some good 'clothes' roles. Better to be a glamour girl than a little Miss Adequate. So I was delighted when they told me I was being loaned to M-G-M for *Susan and God* and that I would wear Adrian clothes."

She was elated that George Cukor was the director, and Joan Crawford the star. Anita Loos had written the screenplay, adapted from the Broadway hit which had starred Gertrude Lawrence. This was a production with the kind of gloss that was new and exciting to Rita, who was used to the cramped surroundings and working conditions that existed at tiny Columbia.

Joan Crawford, then thirty-six, was not fond of beautiful, younger women, all of whom, in her mind, posed an ever-increasing threat to her own career. But Cukor was running the show, and everything went smoothly. Rita delivered a fine performance as a femme fatale, married to an older man (Nigel Bruce) but attracted to a younger one (John Carroll). She looked gorgeous, and in a party scene, when she dances a rhumba, the entire Rita Hayworth persona is in full bloom.

Louis B. Mayer was very impressed with Rita. In a meeting with his executives he suggested she be cast with Gable, Tracy, and Claudette Colbert in *Boom Town,* Gable's second picture after *Gone With the Wind.* What an opportunity! But Hedy Lamarr, who was under contract to M-G-M, wanted the role—went after it—and got it.

Rita returned to Columbia.

To Judson's dismay Rita also lost out on two big roles that Paramount wanted her for, not because Cohn wouldn't lend her out—he would—but because of the successful politicking of other actresses, agents, and executives. A real plum part, the lead in Cecil B. De Mille's *Northwest Mounted Police,* went to Paulette Goddard. And to play opposite Ray Milland in *I Wanted Wings* director Mitchell Leisen opted for Veronica Lake, who made her debut in the part.

Incredibly, Judson was at this point fearful that Cohn was waiting out Rita's contract and wouldn't renew her next option, since the mogul seemed to have no inclination to build a film around her.

Meanwhile, on the set of the next picture Cohn put her in, *The Lady in Question,* Rita met two men who would be important both in her career and in her personal life: actor Glenn Ford and director Charles Vidor.

Today, Ford recalls the Rita of this period as someone who was *very* shy, but who had a marvelous sense of humor. In their first picture together, there was no explosive chemistry between Hayworth and Ford; Harry Cohn did not sit up in the screening room and take notice of a screen team that would make box office history. (In fact, Ford would shortly enter the navy, when America entered World War II.)

Another screen newcomer, actress Evelyn Keyes, was in the cast, and she has thrown a spotlight on what director Vidor was like. Vidor, a Hungarian Jew, was an extremely attractive man in his midthirties, who smoked a pipe and wore lots of expensive cologne. He was a buddy of Harry Cohn's, and the two men shared an obsessive common interest: women.

The Lady in Question was an excellent "small" film. It did nothing to hurt Rita's career, nor did it advance it.

Cohn next cast Rita in *Angels Over Broadway,* which boasted very special ingredients. It was written and produced by Ben Hecht, codirected by Hecht and top cameraman Lee Garmes, and starred Douglas Fairbanks, Jr. (who also coproduced). Harry Cohn had enormous respect for Hecht—one of Hollywood's top three writers—and Cohn had been the one who suggested Rita be used in the picture.

She was, as usual, incredibly shy when interviewed by Hecht and Fairbanks. While she had the face and body of a gorgeous, sexy woman, she seemed so genuinely innocent and intent on pleasing that Hecht—a hard-boiled veteran of the Hollywood scene—behaved with unusual restraint.

"When Ben Hecht tested me for *Angels Over Broadway* and said the dramatic part of the girl was mine—I gave up wondering about the way they do things in Hollywood," said Rita. "If I had a word of advice to newcomers it would be 'Don't plan anything.'"

Needless to say, Rita didn't become chummy with either Hecht or Fairbanks. She was a total introvert. Yet Hecht liked her and told Cohn that Rita definitely had that extra something. He had heard that she was a wonderful dancer, and Hecht had a wonderful idea—why not star her as Isadora Duncan?

"Who's Isadora Duncan?" asked Cohn. Hecht pursued the idea no further.

Judson was growing impatient—when the hell was Harry Cohn going to produce a showcase film for Rita?

Over at Warner Bros. overworked "Oomph Girl" Ann Sheridan

was making waves. She was tired and underpaid; under no circumstances would she play in *The Strawberry Blonde,* even though James Cagney was the leading man and Olivia de Havilland the other female lead.

It was a juicy femme fatale role, in a story set in the 1890s. The property was based on the hit play *One Sunday Afternoon,* and Warner's top production talent was working on the picture: Hal B. Wallis was producing, Raoul Walsh directing.

While Ann Sheridan was indeed a redhead (in fact, she and Rita facially resembled one another), it has often been assumed that Rita was now summoned to step in because she was Hollywood's other dazzling redhead. Rita was, in fact, still a brunette, and she got the role in *Blonde* because Walsh had seen her on film and thought she would be terrific.

A major change in Rita's appearance was once more in the offing. Early one Sunday morning a wide-eyed Rita Hayworth arrived at The House of Westmore, the elaborate beauty salon in Los Angeles owned and run by Perc Westmore, the head of makeup at Warner Bros. Helen Bore, Westmore's top hair colorist, was also there. Perc, Helen, and Rita were alone. There would be no disturbances on this special Sunday. Rita was patient, uncomplaining, cooperative, and quiet. At the end of the day Rita's transformation—it had taken *hours*—was complete.

Helen Hunt explains that, prior to this, Rita's brownish hair had been given red rinses, but had never been dyed, because in those days it was against the law for people to dye hair at the studios—they had to go to a professional, licensed beauty salon to have it done.

Now Rita's hair was "strawberry blonde," a basically blond shade with red highlights. Offcamera it was a slightly peculiar tint: on film, it was perfect.

During filming of *The Strawberry Blonde* James Cagney and Olivia de Havilland were rumored to be feuding. Cagney adored Rita, and when it looked as though other far more experienced players were doing some scene-stealing at Rita's expense, Cagney saw to it that Rita was given additional footage. Men always responded to Rita in a positive way; her naïveté was genuine and appealing, and even women, once they saw it wasn't an act, were drawn to protect her.

George Hurrell, the famous portrait photographer who would later work closely with Rita on the Columbia lot, first encountered her at Warner Bros. "She had a nice personality, but could be rather subdued," he recalls. "But if she was experiencing a case of the blahs, all I had to do was place a tango, samba, or rhumba record on the phonograph, and her spirits would perk up and the pot would start to boil."

Warners kept her over for a role in a comedy, *Affectionately Yours,* which headlined Merle Oberon and Dennis Morgan.

Meanwhile, her marriage was becoming strained. Judson had labored long and hard to garner attention for his wife, and now that she was beginning to receive it—and enjoy it—he wanted her to spend more evenings at home.

He could be mean and nasty at times, and still goaded Volga on those rare occasions when he saw her. But he had brought Rita far. She owed him a great deal. No one could or would ever accuse Rita of being disloyal. But no one could or would keep her a prisoner, either. Not anymore.

A major turning point in Rita's life now occurred because a "blonde bombshell" refused to dye her hair red. Over at Twentieth Century-Fox, Darryl Zanuck had assigned Carole Landis to be Tyrone Power's leading lady in *Blood and Sand,* the classic Ibañez tale of good and evil—a bullfighter (Power) in love with a pure girl (Linda Darnell) falls into the clutches of a femme fatale (Landis).

The role of the siren was one that other well-known actresses in Hollywood had coveted so intensely they had even screen-tested for it.

"It is a part actresses would kill for," noted hard-edged columnist Hedda Hopper, who pointed out that Fox was going all out on production, and the film would be in Technicolor.

Pinup girl Landis was under contract. Zanuck liked her and was giving her the buildup. When she refused the role—"I'm a blonde, dammit, not a redhead! I'll play it as a blonde!"—Zanuck was furious.

Meanwhile, Rita's dazzling look in *Strawberry Blonde* was already the talk of the private screening room circuit. Her dazzling smile, the plunging necklines of her revealing costumes, and the sensuous, easy way she moved, stole every scene she was in. Yet Rita could hardly believe it when she was summoned to an interview with director Rouben Mamoulian to discuss the role of Doña Sol in *Blood and Sand*.

"*Me?* You think they really want *me?*" she kept saying to Ed Judson. Since the shock of losing *Ramona,* all matters pertaining to casting filled Rita with misgiving. In this case her fears were unfounded. "The moment I saw Rita Hayworth walk, I knew I had my Doña Sol," said Rouben Mamoulian. "She was a dancer, so naturally I expected her to be graceful, but she had something more than that—a feline sort of movement that was subtle—and insinuating—exactly the kind of animation I imagined Doña Sol would possess."

Rita Hayworth would be working for Zanuck, the man who had taken *Ramona* away from her. Said she'd never be big in pictures. And now he had to negotiate for her services in his studio's top picture of the year.

The Gordons, a writing team, knew Rita at this time. "We walked on the set of *Blood and Sand* the first day of shooting. Rita Hayworth was wearing slacks. She was shy but friendly and ever so young. She was frightened, and this was strange for she'd been in many films. . . . She appeared quiet, even languid, but she was intensely disciplined. She was consistently easy to work with. She had no pretenses, no temperament. She had a smile for everyone. She never failed to thank people and show her appreciation."

Rita registered on film like a live current of electricity. The rushes of *Blood and Sand* indicated that it might turn out to be *her* picture! But her moment of professional triumph was blemished, because Rita was now totally disillusioned with her marriage. Henry Rogers tells a revealing story about the relationship of Rita Hayworth and Ed Judson at this time.

"One day Eddie came into the offices with a dejected look on his face. He said, 'You know, Henry, that Rita has just started to work on *Blood and Sand.*'

" 'Yes, I know. How is it going?' I replied.

" 'Well, the picture has scarcely started and Rita is already having an affair with Tony Quinn.'

"I was shocked. A man telling another man that his wife was having an affair was not something to be taken lightly in 1941.

" 'Eddie, that's ridiculous,' I replied. 'You have been listening to idle gossip. Who told you silly drivel like that?'

" 'She did,' said the cuckolded husband. 'You must understand, Henry, I wouldn't mind if Rita had an affair with Tyrone Power or Darryl Zanuck or someone else who could help her career, but Tony Quinn!' "

Rogers sadly notes, "It seemed to me Eddie would have sold his wife to the highest bidder if it would have enhanced her career."

And Judson *still* felt her position at Columbia was insecure. As Rogers tells it, Judson actually went to him and said, " 'Henry, I need your advice. You know that Rita's option is coming up. Everything seems to be going nicely, but I'm not sure that Harry Cohn is going to exercise that option. He invited us to spend the weekend on his yacht. He said we would all take a cruise to Catalina. What would you think if I took conveniently ill just before we were ready to leave? Then I would insist that Rita go alone. If Rita and Harry Cohn spent the weekend together, there is no doubt that he would exercise her option for another year.'

"I advised him not to get conveniently ill and that he should accompany his wife on the yacht. I told him that Rita had already displayed enough talent and that her career was moving ahead quickly enough. She didn't have to sleep with producers to get ahead. I never asked whether Rita went on that weekend trip alone or with her husband. The fact is that her option was picked up and she went on to great fame."

The Strawberry Blonde was a topnotch film and a big hit. It was the beginning of Rita Hayworth's career as a first-magnitude star—few people realize that she was billed below the title when the picture was initially released. *Blood and Sand* firmly established Rita in the role of femme fatale, although she was billed below the title in that film as well.

Variety noted, "Rita Hayworth takes another stride toward her assured position among the stars in demand." She was named "Star of Tomorrow" by the respected Quigley Poll. It was ironic that Warner Bros. and Twentieth Century-Fox had done for Harry Cohn what he could not possibly have done for himself—Columbia owned no theater chains and relied on the chains of rival studios for playdates. But Cohn, by allowing his competition to utilize Rita Hayworth in their own films, had enabled her to be seen by virtually all moviegoers throughout the nation.

Rita's impact in *Blood and Sand* was undeniable and affected millions of men, but two men who saw the film—one in South America and one in the Middle East—were fated to link their destinies with hers.

THREE

After *Blood and Sand,* Harry Cohn finally took the big step with Rita. At last the poverty row studio had its own star, and *You'll Never Get Rich* was a project even Rita rejoiced about. "No one was more surprised than I," she said. Fred Astaire had been a long-time idol of hers, and the film would team Astaire and Hayworth! According to Rita, Fred had *asked* for her. "He knew I was a dancer. He knew what those dumb-dumbs at Columbia didn't know." Of course Astaire had known the Cansino family since his early days in vaudeville.

The plot line of *You'll Never Get Rich* was pure boy-meets-girl fluff, Astaire-style, but with a contemporary touch: military life provided the background for the story.

Cohn was delighted to have Astaire—"*real* class"—on the lot. The mogul saw to it that everything about *Rich* was top-drawer. The score was by Cole Porter. Sidney Lanfield was signed to direct. Robert Alton was working with Astaire on the choreography. Humorist Robert Benchley had a featured role. Rita had a fabulous wardrobe, and Helen Hunt coiffed her hair in a classic, non-lacquered, free-flowing style that could have been designed today.

Astaire at this point was thinking of retiring. He was over forty. The partnership with Ginger Rogers was over, and although he had made a film with Eleanor Powell and another with Paulette Goddard, the public still thought of him and Rogers as a team.

The press wondered if Fred would click in a new partnership with red-haired Rita.

What did Rita think about "replacing" Ginger Rogers? The Astaire-Rogers duo was, after all, beloved by millions. "I just didn't think about it at all," Rita said. "Oh, I thought about it at first, but then I put it out of my head so it wouldn't inhibit me." Rita was actually a far more accomplished dancer than Ginger, and her discipline, acquired from Eduardo, was invaluable. Astaire, too, was a perfectionist.

Astaire had been concerned that Rita might be too tall for him. At one of their early rehearsals (to which Judson accompanied her, at Rita's request), both Rita and Fred were in flat heels and Astaire has recalled, "I was easily three inches taller and I told her I hoped she didn't have to wear very high heels with me. She said, very quietly, that she didn't think she had to."

Astaire was aware of her nervousness and went out of his way to put her at her ease, clowning with her, getting her to laugh. And he was fascinated at how she lit up when the camera was turning, and executed her steps with an intensity and energy that had not been at all evident in rehearsal.

According to Astaire, "She learned steps faster than anyone I've ever known. I'd show her a routine before lunch. She'd be back right after lunch and have it down to perfection. She apparently figured it out in her mind while she was eating."

Life magazine, inspired by the furor over Rita in *Blood and Sand*, decided to do a feature on her. Henry Rogers recalls, "Maggie Maskell, in charge of magazine publicity for Columbia, came up with the idea of posing Rita in a black-and-white, lace-and-satin nightgown. We were at the Judson house, shooting 'Rita Hayworth at Home,' when the photographer said, 'Rita, get on the bed—yes—on top of the bed cover—get on your knees, give your body a half-profile to the camera, and give me a provocative look.' Rita, always willing to comply, jumped on the bed and struck the proper pose as Maggie, Ed, and I stood by watching. Click, click, click, went the camera. Three weeks later the photo was on the cover of *Life*."

The *Life* cover, appearing August 11, 1941, created a sensation, and the next month *You'll Never Get Rich* was ready for

release, only four months after production had started. What a
year it had been! *Strawberry Blonde; Affectionately Yours; Blood
and Sand;* and *You'll Never Get Rich.* All released in a nine-
month period! Cohn saturated the trade press with ads for *Rich*
that boldly proclaimed Rita as "The Most Exciting Girl On The
Screen." For once Cohn wasn't accused of overselling. Rita's popularity was genuine. Her name was already being used—in other
studios' films, in comedians' nightclub routines, on the radio—as a
synonym for sex appeal.

Rita's salary at this point: five hundred dollars a week. Cohn
had paid Astaire a six-figure stipend, Astaire's going rate, and the
film would reestablish him as a draw without Ginger.

"I should be taking singing lessons if I'm going to be doing a lot
of musicals. Why can't I do my own singing?" Rita asked Judson.
Harry Cohn's response to Judson: "Tell her to forget it."

"Isn't it insane?" observes a top manager-agent today who
knew Rita and Judson back then. "Cohn didn't want to pay for
singing lessons!"

Ed Judson was still in the picture and functioning as a buffer
between Cohn and Rita. But within a few months everything
would change. And change dramatically.

Time magazine featured Rita on its cover in November 1941,
when *You'll Never Get Rich* was playing in New York at Radio
City Music Hall. A star had indeed been born. She was *the* girl,
the beauty, *the* new cinema goddess of the year.

"Christ, send her to New York. The press will go *wild!*" decreed Columbia publicity executives, and Rita and Judson were
dispatched to Gotham, where Rita's every move made news. The
armed services were of course on the front pages, so astute Columbia publicity man Frank Rosenberg arranged for Rita to appear everywhere with a soldier, a sailor, a coast guardsman, and a
marine. And she went everywhere. The Stork Club. El Morocco.
The Rainbow Room. The Statue of Liberty.

"Who's that guy?" photographers would sometimes ask when
spotting a middle-aged, balding man who seemed always to hover
nearby.

"That's Rita's husband," was the answer. Judson was unusually
silent on this jaunt, for obviously his Trilby was disenchanted with

him. "Rita the rebel," he sometimes called her, half-jokingly. They made it through the trip, smiling for photographers, and were back in Hollywood by late November for Rita to report to Fox for *Tales of Manhattan*.

The Judsons separated.

"The Girl of the Moment" was abruptly bumped off the front pages when an event affecting all Americans took place: on December 7, 1941, the Japanese bombed Pearl Harbor and America was at war.

Rita was back at Fox for the second picture, *Tales of Manhattan*, under a three-picture deal Cohn had made with Zanuck. People had a different attitude about Hayworth now. She was treated with a certain deference, although she was definitely the same girl: shy, quiet, waiting to be told what to wear, where to stand, what to do. But now, instead of "Stand here," "Do that," it was "How do you feel about doing it this way?" or "Would you like some more time to get ready?" "Are you pleased with the way the costume looks?" Rita accepted it all with her natural, characteristic reserve.

With the advent of the war, not all the eligible young male actors were drafted into the service immediately. Hollywood's social life, momentarily, remained status quo. But production was escalating to an all-time high at Fox and all the other studios, as they geared up to satisfy the virtually insatiable appetite of a public seeking fantasy and escape to a greater degree than ever before.

Tales of Manhattan was a platinum package which placed Rita Hayworth on a par with the biggest stars in the business. She was top-lined with Ginger Rogers, Henry Fonda, Charles Boyer, Charles Laughton, Edward G. Robinson. The great French director Julien Duvivier was at the helm. Each episode in the multistory drama featured different stars. Rita portrayed yet another femme fatale, a woman who was married to Thomas Mitchell and having an affair with Charles Boyer.

Then she went right into *My Gal Sal*, a lavish Technicolor musical set—as was *The Strawberry Blonde*—in the 1890s. The carefree turn-of-the-century era would be a surefire draw for audiences during the war years. It was incredibly uncomfortable working under the brutally hot lights necessary for color photography, wearing heavy costumes, in pictures like this. But, as always, the public was kept unaware of the difficulties of filmmaking. And Rita performed without complaint.

Ostensibly a biography of songwriter Paul Dresser, *My Gal Sal* presented Hayworth as Broadway star Sally Elliott. Carole Landis —the girl who had turned down *Blood and Sand*—was relegated to the second female lead, courtesy of Mr. Zanuck.

"Carole was ready to pull Rita's hair out, even though Hayworth had had nothing to do with Landis's ill-advised move not to do *Blood and Sand*," recalls a makeup person employed at Fox at the time. "But Rita was not a bitch, and that defused Landis. There were no further problems between them."

Since Rita had separated from Judson and initiated divorce proceedings, she had no reason not to respond openly to her leading man's interest. What young woman wouldn't have? The leading man was Victor Mature, the "Hunk." Movie magazines were making as big a fuss over him as they did over Tyrone Power, Errol Flynn, and Clark Gable.

Mature, the son of an immigrant who owned a profitable refrigeration company, had come from Kentucky to California at nineteen to seek fame and fortune via films. Tinseltown wasn't instantly bowled over.

He landed bit roles in B movies, but it wasn't until a few years later, when he played a scantily clad caveman in *One Million B.C.,* that people began to take notice. Then he returned east to appear on Broadway in Moss Hart's and Kurt Weill's *Lady in the Dark* opposite Gertrude Lawrence. The play was an artistic and commercial triumph for all concerned.

A line of dialogue from *Lady in the Dark* became his personal trademark: "His voice goes through you like a pound of cocaine! Oh, what a beautiful hunk of man!"

Rita had first met Mature back in 1941, when she was making *Blood and Sand*. But at the time she was having her affair with Tony Quinn, and Mature's name was being linked with Betty Grable's and Lana Turner's. When he returned to New York, he married Martha Stephenson Kemp, a young widow with a three-year-old daughter. Now, only six months later, working with Rita on

My Gal Sal, he was entranced by her. She possessed a genuine sweetness that was a rare commodity in the Hollywood jungle—and was even rarer in a top star, which Rita had now become.

The couple became the "dream team" of the moment, which did not make Darryl Zanuck unhappy. Mature was, after all, a Fox contract player. This duo was news. And Rita liked Mature very much. He had the kind of outgoing personality Rita always responded to. He wanted to impress her, amuse her—and did. But she was hardly about to rush into another marriage.

Speculation in the columns ran rampant. Powerful columnists, including Louella Parsons, disliked Mature and devoted full columns advising Rita not to marry him. What a situation! First Rita had had to contend with her father telling her what to do; then Judson; and now—total strangers dictating to her before an audience of millions!

But Rita didn't care. She was free at last to live the social life she pleased. She was having fun. She captained the Hollywood Leading Men softball team in their charity games against the Hollywood Comedians team, captained by Betty Grable.

Rita dated Errol Flynn, David Niven, and others, but it was her involvement with Mature that was the most fun—a real escapade. For Mature, however, it was much more than that.

Rita had reconciled with her family now that Judson was out of the picture. . . . Or was he?

It soon turned out that Judson had no intention of making a graceful exit. He threatened to publicly ridicule her. Rita couldn't believe how vitriolic he was. She was shocked when he demanded $30,000 to agree to go through with the divorce—"or I'll make quite a stink in the press, my dear."

Where was Rita to get $30,000? That was more than a year's salary!

Rita engaged an attorney, Don Marlin, and at first all seemed to go smoothly. The only statement issued concerning money was "A fair and just property settlement has been reached out of court."

People assumed that Judson had received his $30,000. Some have reported that he got the sum from Harry Cohn. But the facts are that in February 1942 Rita had signed a secret agreement with Judson. It gave him virtually *all* of their jointly owned property, including two hundred shares of common stock in Columbia Pictures and two hundred shares of preferred stock in Twentieth Century-Fox, plus $12,000 in cash.

In return, read Judson's agreement, he would "not imply, directly or indirectly, that she had committed an offense involving moral terpitude under federal, state or local laws, or that she has conducted herself in any manner which would cause her to be held in scorn, or which would damage her career."

At first she had refused to sign. But there was an inducement for her to do so. Judson agreed to turn over to Rita "all written documents bearing her signature in his possession or under his control." It stated he had "not retained any copy, photostat or facsimile of the documents." Judson further agreed he would "not sell, publish or circulate any slanderous, libelous or defamatory matter concerning her."

The implications inherent in this secret pact were incredibly illuminating. Judson had apparently been accumulating ammunition for this inevitable and distasteful confrontation. Rita's reputation as an obedient Trilby has to be amended in view of all this evidence.

When the case went to court, none of this information was revealed. The divorce was granted in May 1942. A jittery Rita was in court, her pale and tense mother by her side. Rita stated, "He resented my parents, and although I love them very much, I couldn't see them if I wanted to avoid quarrels."

After the divorce was granted, Rita gave out certain guarded statements. She gave Judson full credit for his contribution to her career but also said, "I never had any fun. I was never permitted to make any decisions. From the first he told me I couldn't do anything for myself. My personality crawled deeper and deeper into a shell."

One of her attorneys declared, "He married her as an investment, for the purpose of exploiting her . . . and he intended to get paid for the time he was married to her."

But Rita softened that with comments such as: "I realize how much Ed has done for me. . . . I never had to do any fighting for myself. He fought for me. Running my career was his only concern, and he gave it everything he had and his efforts paid off. . . . Although we had our domestic differences, he's entitled to a fair return."

Judson hung around Hollywood for a while. He even gave the obligatory movie magazine interviews about their divorce: "I built my wife into a dream of perfection. There were hundreds of grasping hands—outstretched for Rita at every turn. I shielded, protected her as much as I could. . . . But building an unknown girl to a great personality is interesting. I'll probably do it again."

He did not do it again. A few months after the divorce his name did appear in the news when Thomas C. Sommermeier, heir to a cosmetics fortune, claimed that his twenty-six-year-old wife was living with and being supported by Judson. Judson denied the charges and claimed that their relationship was "only platonic." Hollywood gossips assumed he was grooming the twenty-six-year-old for "stardom."

But then Ed Judson disappeared from the Hollywood scene as mysteriously as he had appeared, giving rise to the speculation that Harry Cohn had either paid him off or threatened him with serious bodily harm—or both.

Many years later, Rita looked back on the Judson marriage with less than fond memories. "He helped *me* with my career and he helped *himself*—to my money."

FOUR

Victor Mature and his wife had separated and it seemed certain that Mature and Rita would be altar-bound once they were both free.

The Coast Guard intervened, however, calling Mature into service. He was temporarily stationed in Connecticut, and Rita defied Cohn's orders and went east to visit him.

Harry Cohn learned, as had Judson and, one assumes, Eduardo Cansino, that Rita kept silent and allowed the men in her life to think they were calling the shots. But in actuality she did exactly what she wanted to do.

When Rita arrived in New York en route to Connecticut, Cohn's New York publicity executives met her. Frank Rosenberg pleaded with her to follow Cohn's orders. She seemed to acquiesce. All assumed she agreed that it was best not to go to Connecticut. But she went.

Harry Cohn was livid. "Actors! Christ, don't *any* of them have any common sense?"

Cohn expected his new Galatea to exclude such nonsense from her life and to concentrate her entire existence on making films and making money for Cohn and Columbia. Another major film with Astaire was in preproduction.

And though Cohn would deny it, it seemed to several of those close to him that the mogul continued his unrequited yen for Rita. And she continued to make it clear she was *not* available to Cohn *at all*.

Rita said decades later, "I think if he could ever have been in love with anyone, he was secretly in love with me."

No one will ever know if he wanted to marry Rita or strictly possess her. It seems safe to assume that his animosity toward her began during this period, because while she was now painting the town with many men, she still spurned Cohn's advances.

By this time Cohn had finally obtained a divorce from Rose. He married Joan Perry on July 31, 1941. But apparently this did not stop him from, in the words of producer-screenwriter Virginia Van Upp, "verbally raping" all the women on the Columbia lot.

While Cohn wasn't actually having sexual relations with Rita Hayworth, he made sure people *thought* he was. "Of course, he hadn't put a hand on me," Rita subsequently said. "As if I'd let him—but he had to go around saying it."

There are reports that Cohn made these insinuations in front of people in Rita's presence and that her failure to deny them appeared to be a confirmation. But those who knew her well point out that she just wouldn't deign to recognize any of his crude remarks.

Mature was granted leave from the Coast Guard and came back to Hollywood to escort Rita to the premiere of *Tales of Manhattan*. She wore a flashy ring, a gift from Mature.

"Is that an engagement ring, Miss Hayworth?" she was asked.

"No, it isn't!" she chimed, happily. And truthfully.

Rita couldn't, of course, marry anyone until May 1943, when her divorce became final. During the year, Rita continued to be seen with others, and was at last happy with the kind of movie projects Cohn had in mind.

You Were Never Lovelier was a joy to make. She looked forward to her rehearsals with Astaire, and up to this day looks back on the two films she made with him as the "jewels" of her career.

Astaire was fond of her as well. "I remember I went to Fred Astaire's dressing room to help him put on his toupee," recalls Helen Hunt. "He said, 'I've got a present for Rita. I'd like to show it to you. See if you think she'd accept it. You know she's kind of

. . . she doesn't . . .' He was fumbling. . . . Finally, he blurted out, 'Do you think she likes me?' "

"Oh yes," Helen said, "she admires you very much. She always looks forward to rehearsing with you." Astaire took out a jewel box which contained a beautiful pin in the shape of a Spanish dancer, studded with diamonds, rubies, and sapphires. Helen remembers, "The figure was a girl on her toes, wearing a skirt, whirling around. It was just beautiful. Fred told me, 'I want to give it to her, but I don't want her to feel I'm after her in any way. You know how it is. She's got so many admirers.' " Helen reassured him that Rita would accept the gift in the spirit in which it was intended.

The onscreen chemistry between Hayworth and Astaire attests to the feeling of warmth and camaraderie between them. In later years Astaire viewed Rita Hayworth, not Ginger Rogers, as his "favorite dancing partner." Of course, it must be mentioned that Rita never attempted to upstage anyone.

In *You Were Never Lovelier* Rita portrayed Maria, the most romantic and beautiful of Spanish aristocrat Adolphe Menjou's three dazzlingly gorgeous daughters (Leslie Brooks and Adele Mara were the other two). Maria was patiently waiting for her prince charming, a knight in armor on a white horse, to enter her life.

"Not unlike Rita herself," observed a screenwriter who knew Rita during these years.

Directed by William Seiter, the movie was pure fantasy, a story so lightweight it could have been the basis for an animated Walt Disney feature cartoon.

The songs, by Jerome Kern and Johnny Mercer, were delightful. Xavier Cugat and his orchestra completed the package, which was perfect entertainment for a nation now totally caught up in the horrible reality of war.

The film opened at Radio City Music Hall in late autumn. It was Hayworth's second film released in 1942, and another smash hit. Rita did not make any more films that year and subsequently had no films in release for 1943. There are many theories about why. One line of thought is that Cohn had decided she was now a big star and should make only one film a year—a la Garbo. This is questionable. Even at M-G-M, $5000-a-week top stars like Gable and Tracy usually made two films a year. True, Columbia needed time to fashion the proper vehicle for Rita—but it was also true that she and Harry Cohn were feuding during this time. She was willing to risk suspension rather than knuckle under to his will. He had not forgiven her for going east to see Mature.

"Cohn wanted a slave-master relationship," says a close friend of Rita's, "and Rita would never give in to that."

Columbia had announced, and a great deal of preproduction work had already been done on, *Cover Girl*, a picture whose plot was perfectly capsulized by its title. Rita and a group of top models had posed for photographer Philippe Halsman for a layout which *Life* featured in its January 18, 1943, issue. Rita, sipping a soda, was on the cover—her third *Life* cover in less than two years. Her femme fatale image was toned down considerably, much more in keeping with the girl-next-door image the studio deemed appropriate during these war years.

While *Cover Girl* was in preparation, Cohn wanted Rita to make another film, *My Friend Curly*. She didn't like the script, and refused.

Often while feuding with Cohn, Rita would sneak onto the lot to have her hair done. "Cohn watched her like a hawk," relates Helen Hunt. "She came into the hairdressing department one day, her hair covered by a scarf, and literally a minute later Harry Cohn stormed in. I guess someone reported her car on the lot. Rita glanced over and saw him. He glared at her. Didn't say a word. She just walked away and stared out the window. He turned to me and said, 'What's she doing here?'

" 'I dunno. She just came in.'

" 'I know. I know.' . . . Then he commanded, 'Don't you do anything for her. Don't touch her hair.' "

Although feuding with Cohn and off the screen in 1943 (except for a brief cameo in a *March of Time* episode entitled *Show Business at War*), Rita was certainly in the news. The press and public couldn't learn enough about Rita Hayworth. She spent the latter half of 1942 and the early part of 1943 touring with the USO, entertaining at military hospitals and army camps, working at the Hollywood Canteen, and doing radio broadcasts for servicemen.

Character actress and comedienne Vera Vague called Rita one day; she was organizing a club called Hollywood's Own. Charter members included Hedy Lamarr, Dorothy Lamour, Patricia Morison, Martha O'Driscoll, Jean Parker, and Frances Gifford (whose brother Frank would later be a football star).

The purpose of the club was to write letters to the movie industry men now in the armed services—not just the actors, but *all* the guys from the studios, including the cameramen, grips, cutters, and publicists. Other actresses in town joined the group, and they all faithfully wrote to the men in uniform.

Along with other top stars, Rita played the guitar and sang in the Hollywood edition of *Charlot's Revue* at the El Capitan theater. It was a benefit which ran for weeks, with all proceeds going to British War Relief. While in the show she met party-giver Elsa Maxwell, a woman who would have a hand in changing the course of Rita's life only a few years later.

Nineteen forty-three was the most carefree year of her life. She was twenty-four and seemed to have the world by the tail. Victor Mature's wife was in the process of getting a divorce. But the "Hunk" was to face formidable competition for the hand of Rita Hayworth.

At the time that Orson Welles decided to marry Rita Hayworth he hadn't even met her. Nor had his friend Jackson Leighter, who was himself to be an important influence in Rita's life. Leighter, a distinguished-looking gentleman who spent a successful career weaving in and out of show business, met Rita Hayworth through Orson Welles. Leighter was then working with Nelson Rockefeller in the Office of Coordinating Inter-American Affairs, part of President Roosevelt's Good Neighbor Policy.

After Welles's big splash with *Citizen Kane* in 1941 the state department had sent him to South America. They were fearful that too many people in Argentina, Chile, and Brazil were sympathetic toward the Nazis so they sent Welles and other celebrities as cultural ambassadors. Of course Welles often created more problems than he solved. Leighter tells of Welles going to a party in Rio given by the German ambassador to Brazil: "Orson began impetuously throwing the ambassador's furniture from the second-story window."

Ostensibly Welles was on the South American junket making a film, *It's All True.* "But as was usual with him, he had reels of magnificent film—but no story," recalls Leighter, who was assigned to get Welles back to the States.

Instead of being unhappy about the recall, Welles was delighted. He had just seen a film which starred an extraordinarily exciting young woman, and he declared to Leighter, "I'm coming back to America to marry Rita Hayworth."

Only a few years earlier, in October 1938, the dynamic, flamboyant young Orson Welles had stunned Americans with his "War of the Worlds" radio broadcast, the first media event to become an overnight legend. Its brilliant twenty-three-year-old perpetrator, whose talent and versatility seemed to know no bounds, also became a legend on that night, but he had been famous as an actor and director even before that.

As critic Stanley Kauffmann has observed, "The critics and audiences of the mid-1930s were so overwhelmed by [Orson's] youth and energy that, in general, they hailed his acting. . . . By the time he was sixteen he was an Alexander who had not even had to conquer the world—it had been handed to him."

Welles would later comment, "I had luck as no one had; afterwards, I had the worst bad luck in the history of the cinema." But Welles's bad luck was still far in the future when he returned from Brazil to meet Rita Hayworth.

His background was so different from Rita's that they might have come from different planets. Born in Kenosha, Wisconsin— his full name is George Orson Welles—he had an unusual and extraordinary childhood. Whereas Rita had been regarded by her parents as a child, a doll-toy, the precocious Welles was always treated by his family as an adult. His parents were divorced when he was six, and his mother, a brilliant pianist, died when he was seven. Thoroughly versed in Shakespeare by the age of ten, he attended several schools. "I never left a school because I found it dull," he has recalled. "I found it difficult and was asked to leave."

The one school he did graduate from was the Todd School for

Boys, in Woodstock, Illinois, where classmate Paul Guggenheim did his homework and teacher Roger Hill encouraged his theatrical interests.

Welles's father, Richard Welles, was an inventor and man-about-town. Orson's old friend and associate, John Houseman, relates that Richard introduced Orson to brothels as well as literary salons. "Orson was sexually and intellectually mature at eleven," Houseman has said.

But the senior Mr. Welles was a tormented human being, and committed suicide in a Chicago hotel room when Orson was fourteen. Dr. Maurice Bernstein became Orson's guardian—no ordinary undertaking.

At fifteen, Orson went to Ireland, to observe and to paint—another of his passions. At sixteen, by sheer force of his personality, he had talked his way into major roles (saying he was twenty-two) at the world-renowned Gate Theatre in Dublin. This was an amazing accomplishment, considering the Gate's lofty standards. But the tall young man from America was a commanding presence, with an incredible voice, which was even then considered his most extraordinary theatrical asset.

Despite his success and talent he was unable to secure an English work permit, and had to return to the United States. Broadway didn't embrace him, but Katharine Cornell recognized his vast abilities and he joined her company. They toured seventy-five United States cities. He was offered a three-hundred-dollar-a-week movie contract, which he scoffed at. "When I enter pictures, I want to be the producer and director as well as the star."

Ladies found Orson Welles exciting—and vice versa. In 1934, when Orson was nineteen (Rita was sixteen, dancing with her father in Caliente), Welles married a beautiful blonde, Virginia Nicholson. She was from a social and wealthy Chicago family. She had met him when she performed in a summer theater festival he staged for his alma mater, the Todd School.

They subsequently journeyed to New York, where the Federal Theatre Project of the 1930s provided Welles with the opportunity to direct plays. His productions were unique, innovative, daring, avant-garde. They included an all-black *Macbeth*. Even when

Welles's efforts failed critically, he was lauded as an extraordinary young talent—a genius.

With John Houseman he founded the Mercury Theatre. Joseph Cotten, Agnes Moorehead, Vincent Price, Edmond O'Brien, and Everett Sloane were among the players. Radio was the hot, growing medium of the day, and Welles established the *Mercury Theatre of the Air*. Radio listeners throughout the country were already familiar with his remarkable voice—he was the star of *The Shadow* and narrator of *The March of Time*. But the highlight of his radio career was "The War of the Worlds."

He went to Hollywood in 1939 (the year Rita did *Only Angels Have Wings*), arriving presold as no other artist before him. Although there have been many lofty treatises as to why Orson made the move to films, Welles has been candid about it: "The Mercury needed dough. We signed a contract and avoided as many columnists as possible."

"This is the biggest electric train set any boy ever had," he said when walking into RKO. Initially he wanted to film Joseph Conrad's "Heart of Darkness" (the basis, forty years later, for Francis Ford Coppola's *Apocalypse Now*), but *Citizen Kane* was the project that went forward.

Welles's personal life always took a back seat. When he left for Hollywood, Virginia left for Reno. She got her divorce (in February 1940), and custody of their three-year-old daughter Christopher.

The grounds for divorce: extreme mental cruelty. "Orson was not cruel at all," Virginia later admitted. "He just doesn't have time for marriage. He works twenty hours a day. Everyone expects him to set the world on fire in everything he does and it's beginning to get under his skin."

After *Kane* Welles filmed *The Magnificent Ambersons,* then *Journey Into Fear,* starring Dolores del Rio, a sophisticated woman ten years his senior. Reports were that they would marry as soon as her divorce from M-G-M art director Cedric Gibbons became final.

Welles stopped in Mexico City to see Miss del Rio on his way back from South America. Then, instead of proceeding to New York as planned, he headed to Hollywood. (By the spring of

1942, Dolores del Rio announced her engagement to Orson was "over.")

Welles told columnist Sidney Skolsky that among the Hollywood girls he didn't know, the one he'd most like to know was Rita Hayworth, and Skolsky repeatedly reminded his readers, "Orson Welles still wants to meet Rita Hayworth."

During Orson's absence RKO had changed management. After extended bickering it was decided that the studio could not afford Mr. Welles's genius. *Citizen Kane,* which has become the most critically acclaimed movie ever made, was not a financial success at the time it was released. *The Magnificent Ambersons* and *Journey Into Fear* were not commercial hits either.

The new president at RKO was Charles Koerner, and Welles quipped to his staff, "Don't worry, boys—we're just passing a bad Koerner." Koerner's rejoinder, which everyone claims to have used at one point or another in dealing with Orson, was "All's well that ends Welles."

Although his career as a producer-director-writer seemed stalled, Welles was certainly in demand as an actor. He could easily have opted for the conventional leading man roles the studios wanted him for, and settled for the "matinee idol" buildup, but, like Laurence Olivier, that kind of approach held no interest for him. He wanted to be different, to do *varied* projects.

Albert Zugsmith, a film producer who worked with Orson later in his career, says, "Welles was so absorbed in playing fascinating, often complex roles . . . that he did not try to project the romantic image he was capable of then, and which was necessary for male stardom in those days."

Twentieth Century-Fox signed him to star opposite Joan Fontaine in the screen version of *Jane Eyre.* Fontaine has recalled that Welles lived up to his image by behaving in the grand theatrical manner both on and off the set.

He traveled with an entourage, including his valet. After disengaging himself from Dolores del Rio he resumed an active bachelor-about-town existence. He was seeing, among others, the beautiful young singer Lena Horne.

But it was wartime, and Welles's draft classification became a matter of some importance. First, the twenty-eight-year-old had been classified 1-B, then 1-A. Then he was reclassified as 2-B—a worker in an essential industry—and given a six-month deferment.

"I said to hell with it and tore up the notice. People had been talking so much about me and the whole idea of deferment for actors that I decided to go into the army. That's where I wanted to be, anyway."

He reported for induction in May 1943 but was rejected "for physical reasons"—back injuries, bronchial asthma, and arthritis.

While all this was going on, Welles was busy entertaining servicemen. He formed *The Mercury Magic Show,* also called *The Mercury Wonder Show: Mysterious, Thrilling, Sensational.* He also did a show called *The Magnificent Orson—Alive.* His friends from the Mercury Theatre would often join him: Joseph Cotten (JoJo the Great) and Agnes Moorehead (Calliope Aggie).

Welles now focused his explosive, persuasive energies—his irresistible charm—on winning Rita Hayworth.

It has been reported that Orson and Rita finally met at a dinner party hosted by Joseph Cotten. Another account is that they met at Lucy's, the famous restaurant located across the street from the Paramount and RKO lots (and down the street from Columbia). It was a favorite hangout of the film elite.

According to this account, Rita was at Lucy's with a friend, Ruth Rose, the night the two met. Rita was fascinated with Welles; he told her of his magic act and invited her to join the company as the woman he would saw in half. She found the idea great fun, and accepted. Their relationship soon became serious. As Jackson Leighter remembers, "When they fell in love, no one saw either of them for a while."

By this time Leighter had taken over as president of Mercury Productions: "The stationery said I was president—Orson was still the boss."

Orson's magic show was a great hit with the servicemen and Rita was with him every night, even though she had returned to work at the studio, to start *Cover Girl.*

Top models had been brought out from New York, and Cohn treated them all royally—almost as if baiting Rita. He housed the girls at the famed luxury hotel The Garden of Allah and gave them each an elaborate screen test, the implication being that he was on the lookout for a girl to replace Rita Hayworth should Hayworth continue to defy him.

Although many of the girls considered Rita aloof, "She was just being herself," notes an intimate. "She was never one to make fast friends. But she was always cordial and polite."

"Since Rita had been the one who clicked," points out a fashion designer active at Columbia and other studios during this era, "Cohn tried to fit all the other girls into Rita's image. 'Dress 'em like Rita, do their hair like Rita's, they'll be just like Rita.'" It was exactly the same thinking which had been applied only a few years earlier to Rita herself, when the studio had tried just as hard to make her look like another Hedy Lamarr.

Gail Gifford, a very personable, chic, and attractive woman, was the publicist who worked closely with Columbia's contract actresses in the mid-forties. She'd help select their clothes, coordinate their photo layouts, plan their publicity. She recalls the Rita Hayworth of this period as "a *very* sweet girl who did *everything* you asked her to do! She was a delight—*never* a problem."

That most definitely wasn't the case with many of the less successful actresses on the lot, some of whom were jealous of Rita and longed for the recognition she had achieved. One of Columbia's leading actresses lamented to an executive, "Why can't I associate with Rita Hayworth?"

"Who's stopping you?" the executive asked.

"We should be going around together," the ambitious girl wailed. Some of the Columbia contract players from this era have boasted that they palled around with Rita Hayworth. This is sheer nonsense.

Rita's natural reserve kept most people at arm's length. Her few close friends were not actors or actresses. But while reserved, she was never rude. "If you asked her a question, she'd never say 'It's none of your business.' She didn't talk like that," a friend remembers. "She was always very much a lady." If people tried casual conversation with her, she'd answer them, "but she never encouraged conversation."

Offscreen Rita was sometimes quite unrecognizable. Very early one morning when she arrived at the studio after a night of partying with Orson, Donald Gordon, a youngster who was working at the front gate, didn't recognize her and wouldn't let her in. "She obviously had had one hell of a night. She was bleary-eyed, her hair was a mess, she had no makeup on, and she was still wearing an evening gown. I didn't know what the hell to do with this screaming, cursing lady. Finally, she went through her purse and found her identification. I couldn't believe it was Rita Hayworth! I apologized profusely and let her in."

To Gordon's relief—and surprise—she was not angry afterward. She found the whole incident humorous.

Gordon was a friend of another Columbia actress, Janet Blair. One day he went into the makeup department and thought he spotted Janet, her back to him, in the makeup chair. He ran over to her, impetuously kissed her, and said, "Happy birthday to the most beautiful woman in the world!"

To his astonishment, it was Rita in the makeup chair. "I'm sorry!" gasped Gordon. "I thought you were Janet Blair!"

The makeup person was furious. "How dare you! You'll lose your job for this!"

Rita just laughed. "Oh, leave the kid alone. I'm happy to know someone doesn't think *I'm* the most beautiful woman in the world."

But most people did, and *Cover Girl* would go a long way toward cementing Rita's "goddess" image. It was shaping up to be a unique and innovative film. The top-notch cast included Eve Arden, Otto Kruger, Lee Bowman, and leading model Jinx Falkenburg. The music was by Jerome Kern. Travis Banton was brought in to design some of the costumes. Beginning with this picture, Harry Cohn became totally involved in every aspect of the creating of Rita's vehicles, from script to costumes. To insure that *Cover Girl* would be the last word in chic, he had engaged beautiful cover girl (and businesswoman) Anita Colby as consultant.

Even more important was the matter of Rita's leading man. Production had actually begun without one, but producer Arthur Schwartz knew who he wanted: "As far as I was concerned there was only one man in Hollywood who could do it, and that was

Gene Kelly. But each time I mentioned this to Cohn, he would explode.

"'That tough Irishman with his tough Irish mug?! You couldn't put him in the same *frame* as Rita!!' Cohn barked. 'Forget it. Nothing doing. Besides, he's too short. I saw him in *Pal Joey* and he's too goddamn short.'"

There is a story that Schwartz went to M-G-M without Cohn's knowledge and borrowed Kelly for four weeks. It is unlikely that Cohn was unaware of what Schwartz was up to, but in any event M-G-M lent Kelly, and the four-week loan-out was extended as production on *Cover Girl* went on and on and on. He came up with exciting new concepts on how to choreograph and photograph some of the musical numbers.

Cohn had a reputation as a troublemaker, and on *Cover Girl* he went to town. According to one story he tried to cow Gene Kelly by bellowing "You're setting up the dances to make yourself look good—you're making Rita look bad!"

But Kelly wouldn't be bullied. He demanded Cohn take back his accusations or he'd punch him in the mouth. Cohn did one of his usual about-faces. He suddenly smiled and said, "Of course you're making Rita look good. I just wanted to see what you'd say."

Phil Silvers was portraying the leading man's "best friend." He had played a similar role in *My Gal Sal* and got to know Rita very well. They remained close friends for many years.

Silvers recalls, "Rita loved anyone who could make her laugh. And I had a compulsion to be clever all the time. She'd wait for me to come onto the set—this was very early in the morning—and I'd tell her the spiciest stories I knew. She loved it.

"During the 'Make Way for Tomorrow' number in *Cover Girl* I was very nervous. I was no dancer. I'd walk off, saying 'I can't do that!' Then I'd come back, full of apologies, and do something to make them laugh. During one run-through with Rita, Gene, and me, Gene Kelly said to me, 'I wonder what she sees in Orson?' 'Gene,' I answered, 'I think he's doing to her what he did to Hearst.'

"Rita needed love so badly—she didn't believe her publicity. To give you an idea, there was this other time when I told her, 'Get me a glass of water.' The way I said it I thought it would get a big laugh—but she got me a glass of water! She was the most decent person I knew. She never knew she was 'Rita Hayworth.'"

For the actors it was a very happy set—they got on wonderfully together and Rita was in a wonderful frame of mind.

Unfortunately, there were new problems at home. Her brothers had been drafted and sent overseas. This was on her mind, and even more so on her mother's.

Volga was not feeling well, and Rita was worried about her. Constantly in a state of concern about her sons, Volga tried to keep busy. She saw Rita frequently but was more nervous than ever and began staying at home, even remaining in bed. Perhaps it was an early change of life, although Volga was only forty-three. Menopause in those days was often undiagnosed, untreated, and kept in the closet; the suffering person sometimes went mad. The bottle was a frequent companion for Rita's mother during this difficult time.

Eduardo was doing his part for the war effort by working days in an airplane factory, and he continued to teach dance in the evenings. But his business was no longer on a scale which could distract Volga, as it used to, from her own problems.

As far as Rita's love life was concerned, Rita followed no one's counsel but her own. She was fiercely independent on this subject, and even her mother didn't interfere. According to the press Victor Mature was still very much in the picture, but Rita's "inner circle" knew the truth. Rita was in love with Orson.

"This is where *life* began for her," Phil Silvers says. "Orson was the first man that showed her womanly attention—what being a woman was all about. She had been so sheltered—her strict family, married to her business manager—but there was a smoldering fire there that nobody knew about. Welles was a marvelous man, a genius. He took Rita and taught her the function of a man and a woman, and then there was no stopping her after that."

Fan magazines, a very powerful force in the forties, portrayed Rita as torn between Victor Mature and Orson Welles. Example:

> Orson started to drop up to Rita's house with some
> of the newest formulas for amateur magic. Then, in the

weeks that followed, Orson and Rita began to be spotted in the quietest corners of the least populated cafes.

Of course, someone told Vic—wrote him—about Orson and Rita and the quiet little cafes.

When Vic was in New York on leave, there was not enough time for Rita to fly back and see him. She was working. So the lovers talked on the telephone.

"He wouldn't let me explain anything," Rita wept. "He wouldn't listen. If we could have been together for just a little while, everything would have been different. I love Vic, and he is the only man in my life, even if he is as stubborn as a mule. But it is no good trying to solve anything over the telephone.

"If I could only tell him how very lonely it has been, I know he would understand. I know in my heart, no matter what he says while he is angry, that we are not through. Not really. We are just waiting."

In such a fashion did publicity of the day provide a sympathetic framework to explain the sometimes sudden changes of fancy which affected the gods and goddesses of Tinseltown. It was a remarkably effective smokescreen, because it went a long way toward explaining the unexplainable to the public, of meshing the private lives of the stars with the professional images of them the studios had created and marketed.

The sad part of this sham was that no effort was made within the confines of the studios to help the participants in these personal dramas to understand why they were doing certain things— and perhaps help them to avoid many avoidable mistakes.

People in Hollywood scoffed at the alliance of Hayworth and Welles. After all, Lana Turner's marriage to the "intellectual" Artie Shaw had been a short-lived and acrimonious disaster. What on earth did this "Beauty and the Brain" couple have in common?

Many years later Rita was asked, "Weren't you overwhelmed by Orson Welles?" She looked the interviewer straight in the eye and answered, "*He* was overwhelmed by *me!*"

Obviously they overwhelmed each other during the courtship. Orson's many interests impressed and fascinated Rita. He let her be herself. There was no "wear this, wear that, do this, do that." He was a dazzling fountain of ideas. A three-ring circus performing just for her. She had never met anyone like him before. He not only had an exuberant joie de vivre of his own but he brought out the same quality in her.

Orson, a monumental extrovert even by Hollywood standards, was always surrounded by college professors, artists, political activists, columnists, writers. Rita sometimes felt uneasy. She once said to Lenore Cotten, "All those people are staring at me because they think I'm a dumb woman."

"They're staring all right, darling, but it's not because you're dumb," Mrs. Cotten explained.

Reports are that during these years Rita and Orson drank moderately, "though Orson would go on occasional binges to celebrate a film or a radio wrap."

As one of his associates recalls, "He would fill up a tumbler with scotch, and drink it like water."

People sometimes thought Rita was drunk when in fact she wasn't. She would often have a vacant look on her face, but as one of her friends conjectures, "The vacantness in the early days was neither alcohol nor any disease. It was just her method of coping. She knew she couldn't compete on an intellectual level, so she just clammed up."

Work on *Cover Girl* continued. The director, Charles Vidor, was now married to Evelyn Keyes but developed a real crush on Hayworth. She was totally unaware of the extent of his interest, but Vidor seethed whenever Welles came to the set and often took his wrath out on whatever actor was unfortunate enough to be in his line of fire.

Never would he explode at one of the principals, however—they might raise hell about it to Cohn. On one occasion when Vidor reprimanded a player in a nasty fashion, Rita left the set and refused to return. "When he stops that, and apologizes, I'll come back." Rita never stayed angry for long—not now. During this period filmmaking was not a chore.

With Kelly and Silvers on the set, and Orson in her life, Rita was experiencing the happiest moments she had known. But Harry Cohn wasn't pleased. In his opinion, Rita couldn't have chosen a suitor who could have had a more destructive influence on her career. Welles had infuriated the most powerful private citizen in the United States—William Randolph Hearst—with *Citizen Kane,* and the Hearst press was out to destroy him.

Hearst's powerful Hollywood columnist was Louella Parsons, the woman who had advised Winfield Sheehan not to sign Rita. Ironically, Louella was now Rita's staunchest fan among the press, and Louella was aghast. How could sweet Rita be involved with the scheming monster who had created *Citizen Kane?* Even Victor Mature was a better choice than Orson Welles! Louella sternly advised Rita, in print, that she was pursuing a dangerous course. Louella didn't want to see Rita hurt. "Use your head, Rita," she advised, "not your heart."

On the morning of September 7, 1943, Orson Welles was playing the piano at the home of Jackson and Lola Leighter. Many people don't realize Welles is an accomplished pianist. Rubinstein once told the Leighters that Orson could have been the greatest pianist since Horowitz. However, Welles did not play for the public but for himself, and that morning it appeared to Leighter that while Orson was playing he was meditating on a decision he and Rita had made.

He played all morning. Finally, he played an arpeggio, looked up, and said, "Let's go." Leighter was ready. "We headed for the studio at noon to pick up Rita."

Rita was taking no chances on having Harry Cohn louse things up. She had reported to work on *Cover Girl* in the morning, as usual. No one on the lot was aware of anything about to take place. As lunchtime approached, she walked into a friendly executive's office and announced, "I'm going to marry Orson Welles."

She quickly changed clothes and washed her face, but traces of the heavy pancake makeup she wore for the cameras still clung to her skin. She briskly hopped into the waiting automobile, and the trio began their drive to Santa Monica. "Let's get Joe," Orson said. So they drove to Pacific Palisades to pick up Joseph Cotten. Ironically, they arrived as Lenore Cotten was storming out of the house, threatening to file for divorce. (The Cottens didn't divorce.)

Orson and Rita were married by Judge Orlando H. Rhodes,

with Cotten and Leighter as witnesses. Welles had trouble removing the ring from its box, and was so nervous he couldn't seem to slip it on Rita's finger. "Hold her finger with your other hand," the judge suggested.

Welles followed Rhodes's advice. Rita began to weep. Welles kissed her several times—photographers had arrived and were begging for additional shots.

"Orson, you've got lipstick all over your face," noted Joseph Cotten. Welles wiped it off.

Then Orson and Rita took the elevator down to the street, where Rita told one and all, "I've gotta get back to work!"

"Will you take a honeymoon?" reporters asked.

"Are you kidding?" answered Welles.

All accounts of the Welles-Hayworth wedding mentioned that Rita had been expected to marry Victor Mature.

Rita's mother, reached at home, said the marriage was news to her. "Goodness," she said. "I wish she had let me know. I was supposed to have dinner with her tonight."

After completing the rest of the day's shooting at Columbia, Rita appeared with Orson in his magic show that evening.

Victor Mature, still with the Coast Guard but on a bond-selling tour in Chicago, was bowled over. "I was shocked, surprised, and grieved when I heard Rita and Welles were married. You know, when I went away, she and I had sort of an understanding," Mature said.

Harry Cohn was also grieved. But once the shock wore off, Cohn was relieved to find that Welles, totally caught up in his own career, seemed uninterested in becoming involved with Rita's. Rita's films were hardly Welles's type of projects. While she was finishing *Cover Girl,* he completed *Jane Eyre.* There was some behind-the-scenes question concerning whether he would receive coproducer credit (he didn't). Everything he did after *Citizen Kane,* no matter how dazzling or brilliant, seemed pale by comparison.

But for Rita the best was yet to come. *Cover Girl* was a milestone on many levels. The woman who coauthored the script, Virginia Van Upp, became one of Rita's few female friends, and an essential creative element in Rita's upcoming films.

Van Upp and Cohn had known each other for years. She had been a child actress at Universal, then eventually became a screenwriter at Paramount. She had worked on films for Carole Lombard, Madeleine Carroll, Ray Milland, and Fred MacMurray. When she moved over to Columbia, she knew of Harry Cohn's reputation and she knew how to handle him. She wasn't afraid to talk back to him, and she did it without sacrificing her femininity. In addition, she parried his constant sexual overtures with good humor and without hurting his ego.

Van Upp was one of the few who could serve as a liaison between Rita and Harry Cohn, although the woman's loyalty seemed to be with Cohn, whom she found to be a very dynamic man.

Cohn now sometimes referred to Hayworth as "my Rita"—a term of endearment connoting total ownership.

The mighty Darryl F. Zanuck's efforts to borrow Hayworth for the starring role in *Laura* met with a flat no. "She'll do one picture a year," was Cohn's dictum. Her films were to be meticulously and flawlessly produced, each to be an eagerly awaited and carefully planned event.

Rita had come a long way since 1937. But even now, Cohn didn't do anything to make her feel like a star. Her salary was still below what she would have been earning at a rival studio, and Cohn made no effort to renegotiate. At M-G-M when a player clicked, L. B. Mayer would often voluntarily tear up the contract and negotiate a new one that gave the player an increase in salary and the perquisites usually granted to a star. But Cohn was Cohn, and he treated Rita as though she existed in a vacuum.

Cohn's eccentricities are legendary. In the makeup and hairdressing departments at Columbia, actors and actresses were "clocked"—how many minutes they spent having coffee, or going to the bathroom, were noted—so that every second they were on the lot could be accounted for.

While Cohn dealt in million-dollar productions, he always created scenes over what, to other moguls, was only petty cash. George Hurrell was called on the carpet for renting negligees for Rita to wear for a layout that would appear in *Esquire* magazine.

"I can't see spending thirty bucks when we're loaded with perfectly photographable gowns right here," Cohn barked at Hurrell. "If I were you, I'd use our own wardrobe. Savvy?"

"Cohn wouldn't spring for thirty bucks so his top star would look her best," says a former Columbia employee. "That'll give you some idea of what it was like there."

Harry Cohn might have saved himself a good deal of grief if he had shown Rita Hayworth that he appreciated her, rather than allowing his gargantuan ego to dictate his actions. But for the present things were peaceful. Rita was happily married, and work went smoothly. Even workers at the studio had an easy camaraderie with her, almost *too* familiar. She wasn't treated with the kind of fawning obeisance she would have received elsewhere, but then again she did not have the kind of personality or ego that flourish with that kind of treatment. She was most comfortable in a relaxed, family-style atmosphere.

Rita's happiness was rudely interrupted when Ed Judson put her in the headlines by slapping her with a lawsuit claiming she had reneged on their secret settlement. She was supposed to have paid him $12,000 in cash, over a period of two years, in $500 monthly installments. He claimed she had ceased after two payments, and he wanted the remainder of the cash.

"In her answer, Miss Hayworth, now the wife of Orson Welles, admitted signing the property settlement but said she did so only under threat," reported the Associated Press.

Scandal seemed about to break, but it was squelched. Rita's lawyers settled with Judson. Terms of the settlement were never disclosed, but attorneys for both sides described them as "satisfactory."

After this point, Judson virtually disappeared from Rita's life. Forevermore he would be identified as Rita Hayworth's first husband, usually misidentified as an oil man.

His importance in Rita's life cannot be underestimated. Without Ed Judson, there would have been no "Rita Hayworth," despite declarations that she "would have made it anyway." Considering her personality, she could not have made it without someone *like* Ed Judson. His drive and flair and determination to make it happen for her at *any* cost had paved the way. No career as important as Rita's can *ever* exist without a character like Ed Judson feverishly manipulating and hustling behind the scenes.

Judson never lost interest in Rita. Over the next years he would often call Helen Hunt, at home, usually after eleven at night, and say, "I just saw Rita's new picture. How is she? Tell her that I still love her and think of her all the time . . ."

FIVE

At first Rita's life with Orson provided her with the carefree adolescence she never had. Both Rita and Orson loved Mexico and they'd often make impromptu trips there. On one occasion when Welles wanted cash to zip down south of the border, Jackson Leighter drew fifteen hundred dollars from Mercury funds and gave it to him. Rita came in a few hours later and Leighter advanced her another five hundred. Two days later they called him in the middle of the night for more money and he wired it to them. They had started nightclubbing at a hotel in Acapulco, took the musicians all off to another, and led a caravan of taxis and musicians to the Majestic, where they all had one big party. Orson Welles always partied in elaborate fashion.

Orson was very protective of Rita because he knew she was totally unprepared for his kind of life. He tried shielding her from any embarrassment. In fact, during the early days of their marriage he was very attentive. He tried to settle down and take his place in the Hollywood community. He realized that Rita was not on his intellectual level and he did not try to mold or change her, despite myths to the contrary.

"He was actually very creative during his marriage to her," says a close friend. They had a pool house along with the house they rented in Westwood, and he made it his digs. Often, after they'd made love, she'd go to sleep, since she still had early morning calls at the studio, and Welles would go down to the pool house, where he'd paint or write. Much later on, he did see other women—but he was always careful not to hurt or embarrass Rita.

Rita and Orson were in love and were happy. But Welles's awesome creative energies were not getting proper expression. He wasn't receiving offers to make the kind of films he wanted to make. Many years later he would admit that he should have returned to the east and stayed in the theater after his artistic triumph with *Citizen Kane*. Hollywood did not nurture Welles's immense talent, it stifled it.

He was trapped. "A genius in the Hollywood dictionary is somebody who is dead or unavailable," he observed. "The only men in the movies honestly deserving of the title 'genius' are Charles Chaplin and D. W. Griffith."

Welles turned his attention to politics. Roosevelt was running for a fourth term, and Welles, one of his most active supporters, headed up the "Hollywood for Roosevelt" campaign. Welles even contemplated running for Congress himself.

Rita's career climbed yet another notch with the release of *Cover Girl* in March 1944. "Too Thrilling for Words . . . So they set it to Music, Romance, Dance and Song!" ran a key line in the ad campaign. A gorgeous shot of a sexy, long-legged Rita in an evening gown was the major visual utilized—there was no doubt who the key lure for the public in this production was. The models who were brought from New York to appear in the film, Rita's "competition," were mentioned in tiny type at the bottom of the ads: "See 15 of the world's most beautiful women!"

The Welleses went east for a breather—"the honeymoon we never had," said Rita—but in Manhattan the couple could hardly leave the hotel or go to the theater. The crowds descending on Rita were terrifying, and on more than one occasion the actress was in fear of her life.

There was a flurry of bad publicity when Rita's brother Vernon went AWOL.

Vernon and Eddie Junior had a difficult time of it in the service —their sister was the leading sex object in the country, and the boys took a lot of ribbing and baiting. It wasn't easy for two men who had been raised in the Latin tradition to hear remarks about their sister, who was a *lady*. Rita Hayworth may have been referred to in the army barracks as many things, but *lady* wasn't the description usually applied.

The pressures both the Cansino brothers endured during the war changed their personalities. When Vernon went AWOL, he came to New York to see Rita and Welles.

Rita was concerned for the welfare of both her brothers. Although she would never talk about her family to the press, her feelings about them ran deep. Both Vernon and Eddie had listed Rita as their next of kin. Because of Volga's precarious health, they did not want their mother notified first if something happened to them during the war.

The AWOL incident was soon smoothed over, and Rita and Orson happily returned to Hollywood. She had good reason to be beaming, and *Cover Girl* was only part of the story.

"Jesus Christ, she's pregnant!" Harry Cohn was red in the face from rage. This was a possibility even he had not let himself consider. The news came to him from the wardrobe department when Rita was being fitted for her gowns for *Tonight and Every Night*.

Rita was elated. She eagerly looked forward to the event--and to bringing "Orsie" closer to her through shared parenthood.

There was a studio-sponsored baby shower, hosted by Evelyn Keyes, who was so impressed with Rita's radiance that she later said she wanted to become pregnant herself.

Filming on *Tonight and Every Night* proceeded smoothly. The elaborate Technicolor production told a contemporary backstage story set in wartime London (via the Columbia back lot, of course), with Rita portraying a performer. Janet Blair and Lee Bowman costarred. The picture took long hours and many weeks to film, and Rita made two important new friends, who were working with her for the first time: designer Jean Louis and choreographer Jack Cole. Hayworth worked hard, as usual, but she had reason to pace herself and avoid run-ins with Cohn. The film required complicated dance routines—nonetheless, she did them.

On December 17, 1944, Rita gave birth, by caesarian section, to a healthy baby, a daughter, Rebecca. Helen Hunt recalls getting a frantic telephone call from Rita, who was at the hospital, only a day or so later. "These people want to comb my hair and I won't let them touch me!" Hayworth wailed.

Helen went out to the hospital. "She must have had a difficult time of it, because her hair was all matted and tangled. When Rita got home from the hospital a few days later," Helen continues, "she again called me, and I went out to the house." When Helen arrived she found Orson "holding court" with at least half a dozen people. She went directly into Rita's bedroom. Rita seemed very upset, and asked Helen what she knew about birth control. Rita even showed Helen her diaphragm, and wondered if it was the most effective method. Although she was thrilled with "Becky," she didn't want any more children right away.

Their intimate talk was abruptly interrupted when the bedroom door suddenly opened and Welles stuck his head in. "Don't stay in there all alone! Come out and be with us."

He set up a chaise in the living room, and Rita was propped up there while Helen combed out her hair. There were two female secretaries present. Welles was dictating a script to one, and something about his finances to the other.

"There was a man following him around the room talking about yet another project," recalls Helen, "and another man sitting at a table playing cards. Orson would join him every few minutes to play his hand, then bound up and pace around, continuing his dictating. I guess he wanted to impress us with that brain that could focus on so many things at once. But Rita, as always, seemed unimpressed."

"But she *was* happy," says another friend from this period. Rita doted on Orson, even after a year and a half of marriage—however, Orson did not enjoy being doted on. "But when Rita was in love," notes the same friend, "that person was the world to her."

Rita was persistent in her efforts to get Orson to change—to be the kind of stay-at-home husband she wanted her husband to be, unrealistic as that desire may have been. There were ten million men who would have been willing to accommodate her—but Orson Welles was not one of them.

Welles loved the baby, but if Rita had hoped Rebecca would keep Orson home more often, or would in any way alter his lifestyle, she was mistaken. In the words of a former associate, "He viewed Rebecca as an exquisite toy, but his thoughts were always on some project or other."

At Christmas the Cansinos joined the Welleses for a family gathering. Then, after the New Year, Orson left for the East. Roosevelt had been elected to his fourth term and Welles was going to be a guest at the inauguration. Orson had also been signed to write a syndicated column: "Orson Welles' Almanac." He was *way* ahead of his time, advocating that actors should participate in politics.

"Some may ask why a ham actor should be posing as an authority on world affairs. That isn't the important thing. The important thing is that you make people *think*. What does it matter about me personally? . . .

"I don't have the answers to the world's problems and I'm not founding a new religious cult. But I do believe that if I can stir the people to debate and think about our problems, we'll find a way out."

As the new year began, Rita was closer than ever to her mother. The two saw each other frequently, and Volga adored Rebecca.

Then, on a January day in 1945 that Rita would never forget, she received an almost unbearable shock. Her mother, only forty-five, was dead. Volga had been ill only briefly, suffering severe abdominal pains. But there had been so many illnesses over the last few years that this time the cause was diagnosed too late—a burst appendix.

Welles was away. "I called Rita on the phone when I heard about her mother," he said, "and she told me not to come home. I supposed she meant it. I couldn't have got there in time for the funeral, anyway. Well, I daresay that's another instance in which a woman said the opposite of what she meant."

Although Welles was not at Volga Haworth Cansino's funeral, the Cansino family was there in force. Several of Rita's friends from the studio, including Helen Hunt, also attended. Eduardo was devastated. For a while, father and daughter were inconsolable. For many months Rita would begin to weep piteously if someone even mentioned her mother's name. The release of *Tonight and Every Night,* in March, wasn't of much interest to her.

Some say things were never the same between Rita and Orson after this—she was pained that he hadn't rushed to her when her mother died. Although she intellectually understood her husband's actions, Rita, with her Spanish-Irish upbringing and concepts of loyalty and family solidarity, could not forget that he hadn't come through for her when she needed him most.

"When I got back I could tell she was hurt," Welles said. "It was probably a mistake on my part. But the war was on and women all over the world were alone facing their problems and tragedies. After all, I couldn't have brought her mother back. I still don't think it was so terrible of me not to give up what I was doing, because that was very important to me, too."

Welles was back to leading the peripatetic life ingrained in his character, while Rita, ironically, was talking about retiring.

"I'm not going to spend the rest of *my* life on a sound stage!" she declared. And she wasn't speaking without having given the matter a lot of thought. Her discontent was long-standing. She was going on twenty-seven, and she had been working professionally, nonstop, for twenty years. She was weary of the whole trip.

Welles was juggling a dozen projects at once, and it was not in his nature to settle down to home and family.

It had been two years. As Rita and Orson had come together, they now drifted apart.

Some claim that Orson later said that Rita had grown cold in bed. Others assert that their romance "just ran its course." There was no bitterness, no animosity, and the split was very gradual as Orson drifted in and out of Hollywood.

Welles himself has said, "As a lover, I'm the proverbial heel. Women all get tired of me sooner or later. I woo and make love with all the originality and enthusiasm I can muster up and everything goes fine. But women puzzle and frighten me. They always want to go on romancing when love has been won and all questions settled."

Jackson Leighter gives an enlightening insight into Welles's character. "First of all, he *was* a great talent. And you must realize that Orson doesn't think of himself as of this world. Therefore he has no obligation to society. His talent is contribution enough." But Leighter adds, "Orson is a gentleman. *That* is manifest in his character. He would never knowingly or purposely hurt anyone."

People became aware of discord in the Welleses' marriage. The Mocambo was the scene of one incident involving Rita, Orson, and Victor Mature. According to observers, Rita and Orson, entering the nightspot, "ran into" Mature, who was back in civilian garb. Florabel Muir described the encounter: "Rita attempted to introduce the two men, but Welles stalked off, barely acknowledging the introduction, leaving Rita hanging on Vic's words and looking somewhat confused.

"After she joined her husband at their table, there were heated words, and suddenly Rita got up and left. Welles then strode over to Mature's table. Vic, who compares well with Orson in size but has some muscles to back up his weight, got to his feet. Welles changed his mind, turned quickly, and followed Rita out of the cafe."

Miss Muir went on to note, "Mature was quoted later as saying that he still was carrying the torch for Rita, and didn't see how she could live with a big lug like that."

The words "a big lug" were Miss Muir's necessary whitewashing of Mature's description of Welles.

Rumors began flying. Was it true that Welles was seeing another woman? "I've heard gossip of a redheaded girl named Linda Ware," replied the actor-producer-director-writer. "Ridiculous. I met Linda only once and she was with her mother. I have no interest in any woman but my wife. If my marriage with Rita goes on the rocks, I'll tell you one thing. My next wife, if any, will have other interests besides love to keep her absorbed so that she will have neither time nor inclination to worry about me."

His feelings about Rita were remarkably candid and revealing of both him *and* her. "Rita is a beautiful girl, a lovely wife, a perfect mother. When we are together we have wonderful times and she's happy. But I have varied interests and I can't do anything about it.

"I could tell her that I'm going to change my ways. That I'll be home every night at a certain hour. I would try conscientiously to live up to my promises, and I might succeed for several months. But I would be acting. . . .

"A man gets tired of acting. A man can't change himself. I told

Rita before we were married exactly the things she would have to contend with in me. She couldn't possibly have been surprised. But I suppose that, like every other girl, she thought she could change me."

Welles wasn't interested in changing Rita. "I love Rita just as she is! I married her because I loved her and I don't want to change her even a little bit."

And he minced no words on how deep his feelings went. "I've loved her from the time I met her. I want to stay married. I pin my hopes—slender ones—on time. I've begged her to go slow and try to hold things together."

By the fall, although still legally married, Rita was psychologically and emotionally on the loose. The year 1945 was a historic one. Roosevelt died in April. In May, victory in Europe. In September, victory in the Pacific. In Hollywood it was business as usual. Columbia was planning a new film for Rita, and since Orson wasn't interested in staying home, there was nothing for Rita to do but go back to work.

The new production at Columbia utilized the studio's best talent. It was a true community effort but had one glaring problem: an unfinished script. As originally conceived, the picture was a straight drama—no musical numbers. It would be filmed in black and white, a relief for Rita—the lights necessary for Technicolor were unbearably hot. Rudy Maté—whose association with Rita went all the way back to *Dante's Inferno*—would be director of photography, as he had been on *Cover Girl* and *Tonight and Every Night*.

Virginia Van Upp was producing, and some say she was also coauthoring the script. Glenn Ford, whom Rita hadn't worked with since *The Lady in Question* five years earlier, was back from the navy and was cast as Rita's leading man.

Charles Vidor was directing, and Jean Louis designing the clothes. The name of the film: *Gilda*. It was a return for Rita to the pure femme fatale image which had rocketed her to stardom. This "heroine" was no *Cover Girl* or *Tonight and Every Night* girl next door—although by final fadeout, Gilda would of course be proven a "good" girl!

The story was complex—part espionage yarn, part romantic

drama—the concept was quintessential film noir (a term just then coming in to use), with peculiar overtones and undertones. It certainly was an adult love story for the day—for any day.

Critics and film historians would read implications into *Gilda* that the film's creators, in their wildest dreams, never envisioned—most notably, a homosexual undercurrent between Ford's character and Gilda's husband's character.

Ford, today, says he knows of these interpretations, "But it never occurred to us at the time we were filming."

The story called for its stars to act out a heated sadomasochistic love affair. Director Vidor knew just how to create the proper climate and coax the right performances from his stars.

Sometimes, after Vidor had explained, in the most graphic terms, what the lovers should each be thinking, he would say to Rita and Glenn, "Loosen up, children." If he didn't get the performance he wanted from Rita by the third take, he was in trouble. Rita was an emotional actress, as opposed to a technical one. For a role like Gilda she had to call on her innermost emotions.

The script was being written day by day. No one was sure how the picture would turn out—or if the story would make any sense once it was all cut together.

"In one scene I had to smack Rita," Ford remembers. He felt squeamish about doing it, but was convinced by Vidor and Rita to just "let himself go."

Rita told him, "Just do it right the first time. Hit me. Don't fake it."

So Ford hit her and she was stunned. A couple of weeks later, a scene called for Rita to smack Ford across the face four consecutive times.

"Go all out," said Ford.

Rita looked at him and said, "I might."

She smacked him—one, two, he felt something crack—three, four, he felt another crack. "Cut!" said Vidor. What a great take! What acting, everyone thought. Only Ford knew what had happened. Blood began trickling out of the corners of his mouth. Rita had knocked out two of his teeth.

When Ford recounts the incident, he adds, "The picture was about hate being as exciting an emotion as love."

By all accounts, the filmmakers really weren't sure what they were doing, so it was decided to add two musical numbers for Rita. These would not only make story points but would also satisfy fans of her musicals.

One sequence was a simple scene of her as a nightclub performer, looking gorgeous in a bare-midriffed sequined evening gown, singing the Latin-tempoed "Amado Mio." But the second number proved to be something special. "Put the Blame on Mame" was written (by Doris Fisher and Allan Roberts) *after* the film was well into production.

Over Rita's objections, her voice was dubbed (by Anita Ellis). Rita never sang in any of her films, although some claim she did the brief reprise, in this film, of "Put the Blame on Mame." But her *performance* of the song made movie history. The number, brilliantly conceived and choreographed by the great Jack Cole; the way Rita looked in the black satin strapless gown (which started a fashion trend that has never gone out of style); her peeling off of one long, black satin glove and tossing it to the howling nightclub audience witnessing her "soul-baring"; and of course her fantastic, long, wild, flowing hairdo—all became images of unforgettable visual impact.

Rita's hair, which had been her trademark, would receive even more attention with this film than it had before. Helen Hunt reveals, *"I* got fan mail—and hate mail—about Rita's hair! Some clergymen declared that I would go to hell for contributing to evil because of Rita's hair in *Gilda!*

"Rita acted with her hair," Helen observes. "I would be on the set and hear the director say, 'You're angry now. Toss your hair back.' Or 'You're happy in this scene. Use your hair.'"

The spectacular *Gilda* hairdo was achieved without fuss each morning in Columbia's hairdressing department. First Helen Hunt would wash and set Rita's hair. Then two assistants—each holding a portable blow-dryer—would stand on each side of Rita, drying her hair, as Helen simultaneously brushed it out and styled it. Since time was money in Cohn's studio, all of this was done in twenty—maximum thirty—minutes.

"Rita never even looked in the mirror," relates Helen. "You'd think she'd stare at herself, like the other stars did. She'd never even look at her hair when I was through."

Sometimes a frustrated Helen would ask Rita, "Look at your hair, isn't it beautiful?" Rita would look in the mirror briefly. "Oh, yes. Thanks, Helen."

Rita would just stare out the window or look at her nails while Helen worked on her hair. She seemed to be in deep thought or meditation. "She certainly didn't study her script, as the others did," remembers Helen.

From the start of shooting *Gilda* it was obvious that there was a special chemistry between Hayworth and Ford. In discussing Rita today, Ford is very, very solicitous of her. "Yes, indeed I know Rita and would have kind and good things to say about her . . ."

In recent years, a top publisher spoke with Ford regarding an autobiography. Ford told him that of course he had had a romance with Rita—they were wildly in love during the filming of *Gilda*—but that he wouldn't put any of that into the book. When Ford also stated that he would not discuss his first wife, dancing star Eleanor Powell, the publisher was no longer interested.

Ford has, however, revealed a great deal about his relationship with Rita at the time *Gilda* was being filmed. While today he will not confirm their physical affair, he does admit, "There was an electricity on the set and it was translated to the screen."

The more heat the screen lovers could generate on cue, the more commercial the finished product would be. The authenticity of the heat between Hayworth and Ford was the talk of the lot. They became close friends and a relationship continued for over thirty-five years.

Harry Cohn continued with his abrasive tactics. Since rumors of the blazing love affair between Rita and Ford had raced through the lot and soon began filling fan magazines and gossip columns, Cohn had had their dressing rooms bugged. After a long day's shooting, while Rita and Glenn were having a quiet drink, the mogul would barrage the duo with angry phone calls and demand that Hayworth go home.

Ford says today, "Of course, we knew our dressing rooms were bugged. The sound department had tipped us off." He also notes that everything people said about Harry Cohn was true—"but the opposite was also true."

By the time *Gilda* was finished filming, Rita had announced a separation from Orson. He was in New York and flew back to Hollywood, but did not get to see her.

"In the event of a divorce, I shall expect to support our child and have custody of her six months of the year, just as is the case with my other daughter," said Welles. He said *he* didn't want a divorce. "But, frankly, I don't think there's much chance Rita will change her mind."

On December 31, 1945, Rita attended producer Sam Spiegel's annual New Year's Eve party. Tony Martin was also at the party. Martin was back in Hollywood after a stint in the service and a good deal of bad publicity because he had tried to stay out of the army.

According to Martin, he was sitting at the bar in Spiegel's house —in borrowed clothes, since he was short of cash—and periodically a friend or two would stop and chat for a minute, welcoming him back to town, wishing him luck. Then Rita came by and said, "Hi, Tony—how are you?" They hadn't seen each other since they'd made *Music in My Heart* back in 1940. In true Hollywood fashion, during the ensuing time her star had risen while his had declined.

Martin asked Rita to dance, and while they were dancing, agent Vic Orsatti came over and tapped Rita on the shoulder. "Whenever you're ready to leave, just call me," said Orsatti, obviously her date for the evening. Rita surprised both men with "Oh, Tony's taking me home."

Martin was there without a car. But ever resourceful, he scouted around and spotted his pal Sid Luft. "Sid, I'm in a jam. I've got to drive Rita Hayworth home and I haven't got wheels."

"Here—take my heap," said Luft. "Lynn and I came in separate cars. I'll catch a ride home with her." Luft, later married to Judy Garland, was then married to actress Lynn Bari. Luft's "heap" turned out to be a late-model Cadillac.

Making the opening move on Martin seems a contradiction of the demure, ladylike image all Rita's friends paint of her. But it was New Year's Eve. Rita had had a few drinks, which allowed her to drop her usual barrier of reserve.

Martin later said that when they met in 1940 neither he nor Rita was available for a relationship. She was married to Judson, he to Alice Faye. But now they were both free.

Martin telephoned Rita the next morning but was surprised to learn that she'd left for Palm Springs. But the next day Rita was back in town and called Tony. A whirlwind affair ensued. Martin began working again and had money to spend. He bought Rita jewels and even a mink coat. They were seen at nightclubs and at the races. A few weeks later the affair ended as quickly as it had begun.

Tony was to pick Rita up for the races and a weekend at Del Mar, the seaside resort eighty miles south of Hollywood. But he received a quick and curt call. "I'm sorry, Tony, but Orson and I are getting back together."

Martin subsequently asked Rita for the fur coat. Rita, who was not materialistic, was never impressed by gifts. She gave back the mink.

Gilda was such a hit that even Columbia executives were surprised. It was released in March 1946 and its power at the box office was immediate. Like most of Rita's other pictures, it played Radio City Music Hall—a comment on Rita's prestige, since the story line was hardly family fare.

Gilda was, in its way, a milestone film. A sensation because it was a star vehicle that struck a chord with men *and* women by presenting a woman who typified the ideal: the girl every man wanted to possess and every woman wanted to look like.

Women, in fact, liked, responded to, empathized with Rita Hayworth—they have always made up a huge portion of her audience. Even in her femme fatale roles Rita's vulnerability came through. Her likability and vulnerability are essential factors in her appeal. They go far toward explaining the longevity of her career and her enormous and loyal following.

The *Gilda* ad campaign touched all bases. It perpetrated the myth that Rita was a singer: "Great as is her powerful dramatic portrayal . . . Great, too, is this dancing Hayworth—singing 'Put the Blame on Mame.'"

It offered the dramatic Rita, slapping Ford across the face: "I was true to one man once, and look what happened."

It offered the romantic Rita, in a clinch with Ford: "I didn't think I'd be true to a man again as long as I lived."

"There *never* was a woman like *Gilda*," screamed the key ad line, as a full-figure photograph of a devastatingly beautiful Hayworth gazed languidly at the reader (Glenn Ford was billed *below* the film's title). And the ad line was true—there never was a woman like Gilda, because Gilda was an invented character, a fictional person, portrayed by a woman who was in real life nothing like her.

But Rita and Gilda were synonymous not only in the public mind—she would be Gilda to important men soon to appear in her life. She had ascended the uppermost rung of the ladder of success, and people expected her to *be* her screen persona. It was a dilemma few, if any, performers would ever be prepared to cope with.

Welles was back in New York, working with Mike Todd on a Broadway extravaganza, *Around the World in 80 Days*. They were spending money prodigiously. Welles was always in need of money. Against Jackson Leighter's advice, he had sold the Mercury Theatre films to RKO. Among them was all the footage from the South American trip (*It's All True*). It has never been released. Leighter claims that the footage disappeared during Howard Hughes's ownership of the studio but that some of the footage was used in the Brazilian film *Black Orpheus*.

Around the World in 80 Days was nowhere near ready to open, and Welles and Todd had spent every penny. They put out a call for funds.

Leighter, by then executive assistant to New York *Post* publisher Dorothy Schiff, convinced Mrs. Schiff to put $25,000 into the show. They still required more money, so Welles called Harry Cohn. "I need fifty thousand dollars, Harry."

Through the years there have been many versions of what happened next. One story goes that Cohn said no, until Welles offered to direct a picture in return for the money.

"You got a story?" asked Cohn.

"Yes," said Welles, glancing over at a paperback book a ward-robe woman was reading. *The Lady From Shanghai.*

Other versions of this tale are equally dramatic. According to Jackson Leighter, Cohn was mesmerized by a story constructed on the spot by Welles.

Others say no specific story or title was discussed. There are those who claim that Errol Flynn had given Welles a book to read which intrigued him, and which later became the basis for the film.

In any event, Cohn knew he wasn't risking much. The mogul, a gambler, said yes to Welles's plea for cash, and Welles agreed to direct a film for Columbia if the investment went kaput.

Production began on Rita's new picture, *Down to Earth,* in late March 1946. It was a fantasy-musical, based on Columbia's successful *Here Comes Mr. Jordan* of a few years back (in turn based on the play *Heaven Can Wait.* It would be made yet again, three decades later, by Warren Beatty.). Naturally, all the studio's top behind-the-scenes talent was assigned to the film. Alexander Hall was the director.

Rita played Terpsichore, goddess of song and dance, who comes down from Mount Olympus to join the mortal world when she learns that her legend is being turned into a ludicrous Broadway show by a couple of huckster producers.

Rita had been getting superb advice on her career from powerful William Morris agent Johnny Hyde, a physically small man who was every bit as clever and tough in negotiating a deal as any of the ruthless men who ran the studios. With the immediate and phenomenal success of *Gilda,* Hyde had demanded that his glamorous client be given a percentage of the enormous profits sure to come from her next films. Cohn had, after all, made such arrangements with many independent stars and directors who had worked for Columbia.

But when presented with Hyde's proposal, Cohn hit the roof. Rita would have been *nothing* without him and Columbia, he exclaimed. How dare she ask for such a deal! M-G-M didn't even give Gable a share of the profits. The answer was no, a flat no. She had a contract and she had better live up to it.

Rita, who in all the years she'd been working, had always been on time, always knew her lines, and never complained, now found herself on many days simply too "ill" to report to work. Other days she went to makeup and hairdressing, but then—"I'm going home, I'm not feeling well." This did not happen until she had filmed enough footage so that the production machinery could not be halted. Cohn *had* to proceed with the picture, the studio's investment was too great. It was obvious that production delays would make the already high budget on the Technicolor feature soar.

When Rita sent back the script of *Dead Reckoning,* demanding a rewrite, Cohn was livid. He had planned to costar her with Humphrey Bogart, in what was to be Bogart's first picture away from Warner Bros. Cohn considered Hayworth an ingrate. He was giving her the best scripts and the best production the studio could offer.

As the costs of *Down to Earth* passed the two-million-dollar mark (in 1946 dollars—equivalent to twenty million in 1983), Cohn knew he would have to capitulate. He finally agreed to Hyde's terms. Rita would make one more picture under her old contract, then Cohn would pay Rita's new corporation, Beckworth, 25 percent of the profits of her films, plus her yearly salary.

Meanwhile, *Around the World in 80 Days* had opened in New York, limped along for about ten weeks, and closed—a financial and critical disaster. "I made $375,000 disappear in smoke in that show," Welles mused. "That will be enough magic for a while, thank you."

Rita was finishing *Down to Earth.* Her costar was Larry Parks, who had just been catapulted to fame in *The Jolson Story.* Betty Garrett, Parks's widow, recalls, "Larry just adored Rita. She was the sweetest, most generous actress he'd ever worked with. She, Larry, and Marc Platt had a ball doing the film."

At this juncture Rita was the most talked-about, popular, and imitated movie star of the year. In July, her visage adorned the first atomic bomb tested after the end of World War II. This was page-one news, worldwide. The press reported, "When she got the news, that the famous bedroom picture of her taken for *Life* had been glued to the Bikini atomic bomb, Rita broke into tears of real gratitude."

She was in tears, all right, but it wasn't from gratitude. Rita revealed: "It was Harry Cohn's idea to put my picture on that bomb. I was under contract, and they threatened to put me on suspension if I put up a fuss. Harry was . . . the Gestapo at Columbia. I hate war. . . . That whole bomb thing made me sick to my stomach. My two brothers fought in the war; they were never the same when they came home."

(Her brothers, Vernon and Eduardo Junior, sometimes called Sonny, had a difficult time adjusting to postwar life. Although employees at Columbia remember that both wanted contracts at the studio, others, including Vernon himself, claimed that they were independent and did not want Rita's life, although Vernon did bit parts in two of Rita's films. Being related to a successful performer has always been a peculiar—and difficult—situation. People are usually interested in the relatives of a star only to learn more about—or to get closer to—or to get something from—the star. Sonny drove a taxi for a while, and Rita set Vernon up in a restaurant business.)

Orson came back to Hollywood to fulfill his commitment to Cohn at a time when the front office was in a predicament over Rita's next picture. It would be her last under her old contract, and Columbia stood to earn a fortune if it was a big hit. Beginning with the next film, Rita's corporation would receive 25 percent of the profits.

Any project involving Hayworth was Big Business. The Beckworth deal foreshadowed the great Redford and Fonda deals of the seventies and eighties—except that Hayworth didn't control her own professional destiny.

It has never actually been determined who decided that Rita and Orson would now work together. While Welles's talent was not in question on executive row, his commerciality was. He had never had a big movie box office hit. Rita had never made a flop. His films were heavy dramas. Hers were Technicolor musicals—except *Gilda*, of course.

Welles's new project was in the *Gilda* genre. *The Lady From*

Shanghai was a melodrama, with a femme fatale at its core—but, unlike *Gilda*, an unsympathetic and truly deadly one (Ida Lupino had been mentioned for the role).

Following *Down to Earth* with Rita in a drama seemed good commercial thinking. And Welles's film would be in black and white—that was sure to keep the budget within reason.

Furthermore, there was always the chance that Welles's genius would ferret out yet another facet of his wife's screen persona— one which would result in even more money pouring into the studio's coffers.

Not to be overlooked was the publicity angle. It was a natural: glamorous wife and genius husband reconcile, and collaborate on a film. The clinches would be for real. The egghead and the sex symbol would bring *both* their audiences into the theaters. And who would get the credit for this exciting (and potentially highly profitable) venture? Why, that innovator and master showman, Harry Cohn! The prestige connected with this package was the kind of soul food men like Harry Cohn lived for.

The project got the go-ahead, and the publicity department went to town. The newspapers said Welles and Rita were reconciled. Rita's version is somewhat different: "When I made *The Lady From Shanghai* we were separated but were still friends."

Although Welles had not been inactive in Hollywood—he had starred in *Tomorrow Is Forever* and *The Stranger,* which he also directed, for RKO—*Shanghai* marked his return to total creative control of a production. For the first time since *Citizen Kane,* Welles was producer-director-writer-star.

Helen Hunt had taken a vacation and driven to New York. Not a trivial trip in 1946. Almost immediately on her arrival in New York City she got a call from Harry Cohn.

"What are you doing there?"

"This is my vacation!"

"You get right back here. Every studio in town wants to take credit for her hair. And I know it's your hair. And we won't give anybody else a chance to say it isn't. You get back here tomorrow morning."

"But I drove my car here!"

"I'll ship it back. You get here as fast as you can."

Helen took the next plane and found herself at the studio the following morning administering the most publicized haircut since Samson's. "There were about sixteen photographers standing on chairs. Orson was there. I was instructed to cut Rita's hair. Then I bleached it platinum blonde. Harry Cohn had been opposed to the idea, but Orson had talked him into it."

The stories about Harry Cohn's rage after seeing Rita Hayworth's *Shanghai* haircut are apocryphal. Needless to say Welles and Hayworth did not proceed with such a drastic measure without the mogul's full, if grudging, approval.

Rita was delighted with Orsie's plans for dramatically changing her image. At last she'd have the opportunity to be a real actress. "He was trying something different with me," she said. And she respected—*needed*—that. Welles had assembled a stunning cast of character actors to support them, including former Mercury Theatre players Everett Sloane, Glenn Anders, and Ted De Corsia. And Welles was certainly the best actor that Rita had yet played opposite.

The cast and crew of *The Lady From Shanghai* zipped down to Acapulco for location shooting. Rita and Orson seemed to enjoy themselves aboard the *Zaca,* Errol Flynn's yacht, which was used in some of the scenes. Flynn and his then-wife, Nora Eddington, were there. Rita celebrated her twenty-eighth birthday aboard ship, surprised with a cake by her husband, Flynn, Nora, and the crew.

One night publicity man George Lait and Welles were having a few drinks and got into a discussion about how all women, including Rita, looked pretty ordinary in their off-moments.

"Not Rita," Lait said.

"Even Rita," Welles said.

They got a still photographer, startled Rita out of a sound sleep, and snapped her picture, the flashbulb shocking her awake. "See?" said Lait after the picture was developed. "*I* was right."

As the film progressed, problems with the script bogged down production. There was no doubt that Rita had total confidence in her husband's great talent, and she proceeded to deliver a subtle, provocative performance under his direction. On the set they were affectionate toward one another (she called him Papa and he called her Mama), but before long the film was over budget and behind schedule. Cohn's ire was aroused, but he permitted Welles to proceed unfettered.

Shooting continued at the studio and on location: San Francisco's Chinatown and Sausalito's waterfront. Cohn had ordered his tough production manager, Jack Fier, to take Orson in tow. There were constant battles. Welles put up a sign that read, "The only thing we have to fear is Fier himself." Fier retaliated with a sign of his own proclaiming the oft-quoted "All's Well That Ends Welles."

In *The Lady From Shanghai* Rita played the only death scene in her career. It occurs at the climax, when she's been shot and lies struggling on the ground, crying out "I don't want to die!"

Hedda Hopper was on the set the day the scene was filmed. "I was there the day Welles wiped up the floor with his wife," the columnist noted. "That, in my book, is certainly no way to keep a marriage going." She made no comment on Rita's truly fine acting.

In later years, when asked why she had caused so many production delays on *Shanghai*—"People say you were sick a lot, Miss Hayworth"—Rita snapped back, "*I* was never sick. Poor *Orsie* was the one who was sick—Harry Cohn made him sick."

As the year drew to a close, Orson, Rita, and many others had the pleasure of seeing Harry Cohn publicly humiliated. When Charles Vidor married wife number three, Doris Warner LeRoy of the Warner Bros. family, he wanted to join that studio. He tried to break his Columbia contract and sued Harry Cohn, charging that Cohn had verbally abused him.

The suit was a travesty. L. B. Mayer and the other Hollywood moguls deplored it and feared that the negative publicity would overflow onto *all* of them as Harry Cohn's way of conducting himself was exposed in fascinating detail.

The story was avidly covered by the press—it was a wonderful opportunity to hold Hollywood up to ridicule. Vidor lost the suit, but not before the judge observed that both Mr. Cohn *and* Mr. Vidor "inhabit a fictitious, fabulous, topsy-turvy, temperamental world that is peculiar to their way of life. Their standards are not my standards. Let them be judged by those people of decency who inhabit their world of fantasy and fiction."

The fantasy and fiction which made up the story of *The Lady From Shanghai* continued to cause its creator troubles.

When the first cut of *The Lady From Shanghai* was finally assembled, Cohn was not only angry but mystified; he couldn't make any sense of the story. Welles subsequently agreed to Cohn's suggestion that he consult with Virginia Van Upp about "fixing it up so the audience will know what the hell is going on." Some scenes were reshot and the film was reedited to a short eighty-one minutes.

Rita knew she and "Orsie" had collaborated on a movie which would one day enjoy the acclaim it deserved, and she was right, although that day was *many* years away.

In March 1947 Rita announced her official separation from Welles. "Well, what do you expect?" commented her stoic father. "I am personally very sorry. Welles is a fine man. But you can't leave a young girl like Rita alone, while you sit up all night working. You can't go to New York for three months and produce plays." By this time, Eduardo had remarried, and his relationship with Rita was somewhat distant.

Cohn was still mourning her hair. "Everybody knows that the most beautiful thing about Rita was her hair."

In postwar Europe there was a hunger for American films. *Gilda* had been a smash overseas, and there was enormous interest in America's leading siren.

Cohn agreed to send Rita on a European tour, a paid vacation, provided she ended the trip in London for the world premiere of *Down to Earth*. He was almost amiable when they met to discuss it. He even offered to send his assistant, Evelyn Lane, to accompany her. Hayworth accepted the offer. She needed a vacation. And they even laughed that the trip would allow time for her hair to grow back.

She had told friends, "I just want to roam, to live for a while like the natives in each country." This was Rita's first experience traveling abroad. Never one to enjoy flying, she took the train to

New York and sailed to Europe. Her only concern was that she had to leave Becky at home, but the baby was in the capable hands of Rita's aunt Frances, her mother's sister.

Evelyn Lane knew Rita's personality and passion for privacy, so passage had been booked on a small ship. Rita enjoyed the ocean voyage, and she was received royally by her fans in France, Belgium, Amsterdam, Switzerland—all knew her films and greeted her tumultuously. The jaunt climaxed with the business part of the trip: the London premiere of *Down to Earth*.

The British press had been somewhat hostile upon her arrival. What had she done to inflame them so? Unknown to Rita, it was nothing she had done—there was great animosity for *all* Americans and American stars. They represented wealth and a carefree life, while the postwar British were grappling with rationing, inflation, and rebuilding their cities.

Rita was a target for their resentment. Especially since she had disappointed them. "Perhaps," wrote one friendly journalist, "they had expected her to disembark from the ship costumed in a black satin evening gown, and to peel off a long black-satin glove and toss it to the reporters."

Once settled in London, however, Rita liked it—what little she saw of it. A cordon of bodyguards accompanied her everywhere she went.

Sir Anthony Eden and other notables were present for the glittering *Down to Earth* premiere. The elegant audience was very taken with Hayworth in person. Rita looked very glamorous that evening—gowned and coiffed and very much the film star. It was amazing how she accomplished the transformation from shy Margarita to breathtaking Rita when she wanted to.

The audience's reaction to the film itself was moderate. Rita noticed this and determined that her next picture would be of much better quality, story-wise.

Rita was in good spirits when she sailed for America the next week, just as David Niven, whom she had dated before leaving for Europe, was arriving in London. The press made a to-do about how the "lovers would just miss each other, coming and going."

Down to Earth opened in the United States in the fall. The film cost over four million dollars, a colossal amount for the day. But while critics hacked away at the picture's flimsy plot, they went into rhapsodies over Rita's beauty.

It was not only the critics who noticed that Rita, nearing thirty, looked magnificent.

"What does she do? What exercises?" Joan Cohn wanted to know. The various department heads at Columbia informed her that Rita didn't do anything special—she didn't diet, she didn't exercise. "Rita just looks that way, Mrs. Cohn," they said.

In *Down to Earth* Rita's face seemed to reach a peak of physical perfection, although in a few of the musical scenes her usually lithe body looked a bit out of shape. But Rita was in the full bloom of both her stardom and womanhood. Once again she made the cover of *Life,* which proclaimed her the love goddess.

But the glamour goddess was in fact living a somewhat secluded existence for the time being—in a modest house, with no swimming pool, and spending a lot of time with her three-year-old daughter. The *Life* issue appeared on the stands a week before she appeared in court for her divorce.

At the hearing, she was sad. Later she was quoted as saying, "I'm tired of being a twenty-five percent wife. Night after night he left me alone. . . . It was impossible to live with a genius. . . . He's interested in everything about himself and nothing about his wife."

In later years Rita's reminiscences of Welles were more incisive: "He was tormented, possessive, insecure . . . a genius, crazy like a horse, and a marvelous man, completely unaware of reality."

Winthrop Sargeant, writing about Rita in *Life,* captured the Hayworth mystique—but he didn't elucidate on how she varied from it. "The fundamental trait of Rita's character is simply the desire to please people," wrote Sargeant. "Like the ideal, theoretical woman, Rita exerts enormous power by merely existing. She causes or inspires action, but she does not act herself except in response to the desires of others. Males, on meeting her, experience sudden atavistic impulses to flex their muscles or stand on their heads for her benefit. . . . Rita . . . is totally lacking in ambition and is mentally incapable of initiating anything on her own."

Sargeant neglected to point out that, when necessary, she *did* initiate things on her own. For instance, she had decided *she* was through with Orson, not vice versa.

"But somebody has always wanted to launch something for Rita," Sargeant noted. "Her life is a history of masculine effort exerted in her behalf by husbands, directors, producers, publicity men and managers. Rita, at her end, has done what she has been told to do, worn what she has been told to wear, learned what she has been told to learn and said what she has been told to say with infinite patience and good nature. Though the idea of doing anything for its own sake is completely foreign to her, she will accomplish prodigies to please others."

While Sargeant's comments were accurate, Rita was embarking on a period of her life where she *was* determined to please herself. Professionally, Hayworth was never to be happier. She was surrounded by people whom she trusted and who were trustworthy—most had initially worked for Orson. His former secretary, Shifra Haran, was now Rita's secretary. Jackson Leighter was running Rita's Beckworth Corporation (named for Rebecca and Hayworth).

"Orson called and asked me to please look after Rita's interests," remembers Leighter. Jackson and his wife, Lola, were Rita's best friends. Rita had the final decision regarding stories, directors, costars. The contract spelled out that her films *had* to be in Technicolor and cost a certain amount of money, insuring the onscreen quality of the productions.

Rita was wealthy—her income for 1947 would be $375,000 (although taxes would claim a large portion). Her new deal was one that Harry Cohn bitterly resented—and his animosity would know no bounds when Rita was in a more vulnerable position.

Cohn had a large-scale western planned for her, but she put that on hold. For her first Beckworth production she chose instead a story which almost every Spanish girl longed to play—a role for which Rita was ideally suited—one of the most famous characters of fiction. The story of Carmen had all the ingredients for a Hayworth vehicle, but Cohn was leery. He thought the public would have the wrong concept about the production.

The Loves of Carmen (*not* the opera, the ads would point out), reunited Rita, at her request, with Charles Vidor, momentarily reconciled with Cohn. Rita had enormous confidence in the director. He accepted the assignment.

Rita knew the importance of the right man at the helm. "I know a good director when I meet one. He has to believe in you as an artist. It's a tumultuous thing. He has to feed the actor's ego." Statements such as these belie reports that Rita was unaware of—and unconcerned with—such details.

"She was just quiet about it," notes a publicity woman. "People tended to treat Rita like a beautiful kitten, assuming she had no thoughts or opinions. And looking the way she did, and being as closemouthed as she was, who expected her to have any?"

Rita had definite opinions. She entertained thoughts of starring in film versions of plays by Spain's greatest poet-playwright, Federico Garcia Lorca. In Hollywood, this was a pipedream. But with *The Loves of Carmen* she would at least be portraying a Spanish woman, a dancer, and a famous character of literature.

Since Jack Cole had left the studio, there was only one man to choreograph the Spanish dances: Eduardo Cansino. In fact, the film would be somewhat of a family affair. Vernon would play a bit part, and Uncle José Cansino would be one of the gypsy dancers. Rita and her family were again seeing a lot of each other. Eduardo was content in his new marriage, and Vernon and Eduardo Junior were now both married.

While *Carmen* was in preproduction Rita happened to mention to her pal Glenn Ford that she needed a new stand-in.

"I know just the girl," said Ford.

Grace Godino was a pretty young woman, a full-time employee at the Disney studio as a color matcher in the animation department. She was also an actress. She'd been brought up in Santa Monica. Her father had run the M-G-M Café—a coffee shop near the M-G-M studio in Culver City. As a child, Grace had studied dance with Elisa and José Cansino. She met Ford while they were both at Santa Monica High School, and they had remained friends through the years.

"He called me," says Grace, "and I went over to Columbia. When I first met Rita, they were making tests for *Carmen*. Rita's hair was red. My hair was black and pulled back, but we had the same coloring and we looked about the same weight. Then they stood us back to back—we're both five six. I'm also a dancer. Rita asked, 'Would you be willing to dye your hair red?'

"And I answered, 'I'd love to! I've always wanted to be a redhead!'" So Grace Godino became Rita Hayworth's stand-in. She was able to arrange with the Disney studios to keep her full-time job there, with leaves of absence when Rita needed her at Columbia.

"They were still testing leading men for the part of Don José," Grace recalls. "Jerome Courtland did a test. So did Gig Young." Young had been lured into signing a Columbia contract with the promise that he would star opposite Rita Hayworth. But the part eventually went to Glenn Ford (who says today, "It was a ludicrous bit of casting").

A delicate situation developed when Rita, via a studio emissary, chose one of Eduardo's former students to become involved in the staging of the flamenco dances. "It's not that she didn't have confidence in Eduardo—she did," observed a friend. "But she also wanted the advice of someone who specialized in flamenco, and a person who could bring a new perspective to the choreography so that the dances wouldn't look—well—old-fashioned, or wooden."

As filming progressed it became increasingly evident that Glenn Ford was indeed totally miscast. He considers Don José the worst performance of his career, and he never made another costume picture.

All participants had to endure script revisions, delays, and bruised temperaments, as costs mounted. Location shooting was done at Lone Pine, California, at the foot of Mount Whitney. "It was cold as hell. Some days it was below zero," remembers Grace Godino, "but Rita never complained. She was a real trouper."

Only Rita managed to overcome the script and unexpectedly heavy-handed direction of *The Loves of Carmen*. Over twelve weeks of filming had produced a soggy mishmash of cinematic melodrama, but Rita, emoting and dancing in her gypsy costumes, was exciting to see. She played Carmen with fire and verve. It was a performance her fans would enjoy.

Exhibitors were eager to play the film—a Rita Hayworth picture always filled their theaters—and Columbia's coffers. The studio's balance sheet reflected Rita's drawing power. For 1946 and 1947 the profits had reached all-time highs: $3.5 million and $3.7 million respectively, directly reflecting *Gilda* and *Down to Earth*. Profits had been $1.9 million for 1945 and $2 million for 1944.

The one Hayworth loser during these halcyon years was *The Lady From Shanghai,* released now, in April 1948, over a year after it had been finished. Columbia tried to sell it with a provocative photograph of Rita gowned a la *Gilda*, but short-coiffed and blond, of course. "Do All Rich Women Play Games Like This?" asked the ad line. The public wasn't interested in finding out, even when the ad line was made bolder: "The Story of a Reckless Woman." But 1948 was a bad year for almost all motion pictures. A new novelty—television—had been introduced, and it was keeping people at home.

There was no longer a "key man" in Rita's life. Although columnists, movie magazines, and the press in general gave the impression that Rita's existence was one wild nonstop party, this was not the case. Howard Hughes pursued her, but without success. Rita often stayed overnight with her friends the Leighters, and Hughes would sometimes drive up in his car at two in the morning, toot his horn, and try to lure Rita out. On other occasions he sent planes for her, to fly her to meet him for lunch or dinner. But Hughes was definitely not her type, and she never responded to his overtures.

A more typical example of a Rita Hayworth evening has been described by Helen Hunt. It began late one afternoon at the studio, when Rita walked into Helen Hunt's department. It had been a long day, and Helen was getting ready to leave.

"Where are you going now?" asked Rita.

"I'm going home to get something to eat. I'm very hungry," Helen replied. At that time Hunt was living alone in an apartment on Hollywood Boulevard.

"Let me come home with you and cook your dinner for you," Rita said.

Helen was a bit surprised, to think that Rita Hayworth didn't have anything better to do.

"Gee, Rita, all I have in the house is eggs."

"Well, I'll whip up something," Rita said.

"Are you *sure?*" Helen was incredulous. "Can you cook? I can't cook myself."

"Sure," said Rita. "Come on, let's go."

She went home with Helen, made omelets for dinner, and the two women sat in Helen's kitchen until about eleven, chatting about the studio—and life in general.

Unlike many other stars, Rita, as Phil Silvers and others point out, was basically a working girl with no airs about being different than anyone else at the studio. Her evenings were spent quietly with people she felt comfortable with.

Even when Rita did socialize with other stars, it was often as unglamorous as her evenings with her family. Gene Kelly has told of an evening at his Beverly Hills house on Alta Drive when his cook had invited over a pots-and-pans salesman to do a home cooking demonstration. Betsy Blair, who was Kelly's wife at the time, invited Rita, Hedy Lamarr, Ava Gardner, George Cukor, and a couple of other friends over to watch the demonstration. Cukor arrived with his friend Greta Garbo.

"It's one of the evenings I remember most vividly in all my years in Hollywood," Kelly recalled. "Garbo, Lamarr, Gardner, and Hayworth—four of the world's most beautiful women—draped round my kitchen like ordinary hausfraus. I wish someone had taken a photograph." (Garbo bought a full set of the salesman's pots and pans; Lamarr purchased a few pieces; Hayworth and Gardner passed.)

When *Carmen* was finally finished, Rita knew what she wanted to do—return to Europe. Things had gone well there and she enjoyed the constant change of scene. When she told Harry Cohn of her plans, he wasn't pleased. When she asked if Evelyn Lane could once again accompany her, he asked, "How long will you be away?"

"I'm not sure—at least several months."

"What about the new film? You and Holden will be a good team, and you've never done a big western before."

"I'll be back in plenty of time for that. Now what about Evelyn?"

"If you're gonna be gone for months, I can't spare Evelyn for that long, Rita."

Lola Leighter and Shifra Haran went with Rita to New York, where they saw her pal Phil Silvers in his Broadway hit *High Button Shoes*. Then, in May 1948, the women sailed for Europe. Rita thought she would enjoy a relaxed, leisurely return to historic sites, other lands—a welcome respite from the Hollywood rat race. And this time she wouldn't have to publicize a movie or attend a premiere.

Film historians claim that on this trip Rita was intent on wooing Orson, then in Europe, back into her life. Jackson Leighter debunks this theory. By this time, according to Leighter, Rita had totally accepted that she and Orson had gone their separate ways. They would remain friends, but there would be no attempt to reconstruct a family unit.

"Certainly I'm going to marry again," she had told reporters. "I haven't the slightest idea of what kind of man he will be. I want it to be a surprise."

She had searched her soul and there was no denying that Orson Welles had been the great love of her life. She did not anticipate another relationship of that all-consuming intensity coming her way again.

As far as other men were concerned, she had to be on her guard. She knew she was vulnerable and needed to be wary of the many charming, attractive, and unscrupulous men who were always on her trail. She was now not only successful and famous but also wealthy. She had no intention of getting seriously involved with anyone. But she felt most alive when she was in love.

SIX

The arrival of Rita Hayworth in Europe was of enormous interest to the men of the international set. She was not merely a new face—she personified the luscious Gilda herself, the gorgeous wanton who performed stripteases in public and walked around in black satin evening gowns vamping every man in sight.

How surprised they would have been to observe Rita Hayworth on the voyage overseas. It was unlike the trip of the year before. The screen star was gawked at by fellow first-class passengers to such an extent that she grew highly nervous and barely spoke to anyone. She remained in her cabin most of the time.

When she did venture on deck, instead of using heavy makeup and dressing the role of Hollywood star, she wore unpretentious clothing and no makeup. Women who knew Rita well in the late 1940s all make the point that offscreen Rita dressed to please herself, often in slacks, men's shirts, loafers, and bobby socks. She let her hair go, often back to its natural brown, and she would pull it back or hide it under a scarf. Not unlike Garbo and Hepburn. "Rita was never concerned with glamour," emphasizes a close friend of this period.

When they finally arrived in Paris, Rita and Lola Leighter checked in at the famed Hotel George V.

Rita did meet with Welles. They spoke of Rebecca's future. But the hours-long meeting didn't produce the results fans and columnists had anticipated: a reconciliation.

A week later Rita entered a hospital suffering from a viral infection and had to undergo several blood transfusions. If one believed in omens, this was a disturbing way to begin her foreign sojourn. Plans were made for Hayworth to head south to the Riviera, where she could recuperate. There Rita would meet a group of people—a society—of which she had little knowledge. Nothing in her background—not her upbringing, marriages, fame, or success—had prepared her for what was in store.

In postwar Europe there flourished a group of fast-living, fast-moving, fast-talking people who had not only survived but indeed profited from the war. Some were from the oldest families on the Continent and others were nouveau riche, yet they shared a common bond: all flaunted great wealth, inhabited palaces, frequented fabulous nightclubs, hopped from bed to bed, and jumped from one pleasure spot in Europe to another. Currently, many were lolling on the dazzling white beaches of the Côte d'Azur.

It was this group that made up European café society (soon to be known as the jet set). Countless beautiful women—and men—moved in and out of the lives of the people who made up the nucleus of this international set. One of the most sought-after playboys of all was the dark-eyed, exotic, totally westernized and charmingly debonair dynamo, Aly Khan. H. H. Prince Aly Khan.

Few realize the prince was born an illegitimate child. His mother, Teresa Magliano, had caught the eye of the fabulously wealthy young Aga Khan when she was a beautiful young dancer in fairytale-like Monte Carlo in the early 1900s.

The Aga (already married to a Muslim cousin) fell madly in love with Teresa and provided her, their son, and Teresa's volatile Italian family with an opulent, lavish life-style. The Aga, always an aloof and seemingly distant man, loved his young son and saw to it that the boy was properly raised.

The Aga was an Anglophile, and the British politically supported him. Although a religious leader, with his followers scattered throughout the Muslim world, the Aga lived most of his life in Europe, and Aly was sent to tutors in Switzerland and to schools in England. In short, he was brought up as a European, not as an easterner.

The Aga married Aly's mother in 1922, when the boy was eleven years old. In retrospect it is highly amusing that the Aga once feared that Aly, deeply attached to his mother, seemed to be exhibiting effeminate attitudes and mannerisms. It was decided that the fourteen-year-old had better receive a proper introduction into the attractions of the opposite sex.

Apparently, the approach was one hundred percent successful. One of the boy's private tutors reminisced many years later that Aly Salomone Khan, while highly intelligent and basically "of a serious nature," would never be a scholar. His interests were always in other directions.

The young prince's preference was definitely for non-American women. The personality of the American female was far too "pushy" for his taste.

"From the beginning, Aly had the talent of being *several* men—he donned whichever personality he saw the situation called for," notes a friend. "He was the ultimate adventure for many women. Nothing sensible or staid about Aly; he wanted to go everywhere, do everything—and did."

He was "a chip off the old block," as his favorite group—the English—described him. Since the staid and respected Aga Khan had built up quite a reputation as a lover in his heyday, he could hardly complain too loudly of Aly's peccadilloes. To westerners, it was amazing that father and son, two such hedonistic men, were regarded as divine beings, direct descendants of the prophet Mohammad, by the Ismaili sect of the Muslims which comprised their followers. To the Ismailis, the Aga, the *Imam,* was God in human form on earth.

For all of Aly Khan's wealth and position, however, he was regarded by many in elite English society as simply "a colored man." Consequently Aly had taken special pains to win the complete affection of many highly born British ladies and delighted in the fact that haughty British noblemen had to contend with a man they considered "a bloody nigger" sleeping with their wives!

Margaret Wigham, the most colorful English debutante of the late 1920s, had been one of young Aly's most sizzling romances. Then he fell in love with a married woman, ten years his senior, whose husband would not give her a divorce. Then came Lady

Thelma Furness, who at the time was also seeing the Prince of Wales. A close friend of Lady Furness's was Mrs. Wallis Warfield Simpson, who informed the prince about Lady Furness's interest in Aly Khan. Edward's interest shifted to Mrs. Simpson. A short while later, as the world knows, he subsequently gave up the throne of England in order to marry her.

Aly's affair with Lady Furness was the talk of London in 1934. Then a new woman entered the scene—Joan Guinness—and her affair with Aly became a red-hot topic of gossip in all the toniest British drawing rooms; such news was never printed in British newspapers—not when the scandal involved ladies of Mrs. Guinness's social calibre. Joan's husband, Thomas Lowell E. B. Guinness, heir to the brewing fortune, a member of Parliament, divorced her, naming Aly as corespondent. (Guinness won custody of their son, Patrick.)

Aly married Joan (who was three years older than he) in Paris. Eight months later she gave birth to a premature baby, a healthy young son, Karim. Nine months later came a second son, Amyn. Not long afterward, Joan became a Muslim.

Meanwhile, Aly's mother had died. The Aga had remarried, and fathered another son, Sadruddin. By now the world knew of the Khans' incredible wealth, estimated at between one and two hundred million dollars. But the Aga controlled the purse strings, and Aly was always on an allowance.

World War II furnished Aly Khan with a spectacular stage for his derring-do: he served as an intelligence officer in the Allied cause and won highest honors. By war's end he and his wife had drifted far apart, although the two had been together frequently. From the summer of 1945 on, the marriage existed in name only.

With the passage of time, only Porfirio Rubirosa has matched Aly Khan's reputation as an international playboy. Aly drove fast cars, bred and raced horses, was always in the right place at the right time, and knew the right people.

Tales of his lovemaking reached bizarre proportions. Was it true that Aly went to such elaborate lengths as performing cunnilingus on a woman before taking her out on the town so that she would give him her full attention and wouldn't be tempted to flirt with other men?

At thirty-seven Aly was the best-known and most highly sought-after playboy in international society. But his fame was strictly European; few Americans had yet heard his name.

Elsa Maxwell was the empress of international café society. Her dear friend Cole Porter called her "Miss Liar" to her face. Bumptious, overweight, and over sixty, the never-married Miss Maxwell was an incredibly charming, gregarious, clever, and scheming woman whose entire existence was devoted to entertaining the vain and very bored rich at their own expense—and usually at a profit to herself.

She wrote a widely syndicated society gossip column. The Duke and Duchess of Windsor, among many others, were her great friends. If, as many said, she was using them all, *they* encouraged it—and if a person was not on Elsa Maxwell's "A" list, they were definitely de trop in café society.

Ms. Maxwell liked to brag that she had never had a sexual experience in her life, adding that if she ever had to choose one man to be her lover—if she were twenty-five years younger, of course— that man would be Aly Khan. He was her pet, her dearest friend, her darling chum.

Elsa knew everyone, including, of course, the hottest film star of the year. Rita was now on Elsa's turf, but the actress was staying away from all glittering soirees, no matter *who* was hosting them. People on the Riviera made Rita even more ill-at-ease than their American counterparts. Rita was so unhappy—all the staring, the whispering, the envy—she preferred keeping to herself and socializing mainly with Lola Leighter. But she was still Rita Hayworth, an international celebrity, and everyone knew she was there.

Producer Frederic Brisson (husband of Rosalind Russell) was at Cap d'Antibes at this time and he convinced Rita to attend a cocktail party he was hosting for Louella Parsons and her husband.

"Rita was so ill she could hardly make the stairs," recalled Louella. "I remember she reclined on a chaise longue on the terrace, closing her eyes as if she were too weary even to talk to others."

Many considered Rita's behavior tantamount to "snubbing," but Louella defended her. According to Parsons Rita had confided, "Louella, I'm so weak. I wouldn't have come here tonight except the party was in your honor."

Rita was a lonely woman—especially in Cap d'Antibes. Orson had called her from Rome and had driven to the Riviera to see her. "But," said Louella Parsons, "she hadn't been with him ten minutes before she knew that to reconcile with him would just be more unhappiness."

The attractive young Shah of Persia, Reza Pahlavi, was staying at the same hotel as Rita—the Hôtel du Cap. He had begun sending Rita flowers and seeking an audience. Rita kept putting him off.

There were other invitations as well, invitations of all sorts, and she ignored them all—but Elsa Maxwell was a persistent woman. She kept after Rita. She pleaded, implored, and cajoled her to attend a party she was giving on the third of July at the posh Palm Beach Casino. "Please come! There'll be wonderful people there. Lily Pons is coming. You'll have a divine evening!"

"No, no, I'm sorry," answered Rita.

"But why?"

"I don't enjoy parties where I don't know the guests. I don't like parties at all, to be truthful. And—I have nothing to wear."

"There's a *fabulous* dress salon in the lobby of your hotel! They have a white gown in their window that's *perfect* for you! Oh, come on, dear, don't you want to have any *fun*? Haven't you earned that?"

Fun! Rita had given up on having fun. Yet Elsa was a very persuasive woman. "Go buy the dress. Come in late. Make an entrance." She persisted and said she had a very exciting man she wanted Rita to meet. After more cajoling and pleading, Rita finally said yes.

Aly had not been anxious to attend the party either, until Elsa convinced him the surprise she had in store would be worth it.

"I'll never forget it," said Elsa. "Everybody but Rita was there. We were playing a game. Rita came in the door. Everybody gasped."

For once Rita made an entrance looking like the motion picture star she was, gowned in white, her skin a golden tan, her hair red and flowing—in short, a dazzling vision of beauty.

"My God—who is that?" Aly Khan asked.

Elsa answered coquettishly, "She's sitting next to you at dinner." Elsa subsequently recalled, "That's all I had time to say."

Aly Khan flew to Rita's side like a bee to a honeysuckle. His pal Elsa *had* furnished a surprise that was worthy of Allah himself!

Rita had no idea of who Aly was—Prince Aly Khan was an unknown name on the Hollywood social scene—but he certainly had that quality—Orson had had it—which Rita *always* responded to: joie de vivre.

Rita later admitted that after she was introduced to Aly, "I didn't say very much. Then he asked me to dance. We danced and we danced and we danced. I like to think we never stopped."

Yet at first she was cautious—she was not about to get involved with some foreign stranger just because he knew the right things to say. Observers would note, however, that *he* seemed swept off his feet.

Aly was a small man, not Hollywood handsome; yet after spending a short while with him Rita was surprised at how enormously handsome he seemed. His way with words and his take-charge attitude reminded her pleasantly of Orson in their early days together. But Rita had agreed to meet the Shah of Persia later in the week. The shah was persistent too, and an attractive man. Not that looks were terribly important to Rita. She'd see what the shah was like. What did she have to lose? And Onassis. Luncheon dates with both men were coming up.

But Elsa Maxwell knew that Aly Khan was hooked. He had been interested in meeting Rita Hayworth ever since he had seen *Blood and Sand* at an army post in Egypt years ago, and now *Gilda* was his favorite film. Aly was a man ahead of his time in *many* ways—he was a film buff!

It seemed to one and all that Elsa had scored quite a coup. Not only was Aly thrilled with Gilda in the flesh—but how envious his friends were! And the competitive streak in Aly was one of the forces which drove him.

Almost overnight, Aly Khan found himself obsessed as never

before. He had to leave Cannes for a short trip, but he told Rita, "I would like to see you again. I'm flying back from London in a few days. I'll buzz your hotel."

Three nights later everyone in the hotel took cover when they heard a tremendous roar in the skies. In a few minutes the phone rang.

"I'm here," Aly said.

"Yes," said Rita, "I heard you."

Aly was usually pursued by women—not, however, in this case. He was the pursuer, and he had organized his life so that there was nothing to prevent him from spending twenty-four hours a day seducing women, if he so desired.

When Aly Khan discovered that Rita was going to lunch with the shah, his competitive streak dictated his actions. He overwhelmed Hayworth with countless pleas. On the designated day Rita did not lunch with the shah but with Aly.

Aly continued entertaining Rita royally and romantically at his fabulous villa by the sea, the Château l'Horizon. It was just the two of them (and a silent retinue of servants). Rita required total attention from a man if she were to be genuinely interested in him, and Aly Khan lavished total attention on her. And in a fairytale setting, a breathtakingly beautiful vista far surpassing any Hollywood location.

In fact, Aly's attentiveness and sensitivity far surpassed those of any fictional hero ever presented on the screen. Rita later characterized her feelings: "I loved him. He had such an overwhelming effervescence that he sort of devoured you. The world was magic when you were with him."

Rita had asked Elsa Maxwell about the prince, and knew of his playboy reputation. Miss Maxwell later noted, however, that "The Aly would have made a superb film director. He knew exactly how to draw someone out, to get them to react just as he wanted them to."

While Rita Hayworth was a formidable challenge to him, she was not a fool. It is vital, at this point, to put the Rita-Aly relationship into perspective. Aly was pursuing her—wining and dining her, calling her constantly, sending her flowers—and she was responding, but always honestly, as Margarita Cansino, a girl with no artifice, casually dressed, not groomed like a star, whose only interests included being with the man she loved and having a family.

If she was a movie star, that was just a job—it was not her identity. If Aly had an image of her as a sophisticate, she did not engender it. She had every right to assume, if he was falling in love with her, that he was falling in love with *her*—not Rita Hayworth. They were always alone, and he seemed to want to spend every moment alone with her. Perhaps it was foolish to think it would always be this way—but he was telling her it would.

Before long reporters began to snoop around for details about this fascinating new romance. After all, Rita was still a married woman—her divorce wouldn't be final for three more months. And the prince was a married man also, with no divorce pending. But the fuse of the firecracker had not yet been lit. The couple was able to keep just one step ahead of the press. Not a single photo was snapped of them together. Yet.

For a while the lovers' idyll continued undisturbed. They were even able to enjoy quiet dinners at romantic out-of-the-way local restaurants. Then they embarked on a private sojourn to Spain. Just Rita, Aly, and his chauffeur. That was when Aly Khan learned what it *really* meant to be involved with "Gilda."

Aly had been with ladies, duchesses, princesses—he was, after all, a prince himself (although this was a courtesy title), worshiped by Ismailis throughout the world. But never had he been with a queen of the silver screen. A woman whom the public considered its very own property—a person not entitled, as far as her followers were concerned, to even the smallest vestige of privacy. It was one of the few experiences Aly Khan had not yet encountered. With the other married women Aly had squired, the press had followed a hands-off policy. With an Italian countess or a German baroness Aly could travel incognito anywhere he chose. The couple could travel alone and remain alone.

But now he was entranced by a woman whose beautiful face was her passport. There were few people who didn't know Gilda, no matter how quietly she dressed. She could tuck her famous hair under a bandanna and hide her eyes behind dark glasses, but it was only a matter of time before recognition came. It was an experience that no human being could ever really be adequately prepared for.

In the words of Jackson Leighter, "It was hazardous to be in Europe with Rita after *Gilda*."

"It's them!" An exclamation that would eventually strike fear and trepidation into their hearts whenever Rita and Aly heard it. It hadn't taken long. In Madrid they were recognized at their hotel and photographers swarmed about everywhere. With amazing speed, Aly whisked Rita away.

They managed to elude detection in Toledo long enough to get to a bullfight. But once they were seated in the grandstand Rita's instincts picked up on the buzz of recognition. It always began slowly, politely, then built to a frightening crescendo.

There are few things more harrowing than a mob possessed of a single purpose. How many times had she found herself surrounded by a huge crowd which behaved as one person, with a solitary aim: to touch her, to take a souvenir of the experience, a button from her blouse, a thread from her skirt—anything one could reach out and grab, including her hair!

But on a personal appearance there were bodyguards provided by the studio; at a premiere there was police protection. Here there was only Aly and the chauffeur.

"Gilda-Gilda-Gilda" chanted the mob, and Rita began to panic. "You don't know what they can be like," she said to Aly, her complexion drained of color. "We'd better get out of here—we'd better leave—" She felt she was going to faint.

"Calm down, relax," he assured her, his voice tense. The resourceful Aly Khan never lost his cool. Crowds closing in to pay homage were not new to Aly, who had been an object of worship amidst crowds of Ismailis for years. But people would never have dared to try to tug at his clothing or pull at his hair. Rita inspired a different kind of adoration and frenzy.

Somehow Aly and Rita managed to extricate themselves from the situation unharmed. Some of their escapes, in Spain and Portugal, and later on, were like Keystone Kops episodes, amusing in retrospect but harrowing and dangerous at the time.

In Seville, pandemonium ensued once again, but Rita and Aly managed some quiet moments visiting members of the Cansino family, including Padre, who had returned to spend his last years at home.

Rita was in her element among these people; these were her roots, and her shyness disappeared. She danced the flamenco and other traditional Spanish dances with such electricity and abandon that Aly Khan could not believe his eyes. If Margarita Cansino and Rita Hayworth were not the same person under most of real life's circumstances, at this point in time, far removed from Hollywood, entertaining Aly in a setting of home and family, Rita and Margarita certainly seemed one and the same. Seeing her here, in her natural environment, with all of her defenses most definitely down, Aly truly fell in love with Rita.

The press had begun to report on the romance. This presented a massive public relations problem for both of them. Rita was a mother and her divorce wasn't final—women in that situation weren't permitted to run around cohabiting with married men—not without paying a severe penalty. A scandal could rob a woman of her dignity and—in the case of a woman like Rita—her career.

There was a clause in her contract with Columbia—standard in all actors' contracts at all studios—concerning "moral terpitude." The public would forgive a sex symbol many indiscretions—but there were certain boundaries of behavior never to be crossed.

When Rita and Aly returned to Cannes from their Iberian peninsula sojourn, reporters and photographers swarmed around them: here was the kind of story that would sell newspapers throughout the world. The journalists were disheartened when, in September, they discovered that Rita had returned to Hollywood. Less than ten weeks had elapsed since the evening Rita and Aly had met. But the romance seemed to be over.

The Loves of Carmen was ready for general release. Rita went to Manhattan for the gala premiere and Helen Hunt went with her.

On the evening of the premiere, Rita wore a designer dress of green velvet with ermine around the shoulders.

"It looked lovely and Rita knew it did," recalls Miss Hunt. "There was a mob outside the theater and people were grabbing at her. One man almost got hold of her but a policeman intervened just in time." As they entered the theater after photos had been taken, Rita removed the diamond necklace and bracelet the studio had rented for her to wear, and handed them to Helen.

"Would you take care of these and put them in the safe when we get back?"

The jewelry didn't interest Rita, but the green dress did. The next morning she said, "I just love this dress, Helen. I want it so bad. Would you call Harry Cohn and see if I can have it?"

"I'll get him on the phone," Helen said, "but *you* talk to him."

"I can't," she said. "He's not speaking to me."

"Oh, heavens," said Helen. "Well, I'll do it, but I don't know how far I'll get." Eventually, Hunt got Cohn on the line. She described the dress and suggested that if he and Rita were feuding, this would be a good way to make up.

"All right," barked Cohn, "tell her she can have the dress."

This episode is typical of Cohn's and Rita's seesaw relationship.

At the moment, Cohn was being cautious. Rita was supposed to begin a new film soon. In addition, the studio chief recently had had discussions with Cecil B. De Mille, who would pay a fortune to Columbia to borrow Rita (who would also be paid a fortune) for *Samson and Delilah*. Rita's old friend Victor Mature would be playing Samson.

Rita was "hot." In an era when movie revenues were slumping and stars were not maintaining their box office power—even Gable had slipped badly—Rita was bigger than ever. George Jessel, currently a producer at Twentieth Century-Fox, wanted to borrow Hayworth to costar with Betty Grable in a musical biography of vaudeville's famed Duncan sisters.

At Columbia, Rita went ahead with meetings on the western, *Lorna Hansen*. William Holden, Columbia's third big star—Rita and Glenn Ford were the other two—was to be her leading man. The film would be in color, with the usual high budget and long shooting schedule.

But Aly had followed Rita to Hollywood. There were headlines: "Rich Casanova Lured to U.S. by Hayworth on Eve of Her Divorce."

And now Harry Cohn's troubles really began.

Aly's determination to prove to Rita that she was all that mattered had finally broken through her reserve. They were wildly infatuated with each other, caught up in their passionate feelings.

"They knew what they were doing," says an intimate who was with them at the time. "They weren't the first two people to discover they were in love—it was disturbing to them that outsiders were interfering."

Rita and Aly were not seeking the world's attention—but from the start, they had it. There were many important events occurring throughout the world at this time. And in retrospect, a romance between two celebrities would not seem to warrant front-page coverage. But front pages around the world were suddenly reporting on the love goddess and the playboy prince.

It was, after all, the stuff that dreams are made of. Worlds were meeting: Hollywood and the international set. The western and eastern cultures. It was the story of Cinderella, who had worked her way up to the glittering world where she met the wealthy and titled Prince Charming. And they were daring to defy the moral codes of the day!

Unfortunately for Rita and Aly, they could not explore their relationship as ordinary people would. They were not ordinary people. Both of them had long since given up their privacy. He, by birth. She, by career.

But, courageously, they forged ahead. Neither was going to give up the feeling they had when they were with each other. She felt *alive*. He hadn't realized he could still feel this way about a woman.

She was under far more pressure than he—the start date on the new film was imminent—but how could she begin a film? That meant months of hard work. When would she have time for Aly? He wanted her with him. She wanted to be with him. "We plan to see a lot of each other," Rita told reporters.

Aly, too, was being treated as a movie star, without having had to go to the trouble of making the movies. The press pursued him but he handled the situation adroitly. Replying to persistent queries, he finally said to one journalist, "Look here, old boy, I'd like to answer your questions, but how can I when they are so embarrassing!"

Aly seemed as comfortable in the Hollywood social scene as he was at Monte Carlo. He and Rita dined out alone and occasionally with other luminaries, such as Hollywood's social doyenne, Mary Pickford, and her husband, Buddy Rogers.

The prince had rented a house on Rockingham Avenue, near Rita's on Hanover Street, which infuriated columnist Hedda Hopper. Louella Parsons, on the other hand, continued to support Rita in her column. Louella was still an all-powerful newspaper voice, and her approval was most valuable. (At a crucial point in the Rita-Aly scenario, Louella would not permit Rita or Columbia to forget that the star and the studio were very much in her debt.)

The couple escaped from Hollywood and flew to Mexico City. But the press followed. Rita and Aly then fled to Acapulco, where they managed to enjoy some privacy, but the press pursued them there. Never had Rita experienced such public scrutiny before.

Aly's father was particularly distraught at the landslide of publicity, which hardly painted his married son as the kind of man to become the living God for millions of people.

Those who wrote about Rita now fell into various camps. Sheilah Graham observed, "It would really hurt Rita if the prince ditches her. It would kill her reputation for glamorous sex appeal, and without that, what has she?"

At a press conference in Mexico City, Rita, minus Aly, of course, told nagging reporters she had "no plans to be married. My divorce isn't final yet. Can't you all find something else to write about?"

The lovers then went to Batista's Cuba, where they mulled over their predicament and feelings and what they would do next. Persistent reporters awaited the couple when they returned from Havana and landed in New Orleans.

"I really have nothing to say about any romance," Rita exclaimed. "I've just been on a six months' vacation and now I'm going back to do a picture."

Aly chimed in: "I'll talk about anything that is not personal. Ask me about my racehorses. Ask me about my father." When queried why he and Rita were so terse with reporters, Aly answered, "I'm just unhappy. I don't like being stalked."

In December, Rita returned to Hollywood to pick up her final divorce decree and inform Columbia of her decision: she wasn't going to make *Lorna Hansen*.

"He'll take you off salary, Rita," warned her agent, Johnny Hyde. "Your healthy financial position relies on that income." Her base salary was $250,000 annually.

"My mind is made up, Johnny."

She was knowingly giving up a kingdom of her own. She had worked long and hard and was at the very pinnacle of her career. She truly had no peer. There was no other female star in Hollywood who was as big—and reliable—at the box office. No other female star could command the deal Rita had—not Grable, not Turner, not even Garbo got 25 percent of the profits of their pictures.

Many personalities, then and now, downplay their careers, claiming personal considerations are more important. In Rita's case, this was really the truth. To Rita, love *was* all.

Those on the scene note that during this period of their relationship, Aly Khan was totally faithful to Rita. For one thing, they were together almost twenty-four hours a day, and he was as caught up in the passion of their love as she was. His intimate friends scoffed that this fidelity could never last. And how well they knew him.

But for the moment, Aly was totally devoted to Rita, and she would follow him anywhere. Rita, with Rebecca and Shifra Haran, headed east. Rita and Aly rendezvoused in New York, at the Plaza Hotel. They lunched with Elsa Maxwell and her friend Cole Porter, and Elsa asked Rita directly, "Will you be in New York for long?"

"For a while," the always noncommittal Rita answered.

Miss Maxwell, however, knew that Rita was heading for Switzerland—and so was Aly.

A few days later Rita, Rebecca, and Miss Haran boarded the luxury liner *Britannic*. So had Aly. So had reporters. Press coverage had begun to assume ugly overtones. Rita was derided, characterized as a "silly film star." The press was unkind—saying she was "looking as pale and haggard as though she had walked all the way from Hollywood." Aly was described as "Rita's gold-plated boyfriend from mystic India."

Rita, Aly, and their entourage visited Ireland, then went on to London in Aly's private plane. For him, Rita disregarded her fear of flying.

The London press was unrelenting, and Rita had to escape, literally, from the Ritz Hotel. To get out without being seen, she and Rebecca went to the basement and climbed service stairs to an empty restaurant where french windows opened onto a narrow balcony. The management had put down a twenty-foot plank which sloped steeply into the yard below. Rita and Rebecca carefully made their way down the plank, then squeezed through a gap in the fence and rushed to a car that whisked them to the airport. Aly was waiting.

From London the lovers went to Paris. Then on to the Palace Hotel in Gstaad, the Swiss ski resort, where Rita came embarrassingly close to meeting Aly's wife, through no desire on either woman's part. Joan Khan was staying at the Palace while visiting her sons, who were at the Le Rosey school. Joan barely managed to depart before Rita and Aly arrived. Journalists described it as "The Great Escape."

The cosmopolitan Aly saw no reason why the two women *shouldn't* meet. But Rita was opposed to the idea. She didn't realize that Joan and Aly had an arrangement. He was permitted complete freedom, since both parties knew discretion was Aly's byword—or had been, up to this highly unexpected point.

Joan was reported to have received an exceptionally large settlement for her cooperation at the time their separation occurred, and in fact was willing to grant Aly a divorce anytime he wanted it. *If* Aly wanted a divorce, it was his for the asking.

It was in Switzerland, with the breathtaking beauty of Gstaad for a background, that Rita discovered yet another facet of Aly's personality: his talent as a father. Karim and Amyn adored their dad and Rita was delighted at how well Rebecca got along with Aly and the boys. This was the kind of family life she had dreamed about. This was a man she could love forever.

But there were arguments as well as moments of passion. Some say Rita was concerned about Rebecca. What effect was all this running around going to have on her? Others said Rita was puzzled as to why Aly hadn't begun divorce proceedings from his wife.

"Rita wasn't a victim, as she's sometimes been painted in her relationship with Aly, but she certainly was a romantic," says an associate of Aly's. "If she was a victim of anything, it was of her own dreams of what things should be like, instead of what they were like."

In Switzerland, Rita and Aly tried their best not to be photographed together because that would enable the press to pull out *all* the stops. As long as the lovers were not photographed, all that was written was technically innuendo and hearsay. However, avoiding the press, even in Switzerland, was a task guaranteed to cause constant, unrelenting tension. And it did.

Back in the United States women's groups and church groups were beginning to publicly scold and vilify Rita. Cohn was aghast —but powerless to prevent the outrage that was building.

Rita and Aly were a "liberated couple," at a time when it still took daring and courage to be a liberated couple. But their daring and courage were hardly the qualities inspiring the news stories about them.

The most shocking rumor now being circulated was that Rita was pregnant. This was still considered scandalous in the 1940s and could be devastating for careers that depended, as both Rita's and Aly's did, on mass public approval.

Time would prove the allegations, at this point, untrue, but there were legions of people who believed them. One person who believed the rumors was the Aga Khan. He sent the Begum, his fourth wife and Aly's current stepmother, as an emissary, to see exactly what was going on. Then he summoned the couple to his fabulous Cannes retreat, Yakimour.

The old man faced the meeting with feelings of hostility and doubt, but to his surprise and delight he found Rita totally charming. This sweet woman was the femme fatale the press were crucifying for her behavior? Her qualities of sweetness and modesty were rare. The Aga asked the couple if they were "devoted to each other," and when they replied they were, he "advised them to get married."

Aly was relieved his father had been so taken with Rita. The

Aga had never expressed anything other than displeasure with her until their meeting. Now he, too, was won over by the reality of what Rita was—which was the opposite of what the image makers painted her to be.

Aly finally started the machinery for his own divorce in motion and made the announcement the world was waiting to hear. Rita no longer had access to Columbia's publicity department, but the Aly Khans of the world had formidable public relations experts of their own. Aly summoned the press to the Château l'Horizon and gave out "his and hers" typed statements.

His read: "I am going to marry Miss Hayworth as soon as I am free to do so. In these circumstances, I hope that my private affairs will be treated with the consideration which is usually extended to the private affairs of individuals in general."

Hers read: "I am in full agreement" with Aly's statement and have "only been waiting for him to be free to marry him."

"When will that be?" "Where?" "What are your wife's feelings?" "Where is Rita?" "We want to speak to Rita."

"Miss Hayworth has influenza, gentlemen," answered Aly.

"Your Highness, Miss Hayworth is a Catholic. Will she convert?" asked a reporter.

"That will not be necessary," answered the prince.

"Will she continue to make films?"

"That is a question for her to answer."

Rita and Aly soon posed with the Aga and Begum for a "family photograph." Rita looked rested. She was not wearing tightly fitted clothes but loose sweaters and full skirts, once again giving rise to the rumor that she was pregnant.

When the couple attended the races at Epsom Downs, outside of London, the crowds were gaping at Rita and Aly, not the racetrack. Aly seemed delighted by the attention. "Nothing to hide now, old boy!" he exclaimed to a friend. He could display Rita with the pride of a man who owned the greatest Thoroughbred on the track. A Triple Crown Winner. One didn't conceal such a treasure, after all.

At the prestigious Paris Opera, all heads turned to gawk at Rita Hayworth and Aly Khan. It was Rita's first visit to the opera house, and she was amazed that it was *she* who was of the most interest to the glittering crowd. Aly basked in the attention, as usual.

Life in a goldfish bowl was a dismal existence for Rita Hayworth. "However," says a friend, "she felt once they were married, everything would settle down. She didn't see how anyone would want to live at such a pace all the time!"

Rita was totally turned off by most of Aly's European friends. The women were snobbish, haughty, patronizing, or downright hostile. Their barely concealed attitude seemed to be, *This* is Rita Hayworth? Where is the style, the chic, the glamour? This woman is bourgeois—Good Lord, is Aly mad?

"Darling, we will do something about your clothes!" offered Elsa Maxwell. She suggested the leading couturier on the Continent, Jacques Fath, and Rita took her advice. But a chic wardrobe did nothing to alter the animosity many of the females in Aly's set felt for her. She was simply "not one of *us,* darling . . ."

"They were so jealous of Rita," observed a friend. "She had won the prize so many had gone after, and they bitterly resented her." But Rita tuned them all out—their approval was not essential to her happiness. And she repressed any feelings of foreboding she had over Aly's seeming pleasure at having these people around.

During the months they waited for Aly's divorce to become final, the couple argued frequently, then made up. Rita imbibed to release the tension, and Aly scolded her for drinking. That was one of the few vices he denied himself (it was forbidden by his religion).

And over the next couple of months he admitted to Rita, yes, he still on occasion found other women desirable—why couldn't Rita understand this? Surely she understood he didn't *love* any other woman, he simply desired them physically.

She may have understood philosophically—but couldn't comprehend why he couldn't change. He *said* he'd change. There were many loud arguments when it was apparent he wasn't changing.

While Aly could sometimes sneak out on the town, Rita was virtually a prisoner in whatever hotel they happened to be. In the first place, she wanted to remain with Rebecca. But in any case she would not have gone out alone.

On sober reflection, this all-consuming new love of hers left a lot to be desired. What had she gotten herself into? But there was no turning back now. She loved him. She was also stubborn. She didn't *want* to turn back, or return to films. Things would work out.

Rita had almost no friends in Europe (not that she had very many in the United States). She had to be her own counselor. In a situation well over her head, she was determined to survive—and win. Hopefully, her quality of passive resistance, her ability to tune out, would enable her to cope, indeed see her through. After all, she had what she wanted. A man she loved.

"You must not be embarrassed by them, Rita," Aly explained, regarding the Ismailis who sought an audience with him, prostrated themselves before him, and kissed his feet. "You must be prepared to receive the same homage."

As an American, Rita found it weird to think of human beings worshiping at her feet and to think of herself as one who could bless them—she was just as human as they were! But if that's what Rita was expected to do, that's what she would do. She loved Aly, and he had her complete, unswerving devotion.

April in Paris had special significance for Rita Hayworth that year. In the ancient, beautiful, beige-marble City of Light, she told reporters that she expected to be married "within a month." She didn't tell them that the Aga was pressuring Aly to marry as soon as possible—he didn't want the rumors of Rita's pregnancy to prove embarrassingly true.

"Can we avoid a big public ceremony?" Rita asked Aly in private. She was so weary of all the attention.

"Yes," said Aly, who agreed with her wholeheartedly. They had been badgered enough. The press would absolutely be barred from this wedding. "It will be a civil ceremony at the château. That way we will retain control."

Rita was pleased; Aly was a take-charge man, just what she liked. Everything was in his hands—she'd do as she was told. Yes, indeed, things were falling into place very nicely. A husband, a home, no Hollywood or Harry Cohn, and no more publicity—she told herself she was going to be a very happy woman.

Also in April, Aly finally became officially divorced, gaining custody of his two sons. Joan had willingly obliged on *all* counts. No scandal—the name of Rita Hayworth did not appear in the action at any point.

But then Aly broke his ankle while playing with his sons, and for a while it appeared the May wedding would be postponed.

Rita selected her trousseau at the Jacques Fath salon in Paris. Aly accompanied her. The fashions were modeled by Fath's top model, the beautiful, reed-slim Bettina, a woman whom Aly would later fall in love with. But for the moment his thoughts were only on Rita.

That they hoped their marriage would be "private" seems, in retrospect, incredible. The couple had long ago relinquished any possible rights to privacy; the public *demanded* to be a part of the proceedings, and in the end the participants had no choice.

Disgruntled reporters had unearthed an ancient French law which threw a wrench into Aly's plans. No French wedding could be private if any French citizen objected. Naturally, the reporters objected. But Aly thought he could somehow circumvent the law, and was pulling all the strings he could to arrange this. It seemed he would succeed.

The date was tentatively set at May 27. "But why can't we set an *exact* date?" Rita was perturbed—who ever heard of someone not being able to set an exact wedding date?

"Because," Aly explained, "permission has not come through yet from the government to hold the ceremony here at the château. The law says marriages here in France must be held in a public place."

"What about the invitations?"

"They will be printed with a blank space for the date and place. That information will be written in by hand."

Aly was at the center of all the planning. He surrounded himself with the myriad of professionals, all of them his friends, necessary to carry it off. They were the very best the Riviera had to offer.

Rita's business manager, Lee Ellroy, came from Hollywood to help with the wedding plans. It was a task comparable to blueprinting a combination movie premiere—complete with reigning

Number One Superstar—and a private party for a head of state.
An impossible task, at best. At worst, a total disaster.

Aly's passion for his fiancée's films was expressed while he was
planning the menu for a very *intime* dinner for the wedding guests,
which would be held several days prior to the ceremony. The meal
would feature dishes with the names "Cover Girl," "Gilda,"
"Strawberry Blonde." The "Ritaly" cocktail was another creation.
Furthermore, the guests were to be treated to a special screening
of *The Loves of Carmen*.

Aly's friends constituted most of the guest list for the wedding.
His many devoted "friends" could fill a stadium. His family would
be there, of course, his father, stepmother, aunt, his former stepmother, Princess Andrée, seven princes, four princesses, a maha-
rajah, and a maharanee. Whether any of Rita's family were
invited was—and has remained—a matter of speculation. None of
them attended. Neither did any of her fellow movie stars. The
celebrities who were invited to attend—such as Maurice Utrillo and
Edith Piaf—were invited by Aly.

Few people were invited by Rita. Back in Hollywood, Harry
Cohn seemed excited about receiving an invitation. Helen Hunt
recalls, "Cohn was being very vocal about planning to be there.
He and Joan had bought a big, expensive gift."

With the exception of the Cohns, Ellroy, Charles Vidor and his
new wife, Doris Warner, and agent Johnny Hyde, there were to
be no other Hollywood people.

But one Hollywood person who was determined to make it to
the wedding, although she was *not* invited, was columnist Louella
Parsons. All of Louella's cunning and nerve were put into play.
Her rival, Hedda Hopper, snorted, "She won't get within ten miles
of that wedding." But Hedda was wrong.

Louella headed for Cannes, calling Rita from Los Angeles before she left, telephoning Rita again from New York en route, and
trying to coerce Rita in a third telephone call from Paris. Still, by
the time the columnist had arrived in Cannes, all she had obtained
was an invitation to lunch. She brought a unique gift for the bride-
to-be: a lace handkerchief which had belonged to Marie An-
toinette.

Rita faced a dilemma. Louella had been her staunchest supporter from the beginning, but Aly did not want her as a guest at the wedding. No member of the press was going to be a *guest*. However, Louella's prestige and reputation were on the line. She had risked ridicule to come this far. . . .

To Louella's relief and delight, she came away from the luncheon with Rita possessing a pink disk—which only invited *guests* obtained. Later reports, that Rita had feared Louella's vindictiveness, were sheer nonsense. Rita recognized Louella's plight and came to her rescue. If denied an invitation, Louella would have stayed in Cannes and covered the event as a reporter anyway.

As the big day approached, the story was on front pages throughout the world. Then, only two days before the wedding, came bad news from the mayor of Vallauris, Paul Derigon. He personally called on Aly Khan. "Your Highness—the government has turned down your request to be married here in your beautiful château. I am so sorry—in all likelihood, if your fiancée was not such a renowned artiste, we probably could have arranged it—so many people would not have known . . ."

"*Merde!*" exclaimed Aly, angry and disgruntled. Now they would have to be married in the town hall. The press could not be excluded, or very well controlled. And the crowds! "My God, the crowds will be enough to smother us all!" cried the prince. "Let us go to the hall right now and see how we can make things work."

Aly Khan had begun to look haggard and drawn, what with the unending planning, the unrelenting probing by the press into every aspect of his private life. He was truly concerned about his father's growing dissatisfaction. If only this whole thing could be completed with some kind of dignity, then Aly knew all would be well.

The town hall was ugly and *small!* Where on earth was everyone to fit?

"Your Highness," suggested the mayor, "we can have the ceremony here in the *grand salon* on the ground floor, rather than upstairs. Much more room. There is time for fresh paint, flowers—"

"*Oui, oui,*" said Aly.

"And to be sure that we are in control of who goes in and out, I shall personally sign special badges—"

"Good, good."

What he didn't tell Aly was that he would also personally meet with the press to keep them informed of all that was happening, so the world would know everything. Surely that would please His Highness.

The fact that Mayor Derigon was a communist ("Red Mayor Marries Royal Couple," headlines would scream) didn't at all deter him from utilizing a highly capitalistic approach to exploiting the proceedings and jacking up the tourist trade. As a matter of fact, he was looking forward to the royalty expected to attend "this wonderful event."

There was much politicking and backstabbing among the press to get the special passes necessary for admission to the inner sanctum. And the knowledgeable European journalists scoffed at the romantic slant American reporters relentlessly applied to the "smitten prince and the luscious love goddess."

"Aly hasn't changed, believe me," said one *Paris-Match* reporter to another. "I guarantee you he still hits the nightspots way after hours—want to bet? I've heard stories. Shall we try to track him down?"

"Yes, I'll take the bet. My sources tell me he's in love, and that he wouldn't dare to jeopardize the situation. Besides, they know him everywhere. He'd be recognized."

"You can't expect a man who exists on orange juice to stop squeezing fresh oranges simply because he's found one particular orange he likes!"

The reporter was right. In the wee hours—after 3:00 A.M.—the prince had continued to frequent favorite boîtes and gambling clubs, where he was not only well known but friendly with all the help. There were no leaks to the press. The week of his wedding, he happily availed himself of the charms of the beautiful young women who always found Aly Khan alluring—and vice versa.

Rita screamed. The people gathering on the château's rear lawn for the wedding rehearsal were horrified. If this had been a film, only an Alfred Hitchcock—or an Orson Welles—could have dreamed up such a grotesque sight on the day before the wedding:

Above left: Rita, five years and ten months old.

Above right: At thirteen.

At sixteen—before the "transformation."

With her first husband, Ed Judson.

With "The Hunk," Victor Mature.

Remarkably contemporary look in a 1941 photo.

With brother Vernon and their parents.

With daughter Rebecca.

At the very peak of her stardom.

The love goddess
in her spectacular prime.

With Orson Welles.

Above left: With Aly Khan.

Above right: With Princess Yasmin.

With husband number four, Dick Haymes.

With Harry Cohn.

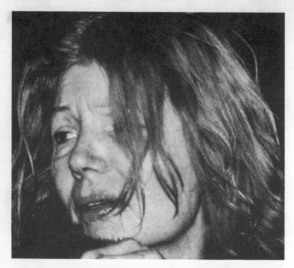

London, 1976: The world was shocked. (UPI Photo)

London, 1976: The next day, looking like her old self. (Worldwide Photo)

1977: With Princess Yasmin.

Above left: With Cary Grant, *Only Angels Have Wings.* (1939)

Above right: With Tyrone Power, *Blood and Sand.* (1941)

With Phil Silvers and Gene Kelly, *Cover Girl.* (1944)

With Fred Astaire, *You Were Never Lovelier.* (1942)

With Glenn Ford, *Gilda.* (1946)

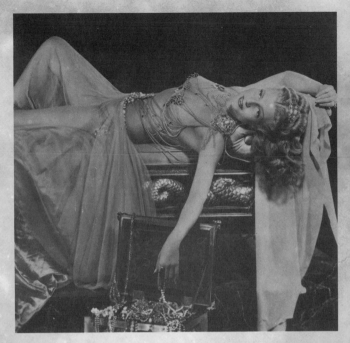

As Salome. (1953)

Above left: With Jack Lemmon, *Fire Down Below.* (1957)

Above right: With Robert Mitchum, *Fire Down Below.*

With Frank Sinatra and Kim Novak, *Pal Joey*. (1957)

With John Wayne, *Circus World*. (1964)

a dead body had been swept in by the sea and was stranded on the rocks below.

"What is it? What is it?" Rita kept exclaiming, her voice trembling, praying that it wasn't what it appeared to be. When the object was identified at close range, a highly distraught Rita took to her bed.

If she had believed in omens, one wonders just what would have happened next. But she was a woman who did what she was supposed to do. She pulled herself together and turned up for the evening screening of *The Loves of Carmen* which Aly had scheduled for their guests.

Again there was a touch of the avant-garde about her clothes: dungarees, white bobby socks, and loafers topped by a chic white suit jacket. Photographers would undoubtedly photograph her from the waist up, and she would appear impeccably groomed; from the waist down, she'd be completely comfortable. It was a trick she'd learned when posing for glamour portraits at Columbia, where she *knew* the shot would be properly cropped. But of course there was no cropping here: photographs of the princess in bobby socks were flashed around the world.

In actuality, despite all the pressure and incredible curiosity and attention, there wasn't much for Rita to do up to the day of the wedding. Aly and his entourage were handling *everything;* it wasn't too different, for her, from waiting for the first day of a film to start production, while others attended to all the details. She might be tense and worried, but there were no dances to learn and no script to memorize.

However, the lady's mood was not one of controlled calm. "I'm so excited. I can hardly think. I'm sort of lost in a dream world. When someone asks me a question, I bring myself to and grunt."

The morning of May 27, the sun rose like a yellow diamond in a sapphire sky. Hollywood's most skillful set designers couldn't have created a more beautiful or charming setting than the little toylike town of Vallauris.

The deceiving quiet was soon disturbed by a low hum, off in the distance, which grew louder and louder. Countless automobiles crammed with French security police began to arrive. In their wake came another fleet of vehicles carrying the press. The village was suddenly overrun with foreigners, pushing, shoving, shouting, jockeying for position. Barriers were set up, and photographers took their posts at the town hall.

The big day had arrived. This latest episode in the history of the world would soon be over. The crowd began to build. It spilled over into the roped-off sectors of the streets.

"Move back—keep the path open!" shouted the *gendarmes*. Over a hundred had been called in from nearby Nice. Why on earth had the damned mayor declared this a holiday? they wondered. Their task would be twice as difficult. The downstairs room of the town hall had been sectioned off: the front for guests, the rear for press and public.

The always-practical Louella Parsons, who would have had an "exclusive" had the wedding been held at the château, reluctantly gave up a prized seat, up front with the guests, for a seat nearest the door. That way she'd be the reporter closest to the telephone, and her story would be on the stands a few hours earlier than anyone else's.

The ceremony was scheduled for eleven. An hour to go, and space already at a premium. The crowd cheered as a formally attired Aly, wearing striped trousers, a double-breasted black jacket, white shirt, and gray tie, unexpectedly arrived at ten. He seemed highly agitated and drew Mayor Derigon aside.

"I have decided I do *not* want the press in the downstairs room, monsieur."

"But, Your Highness—why?! They will scream bloody murder! I cannot evict them now, they would—"

"They will do nothing, monsieur. Have your men ask them to move upstairs. This is an *urgent* request." Aly had learned that his father was very upset that reporters would virtually be breathing down his neck. Derigon complied, securing the ill will of the grumbling horde of journalists.

The guests began to arrive and file into the town hall. The air of expectancy heightened. The Aga and Begum arrived, in a Rolls-Royce, promptly at eleven. And finally the person all had been waiting for. A radiant Rita sat in the back seat of a gleaming cream-colored Cadillac convertible. Her car had been surrounded by an admiring throng the whole distance from the château to the town hall—several miles.

Her up-to-then "secret" wedding ensemble was a simple, tailored, long-sleeved dress of pale blue crepe, with a full, pleated skirt. She wore black gloves. A Scarlett O'Hara-like blue picture hat was perched prettily atop her head. She seemed fine. She was Rita Hayworth today, flashing her love goddess smile and waving politely like a queen, acknowledging the affection of the crowd.

"We can't see her!" screamed the press inside the town hall. "Goddamnit, let us into the big room, Mayor!" Their threats grew loud and ugly.

Inside the crowded *grand salon,* the complaints of the journalists could be heard loud and clear. Aly was sweating. The Aga's face bore a hard, stern expression. The press was permitted to re-enter the rear of the room.

The secretary-general of Vallauris motioned for silence. Then he read the marriage license. Official witnesses were the prince of Orleans-Braganza and General Georges Catroux, former French ambassador to Moscow. Prince Sadruddin Aga Khan, Aly's sixteen-year-old half-brother, was *garçon d'honneur* (boy of honor).

Mayor Derigon rose and faced Rita and Aly, who remained seated. He asked, in French, if they accepted one another as man and wife.

"*Oui,*" said Aly.

"*Oui,*" said Rita. With that word, she became a princess.

It was hot in the room. Aly signed the marriage register, then Rita and the witnesses followed suit. Aly kissed Rita on the mouth, a mild surprise to the French audience. This was not usually done.

Derigon read a long speech he had prepared extolling the wonders of having these world-renowned personages wed in "our little city," and thereby bringing the town to the attention of the entire world. Aly could hardly wait for it to end so he and Rita could escape.

Outside, a wall of flashbulbs exploded in their faces. Protected by police on motorbikes, they entered Aly's convertible and returned to the château. As Rita smiled and waved at the throng, so did Aly. Aly relaxed—it was over! No awful incidents had occurred

—not a single person had been injured. The Aga no longer had anything to complain about. The festivities at the château were almost an anticlimax.

Harry and Joan Cohn had not attended the wedding despite his plans for being there. Some have speculated that his invitation arrived so late that he realized Rita must have been coerced into inviting him. He was, at first, going to slight her by not even responding. But at the last minute he was convinced to send her a telegram of congratulations.

And of course the absence of all members of Rita's family was widely commented on. There were reports that her father received an invitation too late to get there—and others that her relatives could not afford the trip to France. Some say her father and brothers sent telegrams of congratulations and love, while others claim that Rita was in tears because none of her family sent congratulations.

It is true that in 1949 the trip from California to Europe was expensive and time-consuming. There was no Concorde to whisk people across the seas in a matter of hours. It was a trip that required planning, and because the wedding date had been so indefinite, many people who would otherwise have attended—including Elsa Maxwell—did not make it.

At the reception the air was exquisitely fragrant. Hundreds of gallons of perfume had been emptied into the swimming pool, where groupings of flowers spelled out "A" (for Aly) and "M" (for Margarita)—there could be no doubt that Rita had made it plain to Aly that he had married Margarita Cansino, not Rita Hayworth.

Rita and Aly made their obligatory visit to the press. A select number of reporters and photographers from the international press were present, but were confined to a special section and not permitted to mingle with the guests.

A group of musicians—eight violinists, playing selections from Rita's pictures—serenaded the newlyweds by the pool as Aly told reporters, "I know what you want all right—a passionate love scene. But I'm afraid I'm not a competent actor. The acting talent is on the other side of the family."

Rita said she expected to return to California toward the end of the year and make a new picture. "I expect to know the name of it by the end of this month."

Rita was asked why Rebecca had not been present at the ceremony. "She is only a little child, you know."

How was Rita to be addressed? "Rita Hayworth, Princess Aly Khan—*not* Princess Rita."

A table had been set up for the children, and for a while Rita and Aly sat with Rebecca, Karim, and Amyn. It could have been a family grouping at any upper-middle-class wedding.

Many Ismailis appeared at the reception, to pay respects to their prince and new princess. When they knelt and kissed Rita's foot and presented her with offerings, she was mute. The little girl who had gone to grade school in Queens, N.Y., was now a royal personage with worshipers who had never even seen the inside of a movie theater. She had taken on quite a new life. But now that everything was "official," she wasn't quite sure what would come next.

Rita and Aly phoned Elsa Maxwell. Rita got on the phone. "Darling," she told Elsa, "we were not nearly as nervous as the mayor!"

"The mayor did a great job," confirmed Aly. "The ceremony was short. Enthusiasm was enormous."

"Aly gave me the largest diamond ring in the world," Rita told Elsa. And the Aga had given her pear-shaped diamond earrings.

"Don't believe all you hear," said Aly. "I didn't have four hundred cases of champagne. I didn't have four hundred rooms in the Hotel Carlton, and all the hullabaloo didn't really happen. It was very dignified in spite of all the ballyhoo. It was not a real Hollywood wedding in any way. I am very happy, and as you started all this . . ."

Elsa interrupted him. "I'm going to see a happy ending, I know," she said.

It had been a day requiring almost superhuman self-control, and as the hour grew late, Rita was exhausted, as was the Aga. She sat down next to him.

"Too much caviar, Rita, too much caviar," he declared, his enormous belly evident under his impeccably tailored suit.

Despite what Aly had told Elsa Maxwell, the Aga Khan would later comment, "It was a fantastic, semiroyal, semi-Hollywood affair," and noted that he had played his part in the ceremony although he "disapproved of the atmosphere with which it was surrounded."

Louella Parsons, however, approved. "As the reception drew to a close," she reported, "Aly, wearying but still buoyant, dropped on one knee and, with old-world gallantry, kissed Rita's slipper." No doubt Parsons's millions of readers sighed and shuddered with delight. What a perfect ending for the fairytale wedding of Hollywood's most gorgeous glamour girl—its very first princess.

Rita Hayworth had actually found her Prince Charming—he did exist! There were few women who, on this day, wouldn't have wanted to change places with the love goddess.

SEVEN

The next day the brief Muslim marriage ceremony was held at the château. The union was now official in the eyes of the Ismailis.

But then came a jarring pronouncement from the Vatican. The marriage was "illicit" in the eyes of the Catholic Church, and any children from the marriage would be "conceived in sin."

"The Church ignores this marriage," the Vatican spokesman continued. "As a Catholic, Rita Hayworth should know that her civil marriage has no value in the eyes of the Church. For a Catholic, a religious marriage is obligatory when she marries a non-Catholic."

Muslim officials in Karachi, Pakistan, said the marriage was "both permissible and correct" under Muslim law.

There were further denouncements from western religious figures. Father Thomas J. McCarthy of Los Angeles, in his tabloid, *Tidings,* described the Hayworth-Khan nuptials as "the civil union of an Indian prince and his girl friend by a Communist functionary."

Hal Boyle of the Associated Press "reviewed" the wedding as follows: "A strictly grade B script. . . . How bad can times get?"

The interest in Rita and Aly didn't abate. Aly's self-control finally deserted him. "Stop bothering me!" he yelled angrily at photographers waiting outside the château, as he and Rita were about to embark on their honeymoon trip a couple of days after the wedding. According to one report, "the prince rushed at the men, kicking, punching, and swinging his cane, apparently trying to break their cameras" as Rita jumped into the prince's Alfa Romeo at the height of the scuffle.

Another report had Aly saying to the cameramen, "You annoy me! Get out! You're a bunch of bores!" According to one observer, "When the photographers were standing at the side of the road, Aly swerved the car toward them, but all jumped to safety."

Several days later the prince, in formal attire complete with high hat, and the princess, elegantly garbed, were at Epsom Downs for the Derby. Before Rita and Aly arrived, attention had been focused on the Royal Box. King George was absent, but Queen Elizabeth was there with her daughter, Princess Elizabeth, and her new husband, the Duke of Edinburgh.

But the crowd's atttention suddenly moved to the new royal arrivals. The dreaded "It's them!" followed Rita and Aly everywhere. "We want Rita!" shouted the crowd. When the races were over, police had to be called to help them return to their car.

"*Is* she expecting?" whispered the English gentry, observing her figure-concealing coat.

A week later, in Paris: "Rita Faints, Spills Wine on Maurice." It happened at the Festival of Stars, in the Tuilleries Gardens, where Rita had been mobbed by fans and fainted. She had knocked over a bottle of champagne, and Maurice Chevalier was quoted as screaming, "My new suit is ruined!"

Rita, after "a nip of brandy," revived. "No, I'm not expecting," she declared.

At the ultrafashionable Longchamps racetrack in France, it happened again.

"I . . . I'm not feeling . . . well . . ." gasped Rita, unable to catch her breath.

"What's wrong with her?" wondered bystanders. Would a woman faint so frequently if she *weren't* pregnant?

Earl Wilson interviewed the couple, working up to the question everyone wanted answered. He began by asking Rita when she would return to Hollywood.

"We'll see if they have a picture for me," answered Rita. "It requires a lot of discussion. But I will go back when they have one."

"When will the princess have her baby?" asked Earl, noting that it had been widely printed that she would.

"Oh, we're not having one yet," the prince laughed. "God, I hope we have a lot . . . but nothing yet. I'm not trying not to!" He laughed again.

When Wilson asked Rita the question, she answered, "Sometime, of course. But not now." She looked at him with mock fierceness and added, "That's why you came!"

"No, no! But it's been printed," Wilson said.

"Yes," she shrugged. "They printed that I had fainted at the racetrack. I didn't. It was so hot that I put my head back and shut my eyes, and so then they took my picture and said I had fainted."

And when asked how she should be addressed, she told him, "My name is Princess Margarita."

Within a month Rita and Aly were at Deauville. "It is frenetic, *everyone* is here, you *must* come!" Aly's friends had implored him.

"*Must* we go?" Rita had asked her husband.

"You will have a marvelous time, darling!" soothed Aly.

The Aga, the Begum, Rita, and Aly were guests at a fabulous gala in Deauville, at which King Farouk of Egypt was the honored guest. Farouk, like the Aga, was physically immense. "Farouk and the Aga looked like two beached whales," said a snide bystander.

The Begum was ablaze with a treasure of huge diamonds sparkling from her ears, her wrists, her throat. But she and the Aga were distraught because almost a million dollars' worth of her other jewels had recently been stolen.

Rita, wearing a Jacques Fath creation that looked like a maternity ensemble, was miserable and bored and tried to tune everyone out. The vacant look came to her face. Aly knew what that meant. Rita left the party early, a pouting Aly having no choice but to leave also.

Earl Wilson learned that in Deauville "Aly greeted his guests with: 'Well, I suppose you want to know whether Rita is enceinte? She certainly is, and we're both extremely happy about it!'"

From Deauville, finally, came Aly's revelation: "You may officially announce that my wife is expecting a baby. I sincerely hope this official announcement will put an end to all these rumors."

Aly was not about to let Rita's condition dampen his fun at Deauville. In the words of a friend, he painted the town "all colors, and from every end." And while he had previously been sensitive to Rita's moods, he now had no second thoughts about asking his friends—female as well as male—to "drop over" for lunch or dinner, giving Rita no notice. Their marriage was not a total one-way street, he reasoned—she must make some adjustments. Why should she not accommodate herself to his life-style? Rita tried, but she could not suddenly turn into an Elsa Maxwell.

Aly continued to entertain frequently and spontaneously. "This embarrassed her terribly, but Aly was oblivious," notes a close friend of Rita's. "Orson *never* placed her in situations that could embarrass her—Aly didn't seem to mind, now that they were married."

The women Aly invited to their home were in many ways a mixed group, but all were attractive. And they seemed to have one other thread in common: Aly.

Rita eyed them with suspicion but could do nothing. The vacant look came over her face when she was with these people. With Aly, however, she made no effort to repress her anger, but he only laughed. He denied he was having intimate relationships with any of the women—they were all merely "good friends."

To make their marriage even more "open," Aly, to his wife's chagrin, *urged* her to return to work, once the baby was born.

That was not what Rita wanted to hear.

Aly continued to screen *Gilda,* for himself, at least once a month, a fact which certainly backed up Rita's contention to Virginia Van Upp that Aly Khan had fallen in love with Gilda after all, not Margarita Cansino. It was a ludicrous predicament. "It was as if Laurence Olivier had married Vivien Leigh because he thought she was Scarlett O'Hara," observed Charles Vidor.

Furthermore, Aly preferred Rita when she was *angry.* He did not want a placid madonna—he wanted a fiery tigress. When Rita flew off the handle, Aly was usually enchanted. And aroused. Which might have delighted Gilda or Carmen, but was an anxiety-producing situation for Margarita Cansino.

Chauffeur Emrys Williams later noted, "Rita had a shocking temper and flung books about when she was in a rage. She was no angel. At times she had the temper of a wildcat . . . and how wonderful she looked when she was in one of her fiery rages."

Back in Cannes, Rita waited out her pregnancy. Harry and Joan Cohn, accompanied by Jules and Doris Stein, paid Rita and Aly a visit. Stein was head of the powerful MCA talent agency—Rita had agreed to discuss having MCA represent her.

Cohn found the sight of an apparently domesticated Rita somewhat of a surprise. Her hair was almost totally dark, and she wore dungarees and a man's sport shirt. Cohn and Stein subsequently noted that, contrary to "stories" they had heard, there was no antagonism between Rita and Aly—they seemed totally enamored of each other.

While Rita didn't say she would return to work, she didn't say she wouldn't. All knew that no conclusion could be reached until after she had her baby, and that was months away.

Over the next weeks, Rita became more and more nervous. The Aga kept indicating to the press that Rita's baby was due any day. "*Why* does he keep doing that?" Rita complained to her husband. "It's upsetting to me—doesn't he know that?"

"It's because he cannot afford the embarrassment of an *unexpected* premature baby, darling. If our followers realize he *knows* the baby is imminent, then that is in keeping with his knowledge of all things as *Imam*."

To escape the Aga, Aly and Rita went to Paris for the autumn. Aly issued denials that the baby was due in October, as the Aga had predicted, and time proved that the *Imam* had indeed misjudged. However, the estimated month of the baby's arrival remained a prime topic of gossip both in Europe and back in the United States.

The sudden death of one of Aly's closest friends—a man his own age—triggered an extreme reaction in the prince. His pursuit of pleasure increased alarmingly. As Rita grew heavier and heavier in her pregnancy, she remained at home almost all the time, and Aly was almost never at home.

When it seemed her time was drawing near, Rita and Aly went

to Lausanne, as prearranged, and registered at the Palace Hotel (which was owned by Aly's former stepmother, Princess Andrée). The plan was for them to remain in the luxurious hotel until it was time for Rita to go to the Montchoisi Clinic, where an elaborate suite was waiting for them. Most of the royal families of Europe went to this exclusive clinic for childbirth.

There was a touch of the "old days" when the press tried to pry into the timetable of events, but the fourth-estaters were successfully kept at arm's distance.

There was a "secret plan" for the child's birth, almost a military operation: When Rita was ready to go to the hospital, Aly was to notify the police. Then two police cars would escort his car from the hotel to the hospital. There was even a secret password. Another part of the plan was that the concierge at the hotel was to lock the doors, so that reporters staying there couldn't pursue them.

It seemed Aly had thought of everything.

Aly and Rita had left Rebecca in Gstaad, with Rita's aunt Frances. Since Rebecca had been born by caesarian section, speculation was high that Rita would have the new baby the same way. But under the care of one of Switzerland's top obstetricians, Rodolphe Rochat, Rita was having this baby in the natural way.

As often with well-laid plans, something went awry. When Rita went into labor about two o'clock on the morning of December 28, Aly panicked. He forgot about the police and the hotel staff. He threw a mink coat over Rita's shoulders, spirited her out a side entrance of the hotel to his car, pushed his chauffeur out of the front seat, took the wheel himself, and sped to the hospital.

Meanwhile, Aly's servants remembered to telephone the authorities. The screaming police sirens woke reporters, who rushed to the lobby of the hotel only to find that they were locked in—the concierge had remembered his part of the plan. When reporters threatened to smash the doors, a key was produced. The journalists rushed to the clinic, but they were fifteen minutes late. Rita was already inside.

She was in labor for seven hours. At 9:45 A.M., almost seven months after Rita and Aly were married, an infant girl was born. The baby weighed only five and a half pounds.

She was named Yasmin (translation: jasmine).

After the birth Aly sat with Rita for "over one hour, because I wanted to be there when they broke the news to her that it was a girl. . . . You know, an expectant father is just as nervous as an expectant mother, if not more so," he said, tired and relieved. "I feel like I've had a baby, too. I look like the wild man from Borneo."

He was candid. "My wife had a very tough time of it. I was afraid she might have the child in the car racing to the hospital. That is why I jumbled the arrangements I had made to have a police escort and left without waiting for them."

And he apologized to reporters for his earlier behavior. "I blew up completely. You know how it is at a time like this. But my wife is all right now, thank goodness. I am very happy. It is just what I wanted."

Aly described the baby as seven weeks premature, but Dr. Rochat wouldn't comment on this statement, on grounds that he did not want to discuss matters "of a professional nature."

Olga Besson, head nurse of the Montchoisi Clinic, remarked, "She is a very gracious, delightful little girl, with harmonious features and tiny wisps of black hair."

For the first time since she and Aly first met, Rita truly *relaxed*. It was as though the straitjacket of anxiety and tension which had encased her for the past year and a half was suddenly removed and she was a whole, healthy person again.

She, Aly, and the children went to Gstaad for Rita's recuperation, and for Rita this brief period was a happy dream. They were *together*. For Aly, it was a happy time also. What a pleasure that Rita wasn't brooding or complaining. And both new parents *adored* the baby.

Aly often went to Paris on business, but Rita didn't mind because he was never gone long. Momentarily, things were rosy. Aly appeared to have his freedom, and Rita appeared to have the family life she wanted.

Karim and Amyn were not unaware of Rita's celebrity. Michael Korda, who attended Le Rosey at the same time as the Khan boys, and who enjoyed some status at school because of his film industry associations (his uncle, film mogul Alexander Korda, had married Merle Oberon), has recalled that Rita Hayworth was a far more impressive relative. Her visits to Aly's sons at Le Rosey, in Korda's words, "electrified" the school.

When Aly broke his leg in a skiing accident and had to be placed in traction, he thought he would go mad from the hospital confinement. He decided to entertain on a royal scale, continuously, in his hospital room. It was amazing how resourceful the prince could be.

The "rebirth" of the love affair between Aly and Rita was short-lived; neither party was either willing or able to accommodate the other's life-style. It was not in his nature to remain home with her and the children and it was not in hers to be a social butterfly.

They returned to the château. Aly continued with his social meanderings. Rita's passivity, her seeming ability to tune out of unpleasant situations, was her way of dealing with the dilemma. But her feelings were merely repressed, not dissolved. She often remained in her rooms at night alone, dancing and playing the castanets, having a few drinks and then crying herself to sleep. It was obvious the situation couldn't go on indefinitely.

To cheer her up, Aly arranged for him and Rita to join Charles Vidor for a pleasure cruise aboard Errol Flynn's yacht the *Zaca* (the same yacht Orson and Rita had chartered for *The Lady From Shanghai*).

No sooner were they aboard than Aly eyed a girl on a neighboring yacht, and Rita lost her temper. "If Aly had had the same appetite for food that he had for women, he would have weighed seven hundred pounds!" laughs a man who knew the prince closely. Aly Khan was a glutton for sex. He wasn't a superman, however, despite legend to the contrary. He could indulge his appetites to such an extent because reaching climax during lovemaking was not what he required. He derived his pleasure from giving the woman pleasure; consequently, he was able to enjoy many liaisons in the course of a day.

Reports claim he had sexual intercourse three (some said five) times a day but only reached orgasm two or three times a week. But for him, variety wasn't the spice of life—it was the *essential* of life.

Rita and Aly's arguments continued because he could not understand why she could not understand that his love for her and his commitment to family life had nothing to do with his outside interests.

The pleasure cruise was hardly the cure-all for the domestic woes of the prince and his princess. When the *Zaca* occasionally stopped off at a friendly port so the group could shop, Rita was always recognized and the usual questions ensued. When was she returning to movies? "I don't know." One report noted, "Rita herself was busy doing nothing at all, and enjoying it thoroughly."

Vidor felt the time was right for her to start work, get away, put things in perspective. He talked at length on the subject, and Rita was responsive. She finally said she would seriously think about it. She was happy spending time with Vidor, who understood her so well. Except for Vidor and the Leighters, Rita had lost contact with her old friends.

The royal couple returned to London in May, for the Derby at Epsom Downs, where Aly's horses were running. They socialized with Aly's friends and attended the theater. They went to the Palladium, where Rita's former costar Larry Parks was headlining with his wife, Betty Garrett. Garrett remembers that "Rita and the prince created quite a stir when they came backstage. But Rita was very unassuming, very shy and quiet."

In London the prince and princess celebrated their first wedding anniversary. There were rumors she was pregnant again. "No, it's not true. I'm not expecting," she declared.

There were also rumors that they weren't getting along, that the marriage was headed for the rocks. To scotch these tales, and perhaps because Rita *was* ready to return to work, Rita and Aly again met with Earl Wilson.

Rita was definitely and aggressively playing a cat-and-mouse game with Columbia Pictures. "Oh, I have no plans to come back," said Hayworth. "You see, I have a contract with Columbia I'm not satisfied with."

Wilson said, "That kind of statement usually means a demand for more money. Why on earth would the princess Aly Khan need more money?"

"No, it isn't a matter of money," Rita answered. "I want not to have to spend eight months hanging around making a picture. I have to have more free time now.

"Anyway, about the money, there's no sense in me sort of working and working for nothing. After all"—Rita leaned forward as if to make each point carefully, indicating much thought about it—"I don't *have* to make a picture. I don't have to work. I don't have to make a name. As for keeping my name in front of the public—I don't have much trouble."

Wilson noted that this was surely his quote of the month. Rita hadn't made a film in two years, but her name was constantly in the news. Although many suspected, only insiders knew that the marriage was indeed on shaky ground.

She had accommodated Aly as much as she was capable of doing. She had tried to find his friends interesting, she had studied French (her accent was impeccable), she tried to feel at home at the château—even *that* was impossible. The house was always accommodating several of Aly's friends. It was like living at a hotel —except that the other guests seemed more at home than she did!

The obvious speculation was that Rita could no longer put up with Aly's physical infidelities. Ironically, this was not the key issue. It was apparent by now that he was *never* going to change his life-style—and he wanted to travel *constantly*.

Just as Rita finally seemed about to reactivate her career, Aly announced he wanted her to accompany him on a tour of Africa. Rita was skeptical. "First you tell me to go back to films—now to Africa with you—"

Aly explained that he was embarking on this trip to visit the many Ismaili communities scattered throughout that vast continent. "You are my wife, and they must see you too! My father insists that you go. It will look terrible if you don't. *Then* you can go to Hollywood, and I'll go with you."

Aly pointed out that they were hardly going to rough it. This would be a "champagne safari," with all the comforts of home.

Rita was finally persuaded to go, although she wasn't looking forward to it. It would mean a long separation from the children, who would remain at the château. The safari would continue for months. As the princess Aly Khan, Rita would be expected to perform endless official tasks from dawn to dusk; even if the children were to come along, she wouldn't have much time for them.

Jackson and Lola Leighter were living in New York, where Leighter was now the executive publisher of *The United Nations World*. One night they had dinner with Aly. He invited them on the safari, and Aly suggested to Leighter that he make a film of it. "You provide the equipment, I'll provide the crew. Talk it over with Lola. You can meet us in Cairo."

The Leighters joined Aly and Rita on December 20, 1950. They met at the exclusive Automobile Club in Cairo. Leighter had brought along $40,000 worth of equipment and film, which had to be stored in ice. But Aly's crew never materialized. So Leighter, Rita, and Lola went out to the pyramids and the sphinx, where Jackson shot reels of film, which he then air-mailed back to New York for developing.

Aly knew that Lola Leighter's birthday was December 28, the same as Yasmin's, so that night he threw an elegant party. There was the finest champagne, mounds of caviar illuminated by special spotlights, a fabulous dinner. It was a festive affair. "There were just the four of us. He knew how to entertain!" recalls Leighter.

The royal couple seemed blissfully happy. But then, only a few nights later, Aly was back to living a fever-pitch social life—he had rediscovered old friends and acquaintances in Egypt. Aly and Rita argued. At a gala New Year's Eve party, at which King Farouk paid undue attention to Rita—who found him to be one of the most repulsive men she had ever met—Rita was incensed that Aly was boisterous and was flirting with other women.

Emrys Williams has noted, "One of the first causes of Miss Hayworth's unhappiness, in her role as Princess Aly, stemmed from the fact that she nearly always felt like a fish out of water with the prince's friends."

Jackson Leighter gives another view: "Rita was a working girl. In her mind all of Aly's friends were phonies."

King Farouk notwithstanding, she did what she had done at other soirees during the course of the year—she angrily rose from her seat and said to her husband, "I'm getting out of here." Aly went after her—then decided to return to the party.

But they made up and the trip continued.

The group traveled in two planes—Aly's private eight-passenger de Havilland, called *The Avenger,* and a commercial plane, a Lockheed Air Express.

In Nairobi, Jackson Leighter continued making the documentary film of their travels, and in the evening joined Aly for bridge. That Aly Khan traveled with bridge-playing companions is well documented. Jackson Leighter remembers there were at least six players along (Rita didn't play). Leighter, who considered himself a fair player, was a student of the Culbertson method. The others were playing according to the newer bidding theories of Charles Goren. In just a few days Leighter found himself down about two thousand dollars. "I crammed Goren," he says, "and after about sixty days of playing and wildly fluctuating between winning and losing, I ended up five hundred dollars ahead!"

Aly played bridge by night. By day he attended to official duties; these often included ceremonies in which Rita participated. But sometimes Aly would disappear for hours—or even days—at a time.

The highly publicized pilgrimage to Africa was an ordeal for Rita. One day, during a break in the heavy schedule that had been planned for them, Rita wasn't even permitted to take a swim in a hotel pool, although she was in extreme discomfort from the furnacelike heat.

"Please, please, Your Highness, *don't!*" Aly's advisers begged. "It would not be fitting." The sight of the future *Imam*'s wife displaying her body in a bathing suit was something Aly's people were not prepared to cope with, especially with photographers around. Rita didn't go swimming. She was as cooperative in her new life as she had been in Hollywood, where she always knew her lines and always (or almost always) came to the set on time. Her job was to be the wife of Aly Khan, and she was determined to do it to the best of her abilities.

Observing Aly among his followers, Rita was shocked at how her husband seemed to become another person. "I hardly know him when he's like that," she confided. This was not the Aly Khan of Cannes or Paris or Hollywood.

Leighter's documentary film recorded the increasingly unhappy union of the film star and the Muslim prince. Rita was reaching the end of her rope. She couldn't tune out the realities of Aly's nonsense for much longer. When the safari continued to Telek, Rita and Lola stayed behind in Nairobi. In a few days Rita sent a note to Aly, via Lola.

Aly, with the Leighters, flew back to Nairobi. "Rita was *mad*," says Jackson Leighter. "They talked it over, and it was decided that Aly would continue on the safari and we'd go back to Cairo." It was later reported that Rita left Aly "in secret, stealing away in the night," but this was not true.

Aly then flew to Cairo to meet with Rita. She told him she was leaving him, and he was not opposed to the idea. He made no attempt to stop her. They even discussed that she would get an American lawyer to handle the divorce.

Knowing that they would have to contend with the press, Rita and Aly set in motion plans to make reservations, under various aliases, on four or five boats sailing from France to America.

Then Aly rejoined his safari and Rita and the Leighters sailed from Alexandria to Greece. There Rita left the Leighters, flew on to Rome and then to the château at Cannes. The Leighters, driving her Pontiac station wagon from Greece, would meet her at l'Horizon.

Rita spent a week at the château, mulling over her decision. She was happily reunited with Yasmin and Rebecca, but it worried her to learn that the Aga was returning to Cannes from Pakistan. Had he spoken to Aly? Would he and Aly try to gain custody of Yasmin? After all, he had custody of his two sons.

The Leighters duly arrived, and Rita, the children, and the children's nurse went with them to Le Havre. They had secretly booked passage on the luxury liner *De Grasse,* bound for New York.

The press got wind of what was happening. Reporters cornered Aly in Cairo, but he deftly parried their questions. According to Aly, nothing was wrong.

Reporters, photographers, and newsreel cameramen were out in force when the *De Grasse* docked in New York on April 2, 1951. Rita, looking rested and smiling, was prepared to handle the juggernaut of queries.

"Is it true you're separated from the prince?"

"Untrue," smiled Rita. "He is somewhere in Africa now. I think he may come over here."

"What are *you* going to do now?"

"The first thing I am going to do is have a hotdog. Then I want to see all the theater I can."

She said she had rushed to catch the *De Grasse* in order to sail with the Leighters, "dear friends of mine."

Rita did not pose with her daughters, but alert photographers managed to snap pictures of six-year-old Rebecca and fifteen-month-old Yasmin as they were spirited off the ship.

"Now that you're back, do we continue to call you Princess Aly Khan?" reporters asked.

"I just want to be known as Rita Hayworth."

Rita had returned to America a very disillusioned woman. Love hadn't conquered all. She couldn't tune out that fact. She was lonely, depressed, dispirited. What was life adding up to for her? Her looks, her career, her money—what was it all worth if it didn't bring her what she wanted most—the love and companionship of the person she loved?

She told a friend, "The hurt is very deep way down inside me. I can't deny that. I had loved Aly so very much that leaving him was almost unbearable—but it is a step I knew I had to take."

She had given the marriage everything she had—she *wanted* it to work, she forgave him many times more than even she thought she was capable of doing—with *any* man. Yet all her efforts hadn't been enough, and her emotions ran very, very deep.

She checked into the Plaza and stayed in New York for almost a month, giving rise to the speculation that she was waiting for Aly to pursue her. Aly phoned her while she was at the Plaza, but apparently there was no reconciliation in sight. So Rita, with a heavy heart, went ahead with plans for a legal separation.

She was introduced to top attorney Bartley Crum by Jackson Leighter, and Crum began conferring with Aly's Parisian lawyers.

Then she heard from Aly. To placate his father, and because he had no desire for a divorce, Aly sent her a letter in which he tried to soothe her ruffled feathers. He pointed out how for everyone's sake a scandal should be avoided. He loved her, surely she knew that, and a legal separation wasn't necessary, certainly not now. And if, at some future point, she decided she wanted to marry again, well, Aly would not stand in her way. . . .

This was not the urgent love note Rita had eagerly anticipated—it was an insult! No vacant look occupied her face on this occasion. She called Bartley Crum. "I don't want a legal separation. I want a divorce."

This was a serious step but she was determined to survive, for there were two vital factors to consider—two people in Rita's life whom she cared about and *loved,* very dearly and deeply, and without whom she might very well have gone under: Rebecca and Yasmin.

"The girls were *all* she really cared about," say those women close to Rita. "She came alive when she was with them."

"I feel I have so much to live for in my two little girls," said Rita. "I'm going to keep working hard to take care of them and give them the advantages they should have."

In early May, Lola, Jackson, and Rita started a cross-country trip to Reno in a blue Packard convertible. The children and their nurse had flown ahead and were waiting at Lake Tahoe.

At one point, crossing Nevada's deserts, the vehicle was speeding, and police stopped the car. "Rita thought we were going to give her a ticket," said Patrolman Clyde Fields. "She laughed when we told her we just wanted to know how things were."

Rita would have to live in Nevada for six weeks to qualify as a legal resident, and the press conjectured that maybe this dramatic move would shock Aly into a reconciliation—and into changing his ways.

Rita told the public, "There is definitely no chance of a reconciliation."

Would she sue for divorce or legal separation?

"It really hasn't been decided yet."

Why had she left Aly?

"My husband's social obligations and far-flung interests make impossible the kind of home I want and my children need."

Aly's comment: "Those preliminary divorce papers Rita filed at Reno can lie there a hundred years."

Rita resolved that no matter what happened between them, she was determined to have a trust fund set up for Yasmin—a three-million-dollar trust fund. The baby shouldn't be dependent on anyone for her future, reasoned Rita. Aly Khan—and most certainly the Aga—was in a position to see to that.

Rita had developed a fear that the child would be abducted by agents working for the Aga—she was afraid of the incredible influence wielded by the wealthy leader. Many people dismissed her fears as groundless, but not everyone. Some knowledgeable people felt her instincts were on target and told her she had been wise to leave Europe.

Unknown to Rita, the Aga was furious with his son. Why had Aly allowed Rita's discontent to reach such a heated state? Was his eldest son so unaware of who he was and what his responsibilities were? According to rumor the Aga had another, more personal, reason for his displeasure with Aly. He was entertaining thoughts of separating from his current begum, but with Aly in the headlines constantly, the Aga could not make a move without publicity. He most certainly blamed Aly, not Rita, for the couple's breakup, and he feared that Aly would not be able to assume the position of *Imam*. Public opinion was too much against him.

Aly was highly distraught—not that he might not become *Imam*, but that his father might cut off his income.

"We must convince Rita to hold off for at least six months" was the strategy, but Rita no longer trusted him. Her reply to Aly's request that they meet at a Caribbean resort to discuss reconciliation was very legally phrased: "I am unwilling that there be a meeting, believing that delay would be harmful to the interest of everyone."

She agreed, however, to hold off on doing anything for the half-year Aly requested. There was so much for Rita to consider: Yasmin's future was at stake.

Bartley Crum went to Paris for a month of negotiations with Aly's lawyer, Charles Torem. Then both men returned to New York, and Torem declared, "It's difficult to do anything when the two parties refuse to meet. Now we are trying to transfer the question from a legal to a personal basis."

Meanwhile, for living expenses, Rita had borrowed $25,000 from the William Morris Agency. She was running up bills—she had spent a month at the Plaza and two months at Lake Tahoe. She needed money and there was only one thing to do: go back to work.

While much has been made of her money problems at this point, much has also been overlooked. According to one close business associate, Rita was not without funds—and she had brought with her a small fortune in fabulous jewels which Aly—and the Aga—had given her. Furthermore, the Beckworth Corporation was worth a substantial sum, if she had wanted to sell her interest back to the studio. But she did have a cash flow problem.

So in early July she headed for Hollywood, checked into the Beverly Hills Hotel, and informed Columbia that she was ready to return to work. Now Harry Cohn had the upper hand. He would take her back, but not on the old terms.

EIGHT

Harry Cohn could have put Rita in his pocket forever if he had exhibited toward her now one trace of the compassion she desperately required. She needed support and trust from the people who were going to guide her career.

What she got from Harry Cohn was more of the kind of treatment that he had doled out over the years. The kind of behavior that would make people say, years later at his funeral, that they hadn't come to pay their respects—just to make sure he was dead!

Instead of welcoming back the star who would once again earn millions for Columbia, Cohn regarded her as a recalcitrant adversary who must be punished for her cardinal sin: walking out on Harry Cohn.

Cohn was eager to extract his pound of flesh. There was no longer a powerful person in Rita's life to give her the help and protection she needed. Johnny Hyde had died only a few months earlier. (Hyde, before his death, had gone all-out to launch the career of an unknown twenty-four-year-old actress he wanted desperately to marry: Marilyn Monroe. Hyde had even introduced her to Harry Cohn, who invited her for a weekend cruise aboard his yacht. When Marilyn answered "I'd love to join you and Mrs. Cohn for a cruise," Cohn threw her out of the office.)

With Hyde out of the picture, Cohn now insisted that Rita's contract be renegotiated, depriving her of control over her scripts and directors. He argued that she had been off the screen for three years and had aroused public ire. What guarantee did he have that the public would support a Rita Hayworth film? There had been a storm of protest against Ingrid Bergman when she deserted her husband and daughter for Roberto Rossellini, and groups in America had successfully boycotted her pictures. Ingrid had been at least as big at the box office as Rita.

And the industry had changed. People were losing interest in glamour, and new macho males were catching the public's fancy, actors like Montgomery Clift and Marlon Brando, for example. Television was continuing to grow at an alarming rate, and attendance at films had fallen off drastically.

Rita capitulated. She may have been frightened into believing that he was right. Rita wanted to work now, indeed was anxious to work. But it stood to reason that her return to the screen should be in something special, a really *good* picture—that was only good business sense. It would hardly be wise to *rush* Rita Hayworth before the cameras. But that's exactly what Cohn was anxious to do: take advantage of her current notoriety to test her box office lure immediately.

But Rita was tougher than a lot of people gave her credit for. *Affair in Trinidad* was such a pedestrian, skimpy script that she threw it across the room when she first read it.

Vincent Sherman, a director who had spent most of his career at Warner Bros., had recently directed *Harriet Craig,* with Joan Crawford, for Columbia.

"I was one of the few people who liked Harry Cohn," says Sherman today. "I had read *From Here to Eternity* and knew Columbia had bought it, so I called Harry to see if I could get the assignment."

"Come on over," said Cohn. When Sherman arrived, Cohn said, "Never mind *From Here to Eternity.* I've got something better for you. How would you like to work with Rita Hayworth?"

"Who wouldn't?" replied Sherman.

"She has a contract that's still in force, so I hadda put her back on salary."

"Why me?" Sherman asked.

"I *like* you," Cohn said.

"When the bullshit was over," Sherman says today, "he gave me twenty pages to read and said, 'It's a springboard.'"

After Sherman read the treatment, he said: "It's great. It's a deal." They shook hands, and Cohn said, "Go and see Virginia."

Sherman went up to Virginia Van Upp's office, where he introduced himself to Van Upp and producer Bert Granet. "I asked them what the rest of the story was, and they began bandying back and forth. Two hours later I had heard four or five stories. Granet walked out of the office with me and said, 'Boy, what you just got yourself into.'"

Granet soon left the project, since he felt they were getting nowhere. Cohn told Sherman, "Don't you think I know we're in trouble? I need help. I paid Virginia $50,000 for that story and it hasn't worked out. Throw in a few dance numbers. Make it a love-hate story."

Sherman says, "Now I understood. I was sympathetic. Soon afterwards Virginia left the project, and I got Jimmy Gunn to help me. Frankly, we stole a little from three or four pictures. It was a synthetic piece of material. But one of the ideas—the Soviets establishing bases in the Caribbean—later turned out to be true. Six weeks later we had a first draft and we called in Oscar Saul to help with the script."

In the meantime, Sherman met Rita. He remembers her as being very pleasant, but at first she had little to say. Sherman had already directed some of Hollywood's leading female stars in some of their best performances: Bette Davis in *Mr. Skeffington;* Joan Crawford in one of her most underrated films, *The Damned Don't Cry;* Ann Sheridan in *The Unfaithful* and *Nora Prentiss;* Ida Lupino in *The Hard Way.*

Sherman was looking forward to working with Rita. As Sherman and the writers worked on the script, Rita resumed her dance training, with Valerie Bettis, who had been brought to Hollywood from New York. Bettis would also play a dramatic role in the film. Under Bettis's supervision, the Hayworth shape was beginning to regain its old tone.

The outlook on *Affair in Trinidad* wasn't totally sour. Rita's costar would be Glenn Ford, and she would be surrounded by excellent character actors, including Alexander Scourby, Torin Thatcher, and George Voskovec.

"In six to eight weeks," according to Sherman, "she was back in shape and as good as ever. Cohn had told me, 'Now look, don't give her too much dialogue. She's great at reactions.'" Sherman says, "There's no question he was right. But I was also pleased and surprised to find out she had great potential and realization as an actress as well."

One night Rita dropped by Sherman's office.

"Hello, how's the script going?" she asked.

"Fine," said Sherman. He had already been paid for sixteen weeks, at $3500 a week, and they would begin shooting in a few days. Sherman and Gunn were about to go out to dinner. They invited Rita to join them. She called the children's nurse to say she'd be late, and then accompanied Sherman and Gunn to Lucy's restaurant.

"It was small talk at first," Sherman remembers. "Then Jimmy left, and over coffee Rita told me that she had had over $300,000 when she left and now she had nothing. Apparently, Aly spent her money. She told me about the safari, but I was thinking about Gunn, back at the studio, waiting for me, and I said, 'I'd better get back to work!'

"'You're bored with me, aren't you?' said Rita.

"'God, no!' I exclaimed." He recalls, "It was a poignant and telling moment. I heard she felt she could get a man but couldn't hold one. She was very insecure."

Socially, Rita was keeping a low profile. Although on everyone's "A" list, she went only to a few "important" parties. One evening she was a guest at a glittering soiree at the home of Jack L. Warner. The mogul seemed in awe of her because she was a "princess." This only added to the discomfort she always felt when socializing. By this time she certainly might have been expected to be more at ease—but she wasn't, and made no attempt to be.

One of the people she enjoyed spending time with was old friend Robert Schiffer, the makeup man from *Loves of Carmen* and *Lady From Shanghai*. Rita would often spend a free day with Schiffer on his boat.

Grace Godino, who also knew Schiffer, was friendly with people at the Disney studio who had a boat docked next to Schiffer's. "Oh, then you must have met Rita Hayworth," she said to her friends.

The couple remembered that Schiffer had brought a very nice woman over for cocktails, "but she wasn't a movie star. It was a woman named Margarita something or other."

Rita wore little or no makeup away from the cameras. Bob Schiffer has offered some fascinating observations regarding Rita's most recognizable asset: her face. She was a great beauty, a natural beauty—but not a perfect one. "One eye was a little smaller than the other," he noted, "so I used to take a false eyelash and place it at an angle, then glue her own eyelash to it, just to even her eyes out."

The image of facial perfection presented in Hayworth's closeups was, in fact, an illusion accomplished by the combined talents of cameraman and makeup man. Schiffer has recalled, "Rita was always lit, in those early pictures, for one particular closeup." The cameraman would use a baby spotlight and "look for little rings under the eyes—which Rita had a habit of getting—and he'd bring that spot up until he eliminated them, then he'd take a huge key light and bring that up till it shadowed the baby spot. That's one reason she looked so beautiful in those days—they'd throw four or five of these long, static closeups into every picture.

"Once the cameraman had done all that, I'd come in and work around the eyes. I had a little palette with different colors, and they'd wait till I was satisfied."

While filming *Affair in Trinidad,* Rita spent time with old friends like Schiffer and a few new friends, including Vincent Sherman. Rita called the director one evening and asked him to join her and agent Charles Feldman, whom she was seeing, for drinks.

"She was so miserable," remembers Sherman. "I felt sorry for her—she was a big star but she was a lonely woman.

"But in front of the cameras," Sherman confirms, "although she had been absent for three years, and she was at first a bit insecure, it all came back."

Cohn had unnerved her with tactics such as coming to the set and shouting, "She gets one take and that's all she gets!" People at Columbia knew of Cohn's eccentricities and worked around them. Naturally, Sherman did as many takes as necessary.

And then, about twenty days into filming, the first dance number went before the camera. For the first time, it happened—the pre-Aly Rita emerged—electric, sultry, exciting, mesmerizing. The "Trinidad Lady" number is Rita's first appearance in the picture—an unforgettable entrance. "When she was dancing, she was *most* secure," notes Vincent Sherman.

In other scenes, however, Rita at times looked undeniably melancholy. The camera didn't lie—it was photographing a most unhappy lady. Yet, there was more depth now. The vulnerability remained, but it was more intense and poignant. This was a woman who would have been marvelous in *From Here to Eternity;* artistically and commercially it could have been another *Blood and Sand* for her. But "Cohn wasn't ever going to put Hayworth in that picture, it was *never* under serious consideration for her," observes a former Columbia executive.

"That was an all-star job and Harry would never 'waste' Rita's box office that way. Besides, Joan Crawford had the inside track on that role [of the nymphomaniac lover of Burt Lancaster]. Joan was an intimate friend of Frances Spingold, whose husband was Nate Spingold, one of Cohn's most valuable executives—the man who gave Columbia 'class.' The only reason Deborah Kerr, and not Joan Crawford, got that role was because Crawford and the director, Fred Zinnemann, had a 'misunderstanding' about her wardrobe. And Zinnemann really wanted to cast against type, and with Kerr, he achieved that."

The studio publicity machine was working overtime. Production on *Affair in Trinidad* was launched with a special cocktail party for the press and for a special lady in particular—Rita's avid supporter Louella Parsons.

A private party for Louella was held in Cohn's offices, and Louella was "all dolled up for the occasion," recalls a publicity man. But Rita arrived in one of her shirt-and-jeans outfits. It was an ensemble that would have been hailed as a fantastic "personal statement" by the fashion press of the 1980s, but this was late 1951. For the star not to arrive in satin, sables, and diamonds was

—to Harry Cohn especially—a shock. He barely concealed his anger. "God," he seethed. "She's a princess and that's how she dresses!" But Rita appeared oblivious.

She enjoyed a friendly chat with Louella, who wanted answers to very specific, and very personal, questions. In her disarming and sweet way, Louella was an expert fact finder. Knowing the columnist was not out to destroy her, Rita revealed a great many of her inner feelings.

On leaving Aly: "It may have seemed like a sudden thing, but believe me it wasn't. A strain had been building up between us for six months based on the big and little things that made up the difference in our outlooks on life.

"One big difference was, we did not like the same people. I would often say to Aly, 'Why do you have these hangers-on around you? They are not your real friends. They come just to drink and eat your food.' He would always laugh and say, 'They are not so bad. Just unfortunate.' Unfortunately, I did not share his tolerance."

But Rita defended the prince against allegations that he had mistreated her. "It is wrong for anyone to say or think that Aly was cruel to me. He never lost his temper with me, even when my Spanish-Irish-English temper flared up. Aly always treated me with consideration—after his fashion. He has a happy, carefree temperament."

Had Aly spent her money? "That's another subject difficult to explain. Aly was always extremely generous with me. He bought me beautiful, expensive clothes and gave me jewels. But in his own right, he is not wealthy. He is dependent on what is given him by his father, and his allowance does not always cover his tastes.

"But it is absolutely untrue that he ever asked me to spend my own money. I don't know how such stories start."

It was hardly a great mystery as to how the story had started. There had been an item in the Cholly Knickerbocker society column months earlier that read: "It was a common sight to see Rita lift the tab as she and Aly wandered through the Parisian night-clubs and restaurants."

But now that Rita had made her statement to Louella on the matter, she fervently hoped that that would finally be the end of it.

Hayworth met with the rest of the press, and the publicity avalanche was officially in motion. The theme that would dominate the advertising approach to the picture: *"She's Back!"*

Rita's return to Hollywood had fired up the expectations of the town's most eligible men. Victor Mature was in touch with her again. Charles Feldman was obsessed with her. What had started out as a drinks-and-dinner relationship escalated, in Feldman's mind at least, to a major romance. He sent Rita a brand-new Cadillac convertible, with her initials engraved in gold on the dashboard. She sent it back, and Feldman drove it himself until he bought a Rolls-Royce.

Rita did more socializing than usual during this period, but obviously her heart wasn't in it. One evening Helen Hunt came over to the house Rita was renting in Beverly Hills for herself and the girls. From the living room Helen could hear Rebecca, in the next room, telling herself a bedtime story and, according to Helen, constructing an intricate, fascinating plot.

"*I* certainly wanted to know how the story turned out," says Helen. "Rebecca was a very bright child."

Another friend tells a story of the young Rebecca, in a hotel room, sitting in front of a TV. The youngster looked at a program intently for a few minutes, then got up, snapped off the set, and said, "Silly, isn't it?"

Rebecca was a cute child, now about seven. She was taking dance lessons—with whom else but her grandfather, Eduardo Cansino.

Rita's relationship with her father and brothers always appeared, to the outside world, to be somewhat remote. During certain periods of her life she did not see them often, but they spoke regularly on the phone. And when she needed their support, they were always there. With characteristic Cansino reserve, one of her brothers told a friend, "When we have reason to see each other, we do. We believe in blood loyalty."

Rita needed company and moral support during this difficult period. Helen Hunt remembers another evening at Rita's. The star was going out for a night on the town. Helen looked her over and suggested, "Why don't you wear some jewelry? You need some sparkle with that outfit. How about the ring with the big diamond the prince gave you?"

Rita shrugged. "I don't have it anymore."

"You don't have it?!" exclaimed Helen. "Where is it? What happened to it?"

Rita related that one night at a dinner party another woman was flirting with Aly and kept admiring Rita's ring. At one point Aly "took the ring off my finger and gave it to her."

"*What?!!*" screamed Helen. "Didn't you say anything, didn't you do something?"

"No," Rita said quietly.

This story reveals a great deal concerning the character of both Rita and Aly. Material things meant nothing to either of them, but for different reasons. To Aly, because he could always replace them. To Rita, because she never needed or wanted them in the first place.

"That's obviously one of the reasons Aly married her," says another friend from this period. "If she had been one of the other kind of women—the gold-digging kind—there's no way he would have *married* her, no matter what!"

Meanwhile, as the press avidly trumpeted the return to the screen of the world's premier love goddess, what was Aly up to? Did he miss Rita, had the entire Hayworth chapter of his life, the birth of their daughter, changed him, changed his life-style?

To the contrary—he was womanizing to a greater extent than ever, his tastes taking in an even wider spectrum than before. There were *very* young women now, as well as more mature ladies —that is, in their early thirties. Yet it was amazing how Aly, now forty-one, never seemed to change much, physically—he was as youthful-looking as ever. In fact, Rita Hayworth had made *him* a star! He adored the attention.

He dated actress Joan Fontaine only a couple of months after Rita had walked out on him. It was a joyous "fling"—to use Fontaine's description of the romance—and she was delighted with a gift he gave her, a solid gold cigarette case encrusted with diamonds. Fontaine was far too practical to presume the relationship to be anything more than it seemed to be.

At the Cannes Film Festival voluptuous starlets from all over the world were strutting their stuff virtually in Aly's own back yard. During the festival the Château l'Horizon was the scene of many day-and-night revels, a Playboy Mansion years before Hugh Hefner's.

But early in 1952 the Aga suffered a heart attack, and Aly had to assume many of his father's responsibilities. It was now more important than ever that Aly get back together with Rita; the old man felt very strongly about that.

When Aly's lawyers informed him that Rita's lawyers said she was finally amenable to a meeting, and possibly reuniting with Aly, he was pleased. After more phone calls back and forth, it was finally arranged for Aly to fly to the United States in August to meet with Rita in Hollywood.

Rita was looking forward to that date.

Cohn screened the completed *Affair in Trinidad* for his wife, himself, Sherman, and Jimmy Gunn. After the final fadeout, when the lights came up in the screening room, Cohn said, "It's nothing." He turned to Sherman. "But come in and see me tomorrow."

Sherman reported to Cohn's office the next day.

"I want you to know I appreciate what you've done, and I'm gonna give you a bonus." He turned to Ben Kahane, his assistant. "Give him a check for ten thousand dollars."

Sherman, of course, was surprised and pleased. "I hope the picture does well."

"It will."

"She's Back!" The massive advertising and publicity campaign did its job well and Rita Hayworth returned to the screen in a vehicle which left critics lukewarm ("an imitation *Gilda*" was the gist of their comments), but which was solidly successful where it counted most—the box office.

"Don't tell *me* I'm just one more!" exclaimed Glenn Ford, smacking Rita across the face in one of the key ads used to sell the film. It was a very *Gilda*-like campaign, only this time Ford received equal billing with Rita. However, the emphasis placed on her in all the ads enabled Ford to successfully negotiate a contract dispute with the studio since his contract called for *equal* billing on all levels.

Meanwhile, the documentary Jackson Leighter had filmed in Africa with Rita and Aly was released as a short subject, *Champagne Safari*. The featurette was subsequently booked into many theaters playing *Affair in Trinidad*. Leighter states that the little documentary eventually grossed an astounding $800,000.

Rita kept a print of the film for herself—"I think Yasmin might find it interesting, when she's old enough to understand it."

Affair in Trinidad, which had been made for $1.2 million, high for a black-and-white film in those days, eventually grossed over $7 million worldwide. An appreciative Cohn told Sherman, "She owns twenty-five percent but I'm gonna give *you* two and a half percent of our seventy-five percent."

Harry Cohn had his love goddess back.

The studio had gone all-out publicizing its prodigal superstar. This was still a time when a film company could deliver its stars for product endorsements—"Rita Hayworth Uses Lux Soap"; "Rita Hayworth Wears Hanes Stockings"—in exchange for a plug for the star's latest picture.

Nowadays a star of much lesser magnitude than Rita was then would earn well over a million dollars from such tie-in promotions. But in the early 1950s, lending herself to such exploitation—*at no extra pay*—was a standard part of a star's contract. The visage of the Princess Aly Khan was used to hawk a wide variety of items, as the star's return to the screen was merchandised as thoroughly as possible.

The Rita Hayworth "Look"—the bare shoulders, the cascading hair—was still regarded as the height of allure. "The Look," which had been so carefully nurtured by Columbia's artisans, from Rita's musicals with Fred Astaire through *Cover Girl, Gilda,* and *Carmen,* and even now, in *Trinidad,* was still in. Helen Hunt continued to be besieged by people who wanted the Hayworth look. "Xavier Cugat came to me with his then-wife, Abbe Lane, and asked me: 'Make her hair look like Rita Hayworth's,'" remembers Hunt.

Rita, however, even at this point, was truly tiring of "The Image." She knew there was more to her than that—but that was all her employer was interested in exploiting. The industry motto was "Don't change a good thing." Rita was not merely a "good" thing, she was a *great* "thing." In the minds of the executives, a star is truly great if the *grosses* are great. Rita was a giant money-maker as a sex symbol—so a sex symbol she would have to remain. "Harry Cohn would have liked to keep me that way until I was ninety!" Rita observed bitterly many years later.

Writers under contract to Columbia were now under orders to churn out story ideas for many Hayworth pictures to come, although what Rita would do next was always a subject of long debate: "A musical." "A drama." "A comedy." Cohn had wanted her for *Born Yesterday*, but luckily for Judy Holliday, Rita hadn't been available.

Two of the blockbusters of the past year had been biblical epics —*Quo Vadis* and *David and Bathsheba*—both *non*-De Mille spectaculars.

Under contract to Columbia was the writer Jesse Lasky, Jr., who had written films for Cecil B. De Mille at Paramount. While Rita was making *Affair in Trinidad,* Lasky suggested *Salome* as a vehicle for Rita, and Cohn liked the idea. It would even provide her with a dance number ideally suited to her sex symbol image—the dance of the seven veils. Valerie Bettis could choreograph and Helen Hunt and Jean Louis could go to town creating breath-taking hairstyles and costumes. It would be a big budget. Technicolor.

Rita was amenable to the idea, and the project moved ahead. Naturally, in typical Hollywood fashion, the story was altered to suit the star's image—in this version, Salome would dance, not for the head of John the Baptist, but to try to save him. And even more improbable, she converted to Christianity!

During production Rita casually met the man who would turn out to be a negative turning point in her life. A man who would cause Rita Hayworth not only personal anguish and agony but professional embarrassment—and more.

But things couldn't have looked rosier as plans for production of *Salome* took shape. She was back in the swing of things. And pleased that a possible reconciliation with Aly was on the horizon. *Salome* would be Harry Cohn's personal valentine to his love goddess's Technicolor beauty, and a first-rate cast was signed to support her: Charles Laughton as the notorious King Herod and Judith Anderson as his wife, Herodias. William Dieterle would direct.

Special care was to be taken in the creation of the famous dance of the seven veils—this must present Rita at her most voluptuous and seductive, the living, breathing fulfillment of every man's fantasy—perhaps, most of all, Harry Cohn's.

Cohn was now sixty-one, and his health was failing. He bitterly resented all the changes which had occurred in the industry, as did all the old-line moguls. It was a shock to all when L. B. Mayer was ousted from M-G-M, and Cohn knew he wasn't immune to such treatment. There were many at Columbia's tough front office in New York who felt it was time he considered stepping down, or at least choosing a successor.

It was important that *Salome* be a winner. The prospects were great, and to top it all off, it had a built-in publicity angle—a real-life princess portraying a biblical princess! That was almost as good a hook as "She's Back!"

The hot leading man of the moment, M-G-M's Stewart Granger, was borrowed to be Rita's costar.

As the August date to meet Aly drew nearer, Rita grew nervous with anticipation. But *Salome* was certainly a potent distraction. *Never* had she worked so hard. The lighting necessary for Technicolor was still brutally hot. Her hairstyles were gorgeous, and incredibly flattering—but complicated. Jean Louis's costumes were masterpieces, but her get-up for the dance of the seven veils necessitated wearing the designer's ingenious invention, a molded-to-the-figure nylon body-stocking—Marlene Dietrich would spend thousands of dollars for one when she opened her Las Vegas act—and it was highly uncomfortable.

Costume films may be a feast for the eyes, but wearing the costumes is a killer for the actors. After a few wearings most of the garments became what Stewart Granger described as "pongy"—no matter how many times they were dry-cleaned.

And Rita's dance routine was strenuous indeed, the most demanding of her entire career. It was meticulously photographed and necessitated endless takes and retakes. Vincent Sherman was at one point called in as a consultant.

As production progressed, Rita was distressed at occasional reports still appearing in the press concerning Aly's alleged romantic activities. But she gave him the benefit of the doubt, knowing that the press had been wrong about *her* on more than one occasion—Aly was good copy, that's all. She wondered how truly anxious he was to get back together with her. They'd been separated a long time—almost sixteen months.

Just before Aly's visit, Rita was unexpectedly in the headlines herself. There had suddenly appeared on the scene a handsome young singer named Bob Savage. Six foot three, twenty-nine years old, a former officer in the air force, he had been a band singer until Sophie Tucker, in the words of one newspaper columnist, "took him in hand a year ago and suggested he turn solo vocalist."

Savage had met Rita "at a dinner party." It didn't take long for columnists to receive details, courtesy of the very publicity-minded Mr. Savage.

"Did I feel a spark? It was a fire," he said. "She's tempestuous—that Spanish blood. I didn't know that Aly Khan was coming here. Now mine is a torch bit. I'm in for a siege of not sleeping nights. When you run into somebody like this woman, oh, my God!" he sighed. "I don't know what will happen when and if she is free. I can't predict that now."

"Rumor Says Rita's Picked Her Next!" ran one headline. "Singer Bob Savage 'Smitten,' But Her Pals Say Aly's Still The Man . . .'"

Rita had no comment.

Charles Vidor was still a close chum of Aly's—and Rita's—and on that balmy August night all had been waiting for, Vidor met Aly at the airport and took him to Rita's home. It was about midnight. Much to the prince's surprise, and, one assumes, chagrin, he was only permitted to stay a few hours. He returned the next day, and by that time reporters and photographers were grouped around the house. Aly was charming and amiable. Rita wouldn't pose for photographs but said, "I will pose tomorrow if you'll just go away and leave us alone."

Grace Godino, who was again Rita's stand-in, remembers that Aly Khan visited the set of *Salome* and created even more excitement than the Shah of Iran had created when he and his sister had visited Rita on the set of *Affair in Trinidad*.

While the world was awaiting the latest development in the saga of America's princess, an incident occurred that brought the couple closer together. Yasmin, almost three, was a highly curious child; one day she found a bottle on a bedroom table, opened it, and eagerly tasted the contents. . . . She had swallowed sleeping pills. Rita found her unconscious, and rushed her to the hospital. Aly met Rita there. No one knew how many pills the child had taken. The distraught Rita and Aly, his hand tightly grasping hers, were frozen with tension until the doctors pronounced the little girl "Fine!"

Rita agreed to join Aly in Europe as soon as *Salome* was finished. "He must have done some number on her," theorizes a former associate of Rita's, "because she had a lot going for her again—her career was back in high gear, her relationship with Cohn had settled into some cordiality, and life wasn't unpleasant."

But Aly's reappearance had obviously rekindled Rita's hope for a family unit, a full-time father for Yasmin and Rebecca. And the prince certainly must have given her every reason to believe that things would be as she wished, because "her passion for Aly had waned considerably by then," notes a close associate. "Rita would have accepted it then if his visit had simply ended the whole thing."

Perhaps she hoped they could somehow recapture the idyllic days of Gstaad, after the birth of Yasmin. That had been the happiest time of her life with Aly. "It was the one time we were a family," she has said.

Although *Miss Sadie Thompson,* her next film, was already in preproduction, Rita was exhausted and badly in need of a rest. She would journey to Europe, as promised, and try a reconciliation with Aly, but she was proceeding cautiously. She would leave the children at home. Rita went to New York and sailed aboard the luxury liner *United States*. To the world, their on-again off-again marriage seemed on again. As before their marriage, Aly had pursued her to Hollywood, and as before she followed him back to Europe.

When the *United States* docked in Le Havre, she still would not discuss the reconciliation. "That is a personal matter and I cannot talk about it." She said she'd be in Europe for several months and would be busy "picking up clothes."

Aly was not at Le Havre to meet her. He had sent a car. That was strange, but she thought no more about it. When she arrived at their house in Paris, on the Boulevard Maillot, she found that Aly wasn't there either (he was still at the Château l'Horizon) but the house was full of people. Liz Whitney was there. So were Carlos and Theresa de Campos.

Elsa Maxwell sent roses welcoming her to Paris. Rita called to thank her.

"How is your beautiful Yasmin?" Elsa asked.

"What about my beautiful Rebecca?" Rita shot back. Rita always made a pointed effort to get her friends and associates to treat the children equally. Lifelong friends of Rita's emphasize that she never showed partiality toward either one of her daughters.

"It was tough for Rebecca," notes a friend. "Yasmin was not only the baby, she was a princess and everyone made a fuss over her."

Rita told Elsa, "I've left the children in California. I'm here to see Aly."

He didn't arrive until the next day. But when he did, he appeased her anger and won her over. They spent the night together. They posed for photographers the next day, and Rita said she was abandoning her divorce suit "for the time being." Rita noted that Aly was incredibly cooperative and solicitous with the press. What was going on? His old pace hadn't slackened.

"Rita's Latin blood seethed at Aly's behavior. She became angrier than even she thought she could ever be," says a friend. "She felt she had been duped."

Even Aly's buddiest buddy, Elsa Maxwell, hinted at a highly negative facet of Aly Khan's personality, at this point, when she observed that he hadn't tried all that hard to make the reconciliation work. "Aly, with his Oriental philosophy, merely wanted to force Rita to come to Paris to salve his pride. She had walked out on him. No other woman had ever done that and I know it was a great blow to his *amour propre*—the Aly has vanity, which I am sure he, himself, will admit."

Even the Aga expressed dismay over Aly's behavior upon Rita's arrival. "What's the matter with my son? Can't he at least keep away from the blondes and the brunettes while Rita is here? I understand she's at home crying most of the time."

The final straw came when Aly hosted a dinner party in their apartment, ostensibly in Rita's honor, welcoming her home. It was to be followed by an evening at the "in" Paris nightclub, Jimmie's. Rita didn't show up for the dinner, appeared only briefly, later on, at the club—with two "mystery" escorts—but didn't join Aly's party. It was almost like a scene out of *Gilda*.

She moved to the Hotel Lancaster (she had only been in Paris a week), issuing a statement, "I am bored with Aly's entourage.

"When I come to Paris, it's not to live in a house where there are eighty friends of all kinds coming and going, and it's not to dine at Maxim's. I don't leave Hollywood to be photographed in the salons of Paris or at dinner in big restaurants."

She now had to face the hard fact: Aly's attempt at reconciliation had obviously been made solely "for family reasons."

"But I am not abandoning my Reno suit," declared Rita. "The main thing I'm worried about is Yasmin. I don't want any of his money in order to provide for her upkeep. I'll renounce all such claims just as long as I can keep her."

For the first time Rita was candid about her situation. "He is a playboy, while I work all year round in Hollywood. What's more, Aly spends too much, while I have to work for the two of us. He doesn't understand family life. He thinks only of gambling, horse racing, and big-game hunting."

Aly had told friends that being married to the glamorous star was not what it appeared to be. "All she ever wanted to do was slip into something comfortable and stay around the fire. Excitement? She was just a homebody."

But if the world thought that Rita Hayworth would retreat into a shell again, they were mistaken. Rita flew to Spain, where the handsome young bullfighter Luis Miguel Dominguin dedicated a bull to her.

Bob Savage, who had been signed to a Paramount contract, now alerted Louella Parsons that he was flying to Spain to woo Rita.

"Are you going to marry her?" asked Louella.

Savage replied, "Don't you think it's a little early, since she isn't divorced? But if you ask me if I'm in love with her, the answer is yes—but who isn't?"

Rita was furious on learning of Savage's statements. She said she "only faintly remembered" him, and suspected the whole thing of being "a publicity stunt."

Count José Maria Villapadierna, a handsome, forty-year-old Spanish nobleman, a friend of Aly's and Rita's from several years back, squired her about Madrid. Her pet name for him was "Pepe," and she seemed genuinely interested in him. Friends said he seemed to be the only one who "understood" Rita. He even followed her back to Paris.

Suddenly Rita seemed to be leading exactly the kind of social life Aly wanted her to enjoy *with him*—but she was merely showing him she could lead that type of life anytime, anywhere she chose—what she *preferred* was a home life!

The question was, did he care any longer what she preferred, or was he just anxious to end that chapter of his life once and for all? His closest friends knew the latter was most definitely the case.

The second honeymoon was officially over before it had even begun. Rita instructed Crum: "File for divorce."

"Nothing now stands in the way of a divorce except Rita's own agreement to the documents," Crum said. "Aly has agreed to their contents." This turned out not to be the case. Aly had changed his mind.

"Will you turn the handling of the matter over to a Paris lawyer?" reporters asked the weary Bartley Crum.

"No," he said. "We'll handle it by mail."

Then Crum changed his mind. Top Parisian attorney Suzanne Blum was engaged to represent Rita's interests overseas.

The situation grew more complicated. "This has been a tough

case for me to handle," Bartley Crum told Art Buchwald. "For one thing I'm in a rough spot because I'm a Roman Catholic, and according to a recent decree from the Vatican, Roman Catholic lawyers are not supposed to engage in divorce cases. The only thing that saves me there is that Aly is a Muslim and has never been baptized. So in the eyes of the Church this has never been considered a marriage.

"My other problem is that I'm a member of a very respectable law firm, Hayes, Podell, Algase, Crum and Foyer, and this is the only divorce case we've ever handled. Since I started handling the case, hundreds of women want us to get them divorced."

The case had overtones of a Marx Brothers movie. "This is about the fifth time I've flown over," Crum said. "I feel like I'm flying a trans-Atlantic mail route. Last time I was Cupid. I was trying for a reconciliation. This time I came to wrap the whole thing up. The point is that neither princes nor movie stars can stand this much ridicule, and the whole business is getting rather ridiculous.

"Anyway, what we want now is a settlement for Yasmin and a halt to all the publicity. We'd like to give this separation some shred of dignity."

Rita returned to Hollywood furious, frustrated, and in a state of discontent that boded ill for everyone and everything, most of all herself. The stage was set for a frightening change in her life—as she plunged ahead with preparations for *Miss Sadie Thompson*.

Aly Khan began the New Year with a passionate embrace from a beautiful woman he'd met soon after his attempted reconciliation with Rita had failed.

Aly's new infatuation was another actress, an American, a beautiful brunette, a woman Rita's age—Gene Tierney. Tierney and Aly had first met in Argentina, where Tierney was making a film. In her memoirs, Tierney candidly discussed her feelings about Aly; her relationship with him parallels, and illuminates —to an amazing degree—what had happened between Aly and Rita Hayworth.

Gene Tierney has recalled that, for her, it was hardly love at first sight. "In my mind I labeled him a man of trivia. Nor was I taken with his looks. He had a soft face and looked, I thought, like a thinner version of Orson Welles."

Their paths crossed again in Paris. Aly had been sending her flowers all along, and she agreed to have dinner with him and their mutual friends Fran and Ray Stark. (Mrs. Stark was the daughter of Fanny Brice and a leading Hollywood social figure. Her husband, Ray, was to become one of the most successful motion picture producers in the industry.) Tierney has remembered that as she was preparing to meet her friends and Aly, she thought, "That's all I need, some Oriental superstud."

But she soon changed her tune. As he had with Rita, Aly focused all his charm, his dynamic personality, on Gene. As Rita had, Gene realized he was indeed a truly fascinating man. He sensed Gene's ever-changing moods and feelings, and knew just what kind of response a moment called for. When Aly was introduced to Gene's sister Pat, however, Pat's private opinion was that Aly Khan "saw women as trophies."

But to Gene Tierney—whose personal problems would, within a few short years, engulf her—Aly Khan seemed a wonderful solution to her discontent. Just what he had seemed to Rita, four years earlier.

Gene and Aly became seriously involved. "I was his hostess at receptions," she has recalled. "It was easy to be dazzled at first by that role, greeting his rich and important and sometimes royal friends." She even rented a house near the Château l'Horizon.

But how different Gene Tierney was from Rita Hayworth. Tierney was outgoing, independent, a clotheshorse; she thrived on social intercourse. She bypassed lucrative film offers to remain with Aly—she had fallen in love with him. She had recently divorced Oleg Cassini, a man she had loved very much, and realized later, "Anyone who gets divorced, no matter how inevitable it was, goes through a period of wondering if they will ever be able to care so much again—or have that much to give anybody else. Aly Khan, I believed then, was my answer." Those words could have been uttered by Rita Hayworth when, on the rebound from Orson Welles, she had first met Aly Khan.

Elsa Maxwell was in the thick of this love affair, too, and she was candid with her friend Gene: "Don't take him seriously. Only I can afford to love him. I'm seventy and he cannot hurt me."

The relationship between Aly and Gene continued, however, until finally even she grew weary of the constant social whirl. "At one point I kept him out of nightclubs for three months, surely a record for him. I wasn't trying to reform him. . . . But I did hope he would take life more seriously." A vain hope. And again, words that could have been uttered by Rita Hayworth, although Rita *did* try to reform him.

Tierney has also remembered, "I marveled at Aly's ability to become different people. When he stepped off a plane in Ireland, he was completely Irish. With the Islamites he was a Muslim. . . . It was as natural for him to make people feel happy and important as it was to breathe."

The Aga Khan was so disgruntled by Aly's interest in "*another* actress!" that he privately said he would not receive Gene Tierney even if Aly married her! The Aga was upset that the reconciliation had not worked. Rita would not even let Yasmin out of the United States to visit him. The baby had been "the first baby girl to be born in our family for two hundred years," moaned the Aga.

Tierney summed up Aly's personality perfectly: "Aly Khan's life was a constant escape from responsibility. . . . He did not want to succeed his father as the Aga—he was a misfit in that world. He craved excitement, not reality. He avoided the mosque, preferring racetracks and nightclubs. His favorite reading was one of those pocket guides on horse-breeding, so and so out of so and so. He always carried one with him and, in idle moments, would study it."

Tierney recalled that when Aly wanted to visit her in the United States later on, there was still a question about whether he could enter the country: "He was embroiled in a long-distance legal battle with Rita Hayworth over child support and visitation rights."

NINE

Rita Hayworth rang in 1953 by immersing herself in Hollywood nightlife. She dated Kirk Douglas, Victor Mature—and the man she had met while making *Salome*. The man certain people in the industry referred to as "Mr. Evil." The man who saw a glittering opportunity in the person of the particularly vulnerable redhead who had returned from Europe in such a disgruntled state.

Dick Haymes had an unusual, boyish face, with a highly upturned nose and strange, slanted eyes. He had been a close rival of Frank Sinatra's as the most popular crooner of the 1940s, having sung with the Harry James, Benny Goodman, and Tommy Dorsey orchestras. Haymes's recording of "Little White Lies" sold over two and a half million copies in 1943, and prompted Darryl Zanuck to sign him for films. He was successful onscreen, too, in movie musicals like *State Fair* and in films with Betty Grable. During the war Haymes's hit record "You'll Never Know" sold more than a million copies in two months. But at thirty-five his big career days were already behind him. He had been working on a Columbia cheapie, *Cruising Down the River,* when he met Rita, joining her after work in an executive's office for an occasional drink.

"I simply cannot fathom what she saw in him," states a former close friend and business associate of Rita's. "In my opinion she felt sorry for him. She was very vulnerable at that point and he must have struck some mother-instinct chord in her. It certainly wasn't passionate love—nothing like what she had felt for Orson or Aly."

Haymes was thrice married. His first marriage, to Edith Harper, in 1939, had been annulled a couple of weeks after it took place. His second wife was Joanne Marshall (later Joanne Dru); Harry James was best man at their wedding. They had three children, and the marriage lasted through Haymes's peak years. But success had changed him. Former associates say, "Success went to his head. He became a bad man to do business with. He'd walk into a room, and before he left he'd have everyone there hating him."

At the Hillcrest Country Club, Haymes was known as "The Ten Most Evil Men in Hollywood." Another associate notes, "Of course, if his records had kept selling . . ."

Joanne Dru's career blossomed as Haymes's fell apart, and they divorced. Almost immediately he married Nora Eddington Flynn (an old acquaintance of Rita's—they had spent time together when Welles rented Flynn's yacht for the filming of *The Lady From Shanghai*). Nora and Dick were still married, though separated, when Haymes began seeing Rita.

When Harry Cohn learned that Rita was involved with Haymes, he really went on a rampage, and for once it seemed justified. Haymes was bad news—woman problems, money problems—not the kind of influence Rita needed at this point.

"Some men are in the 'woman business,'" says Phil Silvers, who found Dick Haymes the one unexplainable partner Rita became involved with.

Events moved at a fast pace. Within three months after her disastrous Paris debacle with Aly, she was granted a Nevada divorce —on January 27, 1953—and she was a free agent.

"Three times I have failed in personal happiness. Three times I have been divorced. I can't help but think that some of this must be my fault. In some way I have failed—not only others, but myself," she observed.

"I'm in a stage now of trying to work out my future, sensibly and without romantics. I hope some time that I may know the joys of a real and happy marriage. But anything like that is very far in the future. I have to readjust myself to *myself* and to try to make a new life for Rita Hayworth—and her children."

That Rita, or anyone in her position, could accomplish her goal "sensibly and without romantics," was an almost ludicrous hope. Nothing about her life up to this point had equipped her for dealing with matters on anything but a highly "romantic," and emotional, plane.

Incredibly, some people, like Louella Parsons, herself a romantic, still asked the question: *Was* there any chance of a reconciliation with Aly, even though she had received a Nevada divorce?

"That is not possible," answered Rita. "Not now."

"Aly *has* called me many times on the telephone," she revealed. "He knows my decision is final. When we talk, it is usually about Yasmin and how she is growing and adjusting herself to her new life in America.

"I want Yasmin always to feel that her father loves her. I don't want her to feel neglected as Rebecca often has." Louella took great pleasure in reporting that Orson Welles had never even sent Rebecca a Christmas card.

Yasmin's trust fund and her religious upbringing remained highly touchy issues. "Where Yasmin is concerned, I can see the point of view of the Aga Khan and Aly," Rita said. "After all, the Aga is a head of the Muslim religion. It would be a bitter blow to him if his granddaughter were not brought up in his faith. But I want Yasmin to know of the Christian religion—and when she is older, she can decide for herself."

Some of the press had recently been unkind to Rita, but she said, "I'm not even upset at the writer who printed some of the worst articles. I know that she's Aly's friend and the Aga's, too. I, personally, never read what she wrote; but people have told me some of the things she said. Well, I suppose she has to make a living."

Rita was obviously referring to Elsa Maxwell.

While the love goddess sounded like she had her life under control, such was not the case. Personal demons were taking charge.

Rita took the train to New York for the world premiere of *Salome*. Haymes followed. They checked in to the Plaza, in separate suites. Supposedly he was bound for Broadway in the hope of rebuilding his career. Nora was in the process of getting a divorce. She was reported to be willing to settle for eight thousand dollars in cash and a hundred dollars a week, because of Haymes's poor financial condition. She was being squired about Hollywood by Charles Feldman and was seemingly anxious to get things settled.

But then, when she learned of Haymes's liaison with Rita, the picture changed. There were two reasons. First, married to Rita, "he would have new glamour and his career might be reactivated," observed a friend of Haymes's. Secondly, if Haymes married Rita, she might become liable for the alimony Dick couldn't pay. Such a situation had recently been in the news when Virginia Mayo, because of California's community property law, had to pay back alimony to an ex-wife of Mayo's husband, Michael O'Shea.

But as things stood now, Rita had no intention of marrying anyone. And the public was still unaware of her involvement with the crooner. She was in New York to publicize *Salome,* and publicize it she did. She gave interviews, attended the premiere, and even made a live appearance on Ed Sullivan's famous and popular Sunday night show. Sullivan usually introduced celebrities who were, by prearrangement, sitting in his studio audience. The star would stand up and take a bow, and Sullivan would plug his or her latest venture.

Rita Hayworth was much too big a star for a mere audience appearance. She was brought backstage and waited in the wings to be introduced. Even though Rita had no dialogue, she became so nervous waiting that Sullivan instructed one of the production staff to "get her something," and a strong drink was provided to soothe her nerves.

The audience went wild when she appeared.

The Leighters were in New York with Rita during this trip. Jackson Leighter recalls that after lunch at "21" one afternoon, when they were walking up Fifth Avenue back to the Plaza, "People were so struck with Rita's beauty and presence that they stepped back and made way for her to pass." According to Leighter, it wasn't so much that she was recognized as that her grace and carriage were so arresting that people stopped and stared. By simply *being* in New York, Rita Hayworth was creating excitement about *Salome*.

Harry Cohn was in New York for the film's opening, and Rita sat with Cohn and his guests at the lavish post-premiere party. The mogul was a total gentleman that evening. When Rita was about to smoke a cigarette, Cohn quickly reached for a match and lit it for her.

But Rita didn't let down her defenses for a moment, even though Cohn seemed so anxious to be friendly. He had good reason to be. *Salome* had all the earmarks of a big hit, and the studio's statistics compilers, who were remarkably accurate in determining stars' long-time box office value, had figured out that Rita was good for at least five more years of big-time picture making. Rita had already been on top for thirteen years. Perhaps Cohn hoped that now he and Hayworth could at last have a less adversarial relationship.

Rita was wary of his friendly demeanor. After all these years, she wasn't buying any sudden change in attitude on Cohn's part.

She returned to Hollywood and prepared to leave for location shooting in Hawaii for *Miss Sadie Thompson*.

Those close to Rita were glad she would be getting away from Dick Haymes.

The ex-Princess Aly Khan was out of sorts when it was time to leave for Hawaii. For the first time, friends noted she was drinking *heavily*. In Hollywood, Rita's usual ladylike deportment in public had been abandoned on more than one occasion.

Then the day arrived and cast and crew of *Sadie* departed on a chartered plane. A makeup man had become romantically involved with Rita. "He thought he had it made, that Rita would be his ticket to big things," recalls Helen Hunt. Rita and her new consort stayed in the back of the plane, drinking, while the entourage was en route to Honolulu.

When the plane landed an incident occurred which has always puzzled Helen. As cast and crew got off the plane, Hayworth pinched her and said, "Oh, Helen, look!" Then she said, "Don't look at her—I don't want her to see me!"

Miss Hunt explains, "It was a young lady who'd been Rita's

secretary in the early forties—who Rita had been friendly with. Naturally, there was a crowd waiting at the Honolulu airport, and in the crowd Rita had spotted this woman."

Helen was baffled at Rita's behavior, but had no choice but to comply with Rita's wishes. A few hours later Helen got a call at the hotel. The woman was very upset. "Why did Rita treat me that way?"

"I don't know why."

Helen had dinner with the woman and her husband, a military man stationed in the islands, but still had no explanation for Rita's behavior. She now attributes the odd behavior to Rita's drinking. She notes, however, that "Rita never had hangovers—her eyes were always bright and clear."

A personality change was taking place in Rita, due in part to her increased consumption of alcohol, and things became worse when Dick Haymes showed up. The makeup man was out in the cold.

Harry Cohn was on the phone every morning to Helen Hunt. "Is Haymes there?"

"I haven't seen him."

Helen wasn't lying. "They had a bungalow, but Haymes would be out of bed and gone before I got there every morning. And he never came to the set."

Haymes continued to keep a low profile. Fear of Harry Cohn was one factor. And in his own way he seemed to the cast and crew as reserved and stand-offish as Rita.

A production associate recalls that Hawaii was so beautiful that it was like being somewhere unreal and wonderfully fantastic—it was a setting where people's romantic desires had the perfect opportunity for flights of fancy.

The company finally went back to Hollywood to shoot interiors. Rita was often late coming to the set. Producer Lewis Rachmil remembers, "Getting her there was a problem, but once she was there she worked like a Trojan."

One morning when Rita was late, Cohn sent the entire company home and issued an edict that no one was to talk to Hayworth. She arrived on a deserted set, saw Rachmil, and told him her car had broken down. They had been talking for a few minutes when the phone on the set rang. It was Cohn. He screamed at Rachmil, "Didn't Jack Fier tell you not to talk to Rita?"

"No," answered Rachmil, truthfully.

"Oh," Cohn said, and hung up.

Rita's stand-in remembers, "Whenever Jack Fier or Cohn came onto the set, Rita would tune out. She never became angry or exchanged words with them, she would just get that vacant look." It was a look coming to her face more and more often these days.

Rita was astonished at Cohn's stepped-up war against her. They fought over how she looked in the picture. She had put on some weight and Cohn demanded she wear a tighter girdle, which she vehemently objected to. (In this case, Cohn was right—she looked heavy in the film, and it was distracting.)

The only pleasant aspect of the movie, for Rita, was working with her costar, José Ferrer—who had won an Academy Award as best actor for *Cyrano de Bergerac* and who had just completed *Moulin Rouge*. Ferrer had quite a reputation as a ladies' man. Lewis Rachmil remembers, "She and Joe spoke Italian or Spanish on the set."

Rita also enjoyed playing opposite Aldo Ray. But *Miss Sadie Thompson* was otherwise an ordeal, and a dated film even for its day. Curtis Bernhardt, another old pro, was the director, but he wasn't able to do much with the material.

Sadie was filmed in a gimmicky new process which had momentarily grabbed American audiences: 3-D. Today, seeing Rita in the film's three dimensional process is exciting—her facial bone structure is beautiful to behold, and indicates what a stunning and unique beauty she still was.

But she was heading for disáster as production wound to a close. Thanks partly to Cohn's unceasing efforts to break up her relationship whth Haymes, she had made her decision: to stick by him. Rita herself gave an interesting insight to the workings of her mind: "Listen, all my life I've had trouble making up my mind about everything. But one thing's easy. Whenever I'm threatened, I do just the opposite."

Her association with Haymes, and obviously her drinking, were the causes of her alienating many of her friends during this time.

Of all the Romeos Rita could have felt sorry for, Haymes was the deadliest. For years he had been in and out of troublesome situations—of his own making.

"For a long time he'd been running—from his fading career, from business obligations, from wives and kids and himself," noted an observer. Haymes's financial situation could best be summed up by a line from an old Preston Sturges movie: "He was a refugee, all right—a refugee from his creditors."

Then, one August day in Los Angeles, the crooner was approached by two plainclothesmen.

"Dick Haymes?"

"Yes—"

"We're with the FBI. Will you come with us, please?"

Haymes was then booked for deportation as an Argentinian citizen. He was released on five hundred dollars bail.

The nightmare had begun.

Headlines screamed that Dick Haymes was going to be deported, and the lid of Pandora's box had been opened. Since one of Haymes's creditors was the IRS, it is most probable that because of his tax problems, Haymes's background had been thoroughly investigated, and there were revelations concerning other aspects of his life.

Until now the public had been unaware that Haymes had been born in Argentina and had an Argentine passport and alien status. Why was Dick Haymes, former bobby socks idol, a man perceived by the public to be as American as apple pie, now labeled an alien?

The implications were devastating and of a nature guaranteed to bury anyone's career. By retaining his Argentinian citizenship during World War II Haymes had remained exempt from the draft.

"I tried to enlist twice," he claimed, "but was turned down for hypertension." But now it also came to light that he had signed an official document which read, "I am forever ineligible to become a citizen of the United States."

Haymes retaliated to these disclosures by claiming that his wife at the time had been pregnant. "I felt she needed me. I underestimated the importance of that paper." But the damage was done and the ball was rolling: Haymes was inundated with new demands regarding back taxes, alimony, bills—totaling almost $200,000.

One report said that the government hadn't become interested in Haymes's case until he applied for a new alien registration card. When he was casually asked at the immigration office if he'd been out of the country lately, he said he'd been to Hawaii (Hawaii was not a state at this time). He hadn't realized that a recently passed law, the McCarran-Walter Immigration Act, required a reentry permit, even from outlying U.S. possessions.

Haymes's lawyer claimed that the singer's trip had been cleared by the Immigration Service before he left, but the government would not cancel the order for his arrest and deportation.

"I'm torn apart by headlines. I'm prejudged guilty as a murderer," he cried. However, there was one person who not only sympathized with him but understood his plight—and felt somewhat responsible for it. That person was Rita Hayworth. Who better than she knew how it felt to be a victim? Haymes's mounting problems aroused Rita's protective side and her fierce loyalty.

Salome was playing to big business around the country when the Rita and Dick affair, and his deportation problems, made headlines.

A source was quoted as saying, "When Rita's in love with a man, there's nothing she won't do for him. Anybody who thinks that this romance will end because Dick is in a jam is greatly mistaken. If anything, it will bring Rita to his side. If Dick should have to leave the country, Rita is likely to go with him—make no mistake about that."

Haymes's estranged wife, Nora, and his former wife, Joanne both supported him in his fight against deportation. Harry Cohn—who, insiders suspected, may have been instrumental in tipping off the authorities to Haymes's alien status—now wanted to avoid scandal and was putting pressure on Nora's attorney to get her a quick divorce. But the attorney, S. S. Hahn, said, "Nora wanted to go to Nevada for a quick divorce, but I talked her out of that. She got her divorce from Errol Flynn in Nevada, and has had trouble ever since collecting on the financial arrangement made in that divorce. You just can't make anyone live up to a financial agreement made in the state of Nevada.

"If she had a California divorce from Flynn, we could attach his property here to provide for their two children. I don't want her to fall into a similar trap with Haymes."

Meanwhile, Haymes's association with Rita had finally paid off businesswise: he was signed to a singing engagement at the Sands Hotel in Las Vegas. Then, to the consternation of Harry Cohn and to the dismay and concern of Rita's friends, Rita and Dick suddenly announced they would be married there.

Never before had Rita rushed into anything so important so impetuously. It was an alarming development in her personality, and reminded many of the erratic behavior of Volga Haworth.

"Oh, God!"

Rita was horrified. She made a hysterical phone call to Bartley Crum. She had received two notes threatening death to herself and Yasmin unless she returned to Prince Aly. Jackson Leighter said one of the notes warned the actress not to marry Dick Haymes.

"I don't know if this is serious or not," said Crum, "but it would be very foolish to take a chance." The children were immediately placed under armed guard.

"I don't know who would do this, or why," moaned Rita. "I'm not worried for myself, but I am concerned over the welfare of my child. My child must be kept safe and unmolested, regardless of what it costs."

The FBI opened an investigation. Had some Muslim fanatic become incensed when Rita turned down a divorce settlement of a million dollars on Yasmin because she objected to a condition calling for Yasmin to be exposed to Muslim teachings when she reached the age of seven? Rita had also objected to having the child taken to Europe for two or three months each year.

The death threats put Rita's private life more negatively in the press than ever before. Fortunately, she still had the benefit of advice from longtime close business associates, whom Haymes would soon permanently alienate. Many close to Rita thought she was marrying Haymes simply to save him from being deported— any alien married to a United States citizen would eventually be on safe ground. Others thought she had succumbed to the singer's charm, his constant declarations that he would always love and protect her.

Haymes agreed to sign a prenuptial agreement protecting Rita's earnings from any of his debts. He proudly declared, "I love this girl so much that I will do anything in the world to protect her. I intend to stand on my own two feet and take care of all my own troubles. I only thank God that I have her and her love to inspire me enough to work and fight my own battles."

The events that led up to Rita's marriage to Aly Khan seemed like a highly dignified ritual compared to the circus surrounding her involvement with Dick Haymes. Aly, at this point, was also in the news—but on quite a different level—he was in London with Gene Tierney, attending coronation festivities for Queen Elizabeth II.

For Rita and Dick, there came a new development: Haymes's divorce. Nora had obtained a California divorce, but under California law Dick would not be free to marry for a year, so he had obtained a Nevada divorce, which would allow him to remarry after thirty days. He then asked Nora to sign a special waiver permitting him to remarry immediately. She refused.

The only reason the soon-to-be-ex-Mrs. Haymes hadn't signed the waiver, she said, was because "I want to read it and study it first. Then I'll probably sign it. I don't want to be mean about this —I just want to know what I'm signing."

The scene of Rita and Dick's marriage would not be a glamorous European locale. Hayworth and Haymes would be married in the Gold Room of the Sands Hotel, and if Rita had second thoughts about the situation, Haymes saw to it that she didn't dwell on them. He was with her twenty-four hours a day. There was no turning back now.

"Smile, Rita!"
"Over here, Rita and Dick!"
"One more, please . . ."
Jack Entratter, president of the Sands, was best man at the wedding. There seemed to be more press agents in attendance than guests. *Life* magazine noted that while Rita's previous marriage had been champagne and diamonds, this one was "rhine-

stones." Actually, Rita wore no jewelry. Her dress was pale blue linen (the same color she'd worn when she married Aly). Haymes slipped an antique ring on her finger and the "I do's" made their union official. Everything had happened so fast. . . .

Haymes managed to fulfill his singing engagement, with a morose-looking Rita sitting ringside for a few of his performances. To Rita's chagrin, she had discovered that it was expected she would be in the audience at every performance! She missed quite a few, and there was nothing anyone could do about it—though, in private, when drinking, Haymes wasn't shy about shouting his displeasure with her.

He was facing an alarming number of negative situations—not only the deportation proceedings but actions on alimony arrears and hounding by the IRS for back taxes. The combined pressures landed him in a hospital with a "nervous breakdown."

"I'm just tired," he said. "I want to go to my wife."

Rita wasn't doing too well herself.

That fall she had turned thirty-five. She and Haymes traveled a great deal. They were in New York in November and attended a dinner at the Waldorf-Astoria for former President Harry S Truman.

Then, at Christmastime, *Miss Sadie Thompson* opened. The ad campaign highlighted a full-figure photograph of Rita, provocatively twirling a purse, a cigarette dangling from her lips. She was wearing a sexy blouse and a slit-up-the-thigh skirt. "Rita Turns It On In 3-D!" proclaimed the ads (in which her waistline had been amply reduced by the retouchers). But now Rita had to face a professional crisis as new to her as her new husband. *Sadie Thompson* was no *Salome*. It opened in New York to good reviews for Rita, but only fair business, and would prove a financial flop throughout the country.

The new year, 1954, turned into a Kafka-style nightmare for them both.

"We know you're in there. You might as well let us in so we can get this over with."

The female voice from the other side of the door was frightened and plaintive. "Go away."

The banging on the door continued. "We're not leaving," said one of the deputy sheriffs. "We're staying here until Haymes comes out."

This was truly like a scene from one of Columbia's old B movies. But this time the scene didn't end with someone yelling "Cut!" Rita was a reluctant actress in the continuing drama surrounding the life of Dick Haymes. The scene was a barricaded hotel suite in New York's Madison Hotel. The scenario: an ex-Mrs. Haymes was suing her former spouse for over $50,000—an amount due her from a property settlement agreed on four years ago. Authorities were trying to arrest him for alimony arrears.

"Get out of here," Haymes growled through the door. "Just go away and leave us alone."

Bartley Crum was summoned to extricate the couple from the predicament. Running from the law was certainly a new experience for the screen's wearying love goddess, whose predicaments were arousing much shaking-of-heads at the highest levels of Hollywood's echelons.

Then another disaster.

The newlyweds had rented a fourteen-room mansion in Greenwich, Connecticut, in December, and now the landlord claimed they hadn't paid the rent and were preparing to vacate without doing so. He also claimed they had damaged valuable objects on the premises, to the tune of five thousand dollars.

A sheriff was sent to the Connecticut home to be sure the couple's possessions stayed put. Haymes and Rita were in New York at the time this occurred, while the children, their dog, a governess, and a housekeeper were in the mansion, bewildered and confused by all the goings-on.

The "rent troubles" certainly shed light on the dilapidated state of Dick's finances. Haymes's mother had signed the lease, and the landlord had obtained a writ against her. Rita and Dick came up with the $675 rent, and again Bartley Crum came to the rescue.

The wire services reported that Haymes would "return soon to his native Argentina." Crum said this wasn't true.

Trouble seemed to rain down from the skies. The IRS attached Haymes's earnings, claiming he owed them $90,000 in back taxes. Lesser debts—one to a leading men's clothing store, one to a local garage which claimed Haymes owed them eighty dollars for gas—piled additional layers of negative publicity on the embattled couple.

Crum had reason to be glad he had had Haymes sign that prenuptial agreement protecting Rita's money.

Harry Cohn had acquired *Joseph and His Brethren,* the first picture L. B. Mayer would produce away from M-G-M. David O. Selznick had turned down Mayer's offer to be affiliated with the project, as well as his offer to have Jennifer Jones (Mrs. Selznick) play the lead. Selznick had expressed the opinion that the script needed so much rewriting that the project wasn't worth pursuing. But Cohn had long idolized L. B. Mayer, and the opportunity to do business with him—in fact, to be in a position over the legendary mogul—was too tempting to pass up.

Besides, Cohn saw *Joseph* as a commercial project. Biblical epics were reliable box office. *The Robe,* the first picture in CinemaScope, had opened to blockbuster business. *Salome* had proved that Rita in biblical costume was a draw. De Mille was preparing *The Ten Commandments,* a sure winner, which would continue the trend. *Joseph and His Brethren,* starring Rita Hayworth, would be a damned good gamble. Cohn decided to do it.

Meanwhile, the poor box office showing of *Sadie,* as well as all the problems Rita was presenting, forced a reluctant Cohn finally to instruct his casting department: "Let's make another star."

Rita's personal travails continued. If, over the next year and a half, she had spent as much time on the sound stage as she had in court, or as she had in discussing upcoming court matters pertaining either to Haymes or Yasmin, Rita would have had a picture in release every year. The situation was dangerously exhausting for the emotionally drained woman, yet there were more surprises on the horizon.

Observers noted that both Haymes and Rita were like two children flailing around in quicksand, hanging on to each other yet also battling each other. The going got rougher.

The couple needed money, but Rita had refused to go ahead with *Joseph and His Brethren.* She was terrified of another grueling costume picture. She simply couldn't face it. She was placed on suspension.

Even Cohn was aware that there was no way the love goddess could do her stuff in front of the cameras in her current state of health. The studio advanced her $75,000 and lent Dick Haymes $50,000 to help him settle his own pressing situation, so that Rita could have peace of mind and prepare for *Joseph and His Brethren*. (The "loan" would create further complications in the future.)

Another major problem presented itself: Who would play Joseph? Cohn looked on it as a star-making role, a vehicle to launch a new Brando, and a search was begun for an actor to play the part.

Bartley Crum and Dick Haymes, who had become chummy, came up with their own solution to Rita's (and Dick's) continuing financial problems: dissolve the Beckworth Corporation to provide Rita with additional funds.

"It was worth three million, easily," says Jackson Leighter today. "But they convinced Rita to sell for $750,000."

Ben Kahane, a Columbia executive described by Leighter as "a good egg," telephoned Leighter and warned him that Dick Haymes and Bartley Crum were trying to get him out of Beckworth. Leighter resigned from the corporation. By this time Rita had alienated all of her close friends. An associate recalls: "Abe Lastfogel [head of the William Morris Agency] was the last one to try to help her extricate herself from the Dick Haymes situation."

Hollywood insiders considered it an outright joke that Haymes was to be in charge of the new corporation Rita was forming. He was trying to control every aspect of her life. He had even convinced her to change her hair color back, from red to dark brown. "She liked the idea," one insider reports, "because it was a step toward becoming an actress, not a sex symbol."

Rita had agreed to meet personally with Aly's lawyers in April to discuss the matters of Yasmin's support and the trust fund to be set up for her.

This lingering proceeding was extremely embarrassing to the

ailing Aga Khan, because Rita absolutely refused to go along with any of his—and ostensibly Aly's—most important wishes. Rita's lawyers made the most of the fact that Aly hadn't wasted any time in conferring settlements on his two sons by his previous marriage.

"Typical, how Muslim women are treated as second-rate beings," was the gist of Bartley Crum's comments. Very embarrassing indeed for the Aga—and even more so for Aly.

It is to Rita's everlasting credit that despite her frazzled nerves and the many pressures on her she refused to buckle under to any of her former father-in-law's demands. Rita realized the importance of her child being raised in America and as an American. Even the incredible wealth of the Aga Khan could not deliver the dividends which accrued to that.

"Come to Florida with me," said Haymes to Rita. She was by now as fed up with all the lawyers as Dick was. There was a singing engagement for Haymes in Florida.

Rita was tempted. In addition to everything else, she was depressed over current newspaper accounts concerning the love affair of Aly Khan and Gene Tierney. Aly had flown to Mexico to be with Gene. He couldn't enter the United States because Rita's lawyers would serve him with subpoenas. Tierney was filming *The Egyptian* (one of her costars was none other than Victor Mature), and gossip was rife concerning the imminent marriage of Gene Tierney and Aly Khan.

Tierney had given out many statements regarding their close relationship and the probability of their marriage. But the prince continued to maintain his "no comment" attitude. However all the signs seemed to be pointing toward an official union.

The prospect of running away from it all was very tantalizing to Rita, and it didn't take much coaxing from Haymes to convince her to take the trip to Florida. Haymes and alcohol were her constant companions during these difficult days.

During her holiday in Florida with Haymes she received shattering news from Bartley Crum: her daughters had been taken into custody by the Children's Court in White Plains, New York, on a petition of the Society for the Prevention of Cruelty to Children.

Rita was shocked—aghast—they were *what?* Taken *where?* By

who? Were they all right? What . . . what in God's name had happened? Who was to blame? . . . She totally blamed herself, of course.

Crum quieted Rita's hysterical queries. The girls were fine but Rita and Dick would have to rush back.

For Rita Hayworth, this was the nadir. This development certainly sobered her up, no matter how much she wanted to wash it all away. As she flew back to New York, Crum was in the process of contacting both Aly Khan and Orson Welles. Their presence would be essential to the upcoming proceedings.

What had happened was this. Rita had permitted Haymes to enlist the services of Dorothy Chambers, a friend of Haymes's mother, to act as the children's "governess." If Rita had been working on all cylinders, she never would have acquiesced. In terms of references and experience, Mrs. Chambers did not compare with the women previously employed by Hayworth to take care of the girls. Prior to this point it had been a matter on which Rita was a fanatic, but now her judgment was off.

Mrs. Chambers lived in a rather run-down neighborhood in White Plains. Nearby lived a friend who operated an antique shop in her home. Yasmin and Rebecca were permitted to roam about both premises freely—a rather shocking development, considering that Yasmin's life had been threatened not many months before—and the premises seemed none too clean.

Mrs. Chambers had been taking care of the girls for over a month, and it was never revealed who contacted the Society for the Prevention of Cruelty to Children—or why. Mrs. Chambers's opinion: "*Someone* wanted publicity."

"She's here! She's here!"

"Let's get a look at her!" It was like the famous funeral scene in *A Star Is Born* as the limousine pulled up to the White Plains courthouse on April 26 and the mob of curiosity seekers swarmed around it. Photographers and reporters pushed and shoved as the grim-faced star, wearing no makeup, followed by her bespectacled husband, alighted from the vehicle.

"Over here, Rita!"

"Rita—Dick—smile!"

She ignored them all and made her way into the courtroom, Haymes following behind her. Aly had left Gene Tierney's side to be at the hearing, and Orson's attorney had arrived with an affidavit from his client stating how fine a mother Rita was.

There was a three-hour meeting with the judge, behind closed doors, and the children, seeming none the worse for wear, were returned to Rita's temporary custody.

Children's Court Judge George W. Smyth declared, "The case will be continued and retained under the jurisdiction of the court until the court is satisfied that assurances given the court today are fully carried out."

Rita burst into tears as she left the courtroom and almost passed out as the throng pressed close for an intimate view.

The matter was far from over. A scandal magazine had obtained photographs of Rebecca and Yasmin while in Mrs. Chambers's care, and the photos clearly displayed the girls, having a seemingly grand time, playing in what were, no doubt about it, filthy conditions.

Rita, truly shocked, knew what she must do. It wouldn't be easy.

Aly was "uncommonly disturbed" by the charges. "This is a very important matter to the prince," said an associate, "because the princess is fourth in line to the ascendancy of the Aga Khan's title. Also, Princess Yasmin is the first woman in the line in two hundred years. She is very important to the Ismailis. This story is big news to millions of them who are horrified at what is happening to their princess."

Actually, the prince's advisers told him that the scandal might work in his interest: it might help him gain complete custody of his daughter. Unknown to Rita, his lawyers had begun proceedings to *prevent* Rita from regaining custody.

Bartley Crum was in Tel Aviv when he learned of Aly Khan's plans, and immediately flew back to New York. He fired a direct broadside at Aly: "We shall show the court what kind of home life Aly Khan has, and no doubt shall also subpoena his current girl friends, including some of Hollywood's most famous stars."

Aly got the message. Onerous headlines—"Crum Threatens to

Air Aly Khan's Private Life"—convinced the prince not to make a court case about Rita's suitability as a mother. Rita eventually regained custody.

But the scandal had given Aly's lawyers leverage in the discussions about Yasmin's future. Bartley Crum summed things up and tried to take the focus *off* his client's private life: "The main issue has been a matter of security. Aly is to have custody of Yasmin, in any country he chooses, for three months annually. The mother wants to be sure the child will be returned to her after the specified period.

"Various countries have various laws and various police procedures. Mrs. Haymes wants to make sure that she is given sufficient power to invoke police action if the father should attempt to hold Yasmin."

Rita put off signing any document.

Aly confirmed that, according to the proposed terms, he would have custody of Yasmin "for part of the year, not for most of it. She will have her the major part of the year."

Why hadn't Rita signed yet? Bartley Crum explained that his client "wants to go over the entire document and have everything explained to her."

Incredibly, Crum said that Rita was consulting with Haymes on the matter! He added, however, "We do not anticipate any difficulty," and noted that the question of Yasmin's religious training had not been raised in the agreement, and would not be. The question would be decided when Yasmin reached "the age of reason, about seven years old."

The settlement, as with everything in Rita's life during these days, wasn't resolved that simply. Negotiations dragged on for many months more. Finally, in November, there was some good news. The agreement for Yasmin's trust fund and support was very close to being finalized, with only minor details to be worked out. In all, it had been three long years in litigation.

The settlement recognized Yasmin as one of the Aga's five heirs (the others being Aly, Aly's half-brother Sadruddin, and Aly's two sons). Bartley Crum estimated the Aga's fortune at one billion dollars. Therefore, even though, under Muslim law, male heirs generally received double shares, Yasmin's share could possibly come to $140 million!

The agreement provided $8000 a year for Yasmin's support, and $100,000 would be deposited annually in a special account, just prior to Yasmin's yearly visits to Aly. The money would be used to "recover" the young princess if she was not returned to her mother on time, and replaced if this contingency occurred.

The $100,000 yearly deposits would accrue to form the girl's trust fund, reaching maturity when she turned twenty-five. That would amount to over $1.4 million. Furthermore, and of equal importance, the child would be raised as a Christian and an American, although the agreement provided that she would be tutored in the Muslim faith for two consecutive hours each week.

From Aly Khan's point of view, it was a total victory for Rita. It was a humiliating development to the Aga that in addition he was forced to supply a letter guaranteeing Yasmin's return *on time*. The entire agreement had to be validated by French courts, so that Rita could call on the police in France to help her if the agreement was violated. Never before had the illustrious Khan clan ever been a party to such a severe and confining contract.

Rita Hayworth seemed to have achieved everything she wanted for her daughter. Now what about her own life?

Columbia notified Rita that production was at last ready to begin on *Joseph and His Brethren*. She, Haymes, and the children returned to Hollywood.

Preproduction dragged on. "All during *Joseph and His Brethren*—through all kinds of tests—she wouldn't talk with me," says Helen Hunt. "She wasn't mad at me—just not talking with anyone. That *look* of hers never left her face for six weeks."

The picture wasn't ready to go when the announced starting date arrived. Rita promptly sued for her full compensation—reportedly in the neighborhood of $200,000—claiming that the studio had failed to fulfill its obligation to begin the production on time.

She was very unsettled. It was dangerous for her to be idle. She hadn't worked in over a year. She wanted to work. Get paid for it.

Instead, there would be months in which to do nothing but worry, drink, and feel guilty.

The embattled Haymeses smiled for photographers in May 1955, when it became official that Haymes could not be deported. Crum had obtained an affidavit proving that Haymes *was* "entrapped" into leaving the United States for Hawaii when he was courting Rita. It seemed that a former employee of the Immigration Division in Los Angeles had been ordered by his superior not to reveal to Haymes that the singer was in danger of losing his right to reenter the United States.

Haymes, sporting a beard, looked elated when he received the good news. Rita, her hair dark and cropped short, looked awful. In seeing Dick through his series of crises, she had tarnished her own image considerably. She wanted to leave Haymes but wasn't yet able to. He was threatening, abusive. He had physically struck her in front of the children—and even in public. He later denied that he had hit Rita in the eye, saying "We just had a husband-and-wife spat." She was fearful of yet more scandal and ridicule.

With the resolution of the deportation issue a weight had been lifted from her shoulders, but the friction between her and Dick remained intolerable. She wanted to patch up her differences with the studio, but he was making unreasonable demands. As head of Rita's new production company, he wanted to coproduce *Joseph* —and incredibly, he wanted to *portray* Joseph. That was why he had grown the beard. Under no circumstances would Columbia even consider this. The trouble-plagued film was shelved. It would be cheaper to write off all costs to date and not proceed further. Columbia countersued Rita, and the lawsuits dragged on.

Flight was Rita's solution. She took her daughters and disappeared from the Malibu home she shared with Haymes. No one knew her whereabouts, but it was obvious she was finally splitting with Dick. "If I ever needed her, I need her now," whined Haymes to reporters. He literally wept, hysterically, calling Rita "the only love of my life." His explanation of the separation: "We began saying things—things about our careers and our previous marriages."

Rita was *very* troubled, to use an observer's words, about the "bad business advice" Haymes had given her. Her whereabouts were kept from Haymes (in fact she was at the home of Joseph Cotten), and she did not show up in court to face Columbia's attorneys. Her lawyer produced a certificate from her doctor, Fred D. Cerni, stating that Rita's separation from Haymes had been "such an emotional shock that I have ordered her to bed for several days. She was so upset I prescribed sedatives for her. Her health would also be endangered if she were forced to attend the trial."

Haymes, by this time, was so close to another breakdown *he* was given sedatives; his agents feared he would be unable to fulfill a $2500-per-week singing engagement at the Los Angeles Ambassador Hotel, which was "sold out." Vic Damone was standing by just in case.

Haymes showed. He dedicated his first song, "Come Rain or Come Shine," to Rita. But in private, he moaned, "I'm still very, very bitter about Columbia. I'm sure studio officials were behind the Immigration Service's campaign to haunt me."

Rita remained incommunicado. But Haymes kept communicating with her via the press. He told the world, "I don't know what I'll do without Rita. She's wonderful. I can't go on without her. I'm in love with her. A man is only in love once. If she divorces me, I don't know what I'll do!"

Rita filed for divorce, and to get even further away from Haymes, she took her daughters and went to Europe. There she hoped to heal some of the wounds the last few years had etched on her psyche. Perhaps she could somehow bring some order to her harried life, and piece together what was left of her career.

TEN

Rita's appearance reflected her state of mind—there was barely a vestige of youth left on her beautiful face, although she was only thirty-seven years old. The Haymes calamity, and waging war with Cohn, had done severe damage—deadened something inside her. It had been two years of hell.

Now was the time to have sought professional—even spiritual—help. But Rita simply hid from the world—and from herself—and waited for things to somehow sort themselves out.

She did nothing to play up her glamour in public—she wore no makeup or jewels, and wore subdued clothing. Her hair was a very dark mahogany shade, not flaming red or strawberry blonde. For the time being she could be successfully anonymous, in Europe, and the unfamiliar peace and quiet were reassuring companions, although any sharp-eyed observer would inevitably be drawn to the still striking face, the strong jawline, firm as ever, and wonder: Don't I know who that woman is? . . .

Fortunately, the furor over Rita Hayworth's comings and goings had died down considerably—funny how the press could lose interest virtually overnight.

While Rita and the children were abroad, they were visited by the Aga and Begum. Rita made a sudden trip back to the United States in December, leaving both girls with Aly at the Château l'Horizon. It looked as if her dispute with Columbia could be settled.

Los Angeles Federal Court was the setting for a dramatic encounter between Rita and the Columbia lawyers. At one point in her testimony, she broke down sobbing. The lawyers for the studio seemed sad and embarrassed.

After hearing all the testimony, the judge, Benjamin Harrison, finally commented, "I have the impression that Mr. Haymes really is the source of all the trouble in this case. I hope both parties will settle this matter themselves."

They did.

Rita would do two pictures for Columbia—for approximately $300,000—to finish off her commitment. That was $125,000 less than she would normally have been paid for two films, and there would be no percentage of the profits. (Still, this was 1956 dollars —translated to 1980s dollars she was getting almost a million dollars per picture.)

However, the studio had no immediate properties for her. *Pal Joey* was in preparation, but many details had to be worked out.

Kim Novak was now Cohn's princess, Hayworth's replacement. It had taken less than three years. The Columbia machine that had so successfully manufactured Rita Hayworth out of Margarita Cansino had accomplished the same with Chicago-born Marilyn Novak, last of the studio-made stars. Harry Cohn's dealings with "the new girl" were no more cordial than they had been with Rita, except Cohn was now old and sick (he had a severe heart condition in addition to cancer) and Kim Novak was twenty-five, strong-minded, and determined.

Discussing Kim and Rita in an interview with *Time* magazine, Cohn declared that stars "believe their publicity after a while, there's nothing you can do about it. I have never met a grateful performer in the picture business." He railed against Rita: "Hayworth might be worth ten million dollars today easily! She owned twenty-five percent of the profits with her own company and had hit after hit and she had to get married and had to get out of the business and took a suspension because she fell in love again. . . . Think of what she could have made! But she didn't make pictures! She took two or three suspensions! She got mixed up with different characters! Unpredictable!"

What Cohn didn't say was that Rita, like most stars, had discovered that her percentage meant almost nothing—"profits" were notoriously low when it came to the bottom line. Rita had accused Cohn of siphoning off profits from Beckworth to offset losses from other Columbia films.

Now Rita languished in Europe in semiseclusion. Her children were enrolled in private schools. Her finances were apparently still in a tangle, as she now sued Orson Welles for more than $22,000, which she claimed he owed for Rebecca's support.

"In the past eight and a half years he has not paid a penny for her support, though the California courts in 1947 ordered him to pay fifty dollars a week," said Rita.

Bartley Crum noted, "We are hopeful of avoiding the unpleasantness of actually going into court, but so far we have had no response from Orson Welles or his counsel. Frankly, this is not too pleasant a chore."

Film director Robert Parrish, also in Europe, brought Rita a script, written by Irwin Shaw, with a part initially intended for Ava Gardner. Ava had starred in Joseph L. Mankiewicz's *The Barefoot Contessa,* which many people felt was loosely based on Rita's life story—a Spanish girl fiercely independent of both her family and the movie mogul who makes her an international star. There was even a sequence showing the character dancing barefoot among gypsies, much as Rita had danced with her family in front of Aly Khan. Some say Mankiewicz had approached Rita to play the part in *Contessa* and she turned it down because of the similarities to her own life. Ava and Rita were very similar—glamour girls who were willing and eager to do more serious work at the expense of their glamour image.

Rita found the role of Irena in *Fire Down Below* a challenge and was willing to do it.

Parrish called Cohn.

"Is she right for the part?" the mogul asked.

"Of course."

"Does she look okay?"

"Fabulous."

"We'll work it out."

Cohn gave the go-ahead and a big production was mounted: color, CinemaScope, location filming in the Caribbean, and a dance number for Rita at a carnival. *Two* top leading men: Robert Mitchum and Columbia's explosive new young comedy star, Jack Lemmon, playing a dramatic role. The prospects were exciting: "3 of the Biggest in 1 of the Best!" the publicity would scream.

Location work was being done in Trinidad in the spring. Things got off to a good start. While Rita was nervous at the beginning, she was happy to be back at work; she was comfortable with Parrish and grew to adore Mitchum and Lemmon.

The men enjoyed working with her as well. Her earthiness was a welcome change from many of Hollywood's "movie queens." An interesting observation by someone on the set: "Rita was a phenomenon who was never worried about her looks. In her quiet way, she was very sure of herself."

Rita was also a good sport. Offscreen, Rita and the hard-drinking Mitchum found they were most compatible. Mrs. Mitchum soon joined her husband as filming progressed, putting a stop to rumors.

In Trinidad, Rita had a respite from her personal travails, and she blocked out the rest of the world. One day, as she was sitting by the shore with a package of unopened letters, she ripped them in half, letter by letter, and threw them into the sea.

It was virtually a vacation in Trinidad, but when the company returned to England for interior shooting, the mood changed. Rita overheard one of the production executives remark to a lighting technician, "Speed it up! No matter how you light her, she's not gonna look any younger!"

Someone on the set recalls, "Rita froze. From this point on she did her job, but the guard-all barrier was up. She was unapproachable."

Ed Sullivan was in Europe at the time *Fire Down Below* was shooting, and he filmed a guest segment for his show featuring Rita, Mitchum, and Lemmon. The threesome were seated informally outdoors as Sullivan queried them. Rita was as quiet as a mouse during most of the interview. Sullivan turned to her and said, "Rita, you're considered one of the most beautiful women in the world and I have a question—who do *you* consider the most beautiful woman you've ever met?"

Rita hesitated and then answered, "Queen Elizabeth."

Sullivan, surprised, asked her, "Why do you say that?"

"Her skin," answered Rita. "She has the most beautiful complexion I've ever seen."

When Rita returned to the United States, the press heralded her with major stories and photo coverage—but she hardly elicited the same *"She's Back!"* excitement she had only six years earlier. She would have looked more like her old self if she hadn't darkened her hair and subdued her appearance. She didn't care.

There was a new princess in the news. The union of Grace Kelly and the Prince of Monaco had captured the public's attention, and Rita was happy to give up the front page. All she seemed interested in was working.

There was some consternation at Columbia regarding the cast of Rita's next picture. Contractual billing presented a major problem. Rita's swan song for Columbia would be *Pal Joey,* and her contract was crystal clear: top billing, period.

"But Sinatra has to get top billing," exclaimed Cohn's nervous executives. Kim Novak was the third proposed star of the production, but the studio controlled her billing.

As it turned out, Frank Sinatra, then at the very peak of his successful film comeback—launched in Columbia's *From Here to Eternity*—had no objection to second billing. "I don't mind being in the middle of that sandwich," he quipped.

Ironically, the property had been bought for Rita seventeen years earlier, when she would have played Linda, the "young skirt." The project languished for a few years because of censorship problems. After the success of *Cover Girl,* Cohn had wanted to reteam Rita with Gene Kelly, who had played Joey on Broadway. M-G-M wouldn't lend him. Then, in the midfifties, Cohn had wanted Marlene Dietrich for the role of Vera. But Dietrich insisted on Sinatra for the part of Joey, and Cohn refused, again shelving the project. Famed producer-director-writer Billy Wilder was brought to Columbia by Jerry Wald to discuss making *Pal Joey.* Wilder had a great idea—Marlon Brando for the heel, Joey, and Mae West for the older woman. He spoke with their agents and found both Brando and West agreeable. This would really point up the younger man–older woman element of the story. But when Wilder met Cohn to discuss it he found the mogul aghast.

"Doesn't this jerk realize Rita Hayworth has to play the part?" Cohn told Wald. "And what's all this shit about their age difference?"

A few weeks after Wilder's meeting with Cohn, Wald was told the deal was off and he moved out of Columbia.

Sinatra would play Joey, Rita would play Vera, and Kim Novak would play the role Rita had originally been scheduled for.

Although she was "the older woman," Rita, in fact, was three years younger than Frank Sinatra. She felt she didn't look like any "older woman" but was anxious to complete the Columbia commitment once and for all.

With her old friends Helen Hunt and Jean Louis behind the scenes handling her hairstyles and costumes, there was an attempt to create the Rita Hayworth of old. She had even taken to playing basketball to get back into shape. But she was now a different woman indeed. The makeup and hairdressing people had a difficult time trying to transform Margarita Cansino into Rita Hayworth, love goddess. It was a classic situation—the star too old to be a sex symbol, too young for character parts.

During the shooting of *Joey* the cast and crew waited for fireworks between Rita and Kim, but none ever came. It was not in Rita's nature to play "star."

One day during a scene with Rita, Kim Novak was having problems with her costume. Harry Cohn was called. "There was quite a furor. Kim was in tears and it was obvious we were going to be delayed for some time," recalls Grace Godino. "Everyone expected Rita to walk off. She just looked at me, shrugged, and sat in her chair with her 'Call me when you're ready' look."

Some of *Pal Joey* was shot in San Francisco, the rest at the studio. Grace Godino recalls, "At first Frank Sinatra wasn't too chummy on the set—it was as though he were feeling Rita out. He had been wisecracking a lot, and Rita, never any good on the uptake, hadn't been responding."

But Sinatra was standing next to Grace while Rita was doing the striptease number, "Zip." As always, Rita's great personality change in front of the cameras occurred.

"Wow!" Sinatra said.

"His eyes got big, and it was as if he finally discovered what everyone had been talking about," recalls Grace. "Here was the Rita Hayworth that everyone knew from the screen."

George Sidney, an old hand at directing both big stars and big musicals, did a workmanlike job with *Pal Joey,* but the camera-man could have been more creative with Rita. She looked tired throughout most of the film, and positively matronly in the confrontation scene with youthfully radiant Kim Novak. But all the special efforts were aimed at Kim.

There was no competitive bitchery between the two women. "Rita was sweet," said Novak, years later. Rita didn't envy Kim at all—the poor girl was welcome to Harry Cohn and all that came with him. Did *anyone* deserve that?

That spring Rita was contacted by a frantic Aly, asking her to rush Yasmin to the bedside of the gravely ill Aga, who was in Cannes. Rita, of course, complied—the seven-year-old child arrived in time. On April 12, 1957, the Aga died.

Yasmin remained in Europe with her father for a while. That summer, in Geneva, she was presented to female religious followers of Prince Karim, her half-brother, who was the new Aga Khan IV. The child acquitted herself admirably, and many said that Rita could only be praised, not faulted, in her raising of Yasmin—the girl behaved with amazing poise and dignity. There seemed to be no trace of the Hayworth shyness.

Fire Down Below opened in the summer. Although many of Rita's fans were disheartened at her somewhat haggard appearance, at least the old Hayworth fire ignited during the dance number. However, in the rest of the film, her energy level seemed awfully low. When she said "Armies have marched over me," audiences believed her. *Fire Down Below* never got off the ground at the box office, although most critics wrote glowing appraisals of Hayworth's performance.

Pal Joey opened a few months later. The picture was a box office hit, but Sinatra and Kim Novak were considered the drawing cards, even though Rita had top billing. Again Rita's tired appearance was distracting, but her acting won the critics' raves.

She had seemingly made the transition she hoped for: she was being taken seriously as an actress. And as Rita grew older, she did not, as some actresses do, allow the characters she played to become more masculine and aggressive. The women she portrayed remained vulnerable and feminine—they simply grew more womanly. This attitude also reflected Rita's offscreen persona—she still resisted the impulse to run her life as if she were a man.

Rita's vulnerability, the quality which made men want to put her on a pedestal, want to protect her, still existed. The men who had loved her retained fond memories of their feelings for her. In the late 1950s Victor Mature reminisced about his love for Rita and how he had lost her when she fell under the spell of Orson Welles. Others, too, regretted that their relationships with Rita had not culminated in more permanent alliances.

But by this time, because of Rita's marriage to Haymes and her changing life-style, she was circulating in a different social milieu. To the disappointment and shock of many, Rita began to be seen with another man whose name raised eyebrows. He was someone who had a reputation as one of the crudest characters in show business. His excesses were legendary—he had been making headlines for over fifty years for his many marriages and countless romantic interludes with increasingly younger women.

George Jessel had been a top Broadway star in the 1920s. He had a big hit with *The Jazz Singer,* but had turned down Warners' offer to star in the film version—which would be the first talking picture—because he was afraid their checks would bounce.

Jessel continued performing and entered the production end of the movie industry. By the 1940s he was Darryl F. Zanuck's right-hand man at Twentieth Century-Fox. He produced several of Betty Grable's movies and one of Tyrone Power's best, *Nightmare Alley.* Jessel was also in charge of bringing gorgeous, available young ladies to Mr. Zanuck's personal attention, a function which brought him an unflattering nickname within Hollywood's inner circles. His more publicized nicknames were "The Toastmaster General," because of his popularity on the testimonial circuit, and "the schnorrer" (Yiddish for professional beggar), because of his enormous success as a fundraiser for various humanitarian causes (an activity that would win him a special Oscar in 1969).

Rita Hayworth was the kind of woman George Jessel's generation of men adored: beautiful, sexy, but basically willing to be told what to do. And, in addition to being famous and successful, Rita was a suitable age for "the schnorrer." The pairing didn't make him appear like a lecherous old man. It wasn't hurting his reputation to be seen with her. Perhaps he could even produce a couple of pictures with her. Jessel had wanted to work with Hayworth since his heyday at Fox.

He squired Rita about town and to various industry functions. One premiere was televised on the Steve Allen show. It was a "remote"—Allen was back at the studio, interviewing celebrities arriving at the theater via television monitors.

When Jessel appeared on camera, Steve asked him a few questions, and then: "Who's the lovely lady with you, George? Would you like to introduce her to our audience?"

Jessel was surprised. "Who is she? She's Rita Hayworth, Steve! You've heard of her!"

Allen tried to cover his gaffe. "Of course, of course! The lights are blinding my view!"

Rita was wearing her hair in an upsweep, as she had in some scenes for *Joey,* but since it was not the famous hairdo that had become her trademark, Allen's failure to recognize her was understandable. Nevertheless, it was an indication that the love goddess was becoming an unfamiliar face.

The pairing of Hayworth and Jessel generated considerable publicity. Louella Parsons went so far as to say they were "engaged." During one of their many nights on the town, Jessel later recalled, he and Rita "had both imbibed a great deal of sauce, and while we were dancing, I asked Rita to marry me. . . . Rita and I both decided we couldn't make liars out of the gossips of Hollywood.

"She agreed enthusiastically, and we climbed into the back seat of my car for the trip to Las Vegas. Because of the effect of the booze, we fell asleep while George, my chauffeur of many years, started out on the seven-hour drive to Bagdad-on-the-Desert. At Baker, George stopped for gas. It was then that Rita woke up; her head was in my lap, face up. She stretched, looked up at me, and murmured, 'I love you, Phil!'

"With that, I shouted to George: 'Back to L.A.!'"

Jessel noted that many years later Rita and he laughed about that night, "and she said she had never dated anyone she could remember named Phil, let alone been in love with such a person." And Jessel commented, "More's the pity . . . for 'Phil.'"

ELEVEN

 After she completed *Pal Joey*, Rita was, for the first time in twenty years—a free agent, professionally. It was a good time to be freelancing; stars' salaries had just begun their rocket-ship rise to astronomical heights. While Rita no longer looked like Gilda, she had just starred in two major films opposite top leading men, and her name commanded instant attention and respect from agents and producers.

 Independent production was flourishing. One of the prime new "indie" groups was Hecht-Hill-Lancaster, consisting of producer Harold Hecht, screenwriter-producer James Hill, and star Burt Lancaster. Hill, a forty-year-old bachelor, had encountered Rita on several occasions over the years. Around the time *Pal Joey* was in preproduction, their quiet relationship began.

 In his youth, Hill, a native of Indiana, had gone to New York to work as a page boy for a radio network. He eventually went to Hollywood and became a screenwriter and top executive. But until he began dating Rita Hayworth, few outside of Hollywood had ever heard of him. At the time Rita and Hill dated, Hecht-Hill-Lancaster was "hot." *Trapeze,* with Lancaster, Tony Curtis, and Gina Lollobrigida, was an international blockbuster and the company was now preparing a screen version of Terence Rattigan's hit play *Separate Tables*.

 Rattigan had wanted his intimate pals Vivien Leigh and Laurence Olivier to star with Burt Lancaster in the film version, and the casting seemed set. But to Rattigan's consternation, the plans changed. One version of the story was that the Oliviers "dropped out" of the production. But other industry sources indicate that United Artists executives pressured Hecht-Hill-Lancaster to get stars who were better film box office than Leigh and Olivier. David Niven, Deborah Kerr, and Wendy Hiller were signed. But the pivotal role of the aging fashion model was still open, and Hill asked Rita if she wanted to play it. The part, described as a "love-worn woman with an unhappy past and a dubious future," seemed perfect typecasting.

Rattigan, however, was very unhappy, and confided his feelings to one of his friends at the party announcing Rita's casting in the film. The friend had a unique suggestion. "Let's push her off the balcony," said a tipsy Judy Garland. Rattigan persuaded Judy that tossing Rita overboard was a bit too drastic a measure, even for his taste.

Rita's relationship with Hill intensified. Soon she stopped seeing other men. Hayworth's affiliation with Hill *seemed* a step in the right direction. He was hardly a Dick Haymes or a George Jessel. Hill's professional advice made sense. In *Separate Tables* she had the kind of role she wanted to play, she was being paid $300,000, and she was given star billing. Delbert Mann, a top "new generation" talent, was the director.

With *Separate Tables* a new career appeared to be in motion for the former love goddess—with a man to guide it, and her. Rita was a woman who wanted to be married, and Hill had never taken the plunge before. They announced their engagement, but Rita's friends took a "let's wait and see" attitude. Look how the Jessel engagement had proven to be untrue.

Meanwhile, a new public image of Rita was being presented, emphasizing the "out of bondage" theme that was proving useful to many stars of Rita's era, including Clark Gable, Lana Turner, and Robert Taylor—people whose careers had been handled solely by one studio for a long period of time.

Rita told friends that, with Hill, she was happier than at any other time of her life. Hill seemed to love Rebecca and Yasmin and the idea of a "ready-made family."

Rita was raising her daughters with a "no nonsense" attitude.

Those close to Rita emphasize that the girls were given love and attention, but *not* indulged as many children of movie stars were.

"Becky collects stamps and Yasmin collects friends," Rita said. "Both girls started their dancing lessons with my father, as I did."

Family life was an essential part of what Rita wanted. Before marrying Hill she had been seeing him for over a year, although she had said, "There's a big difference between dates and love."

On February 2, 1958, Hayworth and Hill were married in Rita's Beverly Hills home. Her brother Vernon gave her in marriage, and it was by far the most dignified of Rita's weddings. Rebecca and Yasmin were present, as they had been at her marriage to Haymes. Hill seemed a most "sensible" choice for a husband. No grand passions were on the line. Respectability was the keynote.

Rita appeared content. "Marilyn Monroe and Jayne Mansfield can have the headlines. I've had enough! From now on the only headlines I want are on my acting." Despite Rattigan's fears, Rita gave a good performance in *Separate Tables* and won some favorable critical attention. "I'm choosing my own parts now. I want to do pictures that are good, and I want to play women that aren't just beautiful or glamorous—they have to be mature women."

Rita also liked her part in *Separate Tables* because "I didn't have to do any dancing in it." Although she told people she enjoyed appearing in musicals, she also said, "You have no idea how much I always look forward to roles in which I do not have to rehearse and limber up for months. It's always a great relief to be able to come out of rehearsals without the aching limbs and sore muscles of a dancer."

Edith Head designed Rita's costumes for the film. A winner of many Oscars, Head had worked with superstars dating back to Clara Bow. But never, noted the designer, "had I worked with anyone who was less of a problem than Rita. I didn't have to be a diplomat with her, trying to talk her into this or that. She hardly *ever* looked in a mirror, and allowed me *total* carte blanche in creating her character's wardrobe."

The man who had fostered the beautiful and glamorous image known as Rita Hayworth died just a few weeks after Rita's fifth marriage. Harry Cohn's funeral was the source of much black humor. It was reported that "thousands" had turned out for the funeral service held at the studio, and that this was the largest crowd ever at a Hollywood funeral. Red Skelton observed, on his network TV program, "It only proves what they always say—give the public something they wanna see and they'll come out for it!"

Rita did not attend the funeral.

Before her marriage to Hill, Rita had been living in a rented house. Now the couple bought a nine-room one-level home in Beverly Hills, just behind the famed Beverly Hills Hotel. It had been designed by noted architect John Woolf.

"The house is perfect for us," said Rita.

That summer, she and Hill traveled to England aboard the luxury liner *United States*. There was quite a stir when Hill arrived in Southampton with a black eye. Could the couple have been quarreling?

At the time, he assured friends Rita did not give him the black eye. "I slipped in the bathroom and my head hit a revolving door."

But Hill himself subsequently revealed that Rita had given him the injury—"right over the eye with the phone receiver"—because she thought he had been flirting with a girl in the ship's bar.

The couple remained in England for six weeks, where Rita met with Orson, and later with Aly, to discuss their respective children. They were back in Hollywood in time for Rita's birthday, in October 1958. The love goddess was forty. In the 1950s, the age of forty was considered *old*. A milestone, especially for an actress.

How did Rita view herself at forty? "As a forty-year-old woman," she said matter-of-factly. "Why does everybody ask how I feel about having birthdays? Everybody has them. It's natural, and changing your point of view as you mature is natural, too.

"I don't know what the future will be—it depends on what comes along. But I'm happy now. For the first time in my career, I'm a free agent, and I like it. And am I happy in this marriage? I sure am."

"I have no plans for Europe," she told associates. "Jim and I have pictures to do here. Besides, my daughters are in school in Beverly Hills."

Rita, however, didn't want to make any more pictures—Hill convinced her to continue working. She was signed to star with Gary Cooper in a big western, *They Came to Cordura*. Tab Hunter and Van Heflin were also in the cast. "Funny to think I started in westerns," noted Rita. "I was always on a horse in those first pictures—and I was so scared of horses!"

And she was back at Columbia—a Columbia minus Harry Cohn. It was a different atmosphere, and the studio's love goddess was now an *actress*. In *Cordura*, Rita wore one outfit throughout most of the film. "You wear fancy clothes if the part calls for it," Rita pragmatized. "But I'm not a glamour girl anymore." Much of the film was shot on location in Utah.

Separate Tables had opened to excellent reviews, and good business in the big cities. It went on to become one of the top ten films of the year, garnering seven Academy Award nominations. David Niven won the "Best Actor" Oscar, and Wendy Hiller "Best Supporting Actress."

Rita had made her freelance debut in one of the year's prestigious films, and was following it up with another. She was garnering good reviews and upbeat publicity. In less than four years' time, the pendulum had swung her way again. The image of the Haymes years, scandal and litigation, were over. She was no longer a sex symbol—she was now an upper-middle-class married woman with two daughters in school, who had resumed her very lucrative and successful career.

It must be noted that, while married to Hill, Rita was under the protection of the best public relations advice and assistance. She was not at the mercy of Harry Cohn's wishes to have the studio's PR people support her—or abandon her.

Rita was now a part of the Hecht-Hill-Lancaster "family." Her name value was not ignored. She was a judge in a "pin-up girl" contest the company's publicity department dreamed up to publicize their Clark Gable–Burt Lancaster starrer, *Run Silent, Run Deep*, a World War II adventure drama. The stunt got quite a lot of coverage—Rita Hayworth still had many fans in the press.

As far as the public was concerned, this was a relatively tranquil period in her personal life. She and Hill did not go out much. Rita had discovered she loved to paint, and was content to spend a great deal of time—she wanted to spend *all* her time—concentrating on this new pastime; she wanted Hill to devote his energies to writing, not producing.

The couple had a small circle of friends and entertained at home. They were close to Burt Lancaster and his wife, and heavy-drinking Van Heflin and his wife. Occasionally the Hills were seen at a premiere or party, and if a special event was taking place they might attend. They went with Hermes Pan to see the Bolshoi Ballet when the famous company appeared in Los Angeles. Afterward, Rita was bubbling over with excitement—at least she had not lost her enthusiasm for dancing, as she had for so many other things. It was always a pleasure to see Hayworth vibrant and animated.

Nights on the town, however, were rare. "Jim and I don't really need to do anything to be happy together. Quiet evenings at home are some of our most enjoyable moments together. We shall keep our lives as normal as possible."

She told friends Hill had given her cookbooks and hoped that her domestic bent would include the kitchen. Rita tried—there was something deep in her that wanted to be a good wife and home-maker—but she simply was not suited to domestic chores.

Their quiet evenings at home were often not quiet.

Bernie Kamber, who was then director of publicity for Hecht-Hill-Lancaster, has told of an evening he spent with the Hills. "She doesn't entertain much but Rita would like to have you over for dinner," Hill had said. Rita was cooking dinner herself.

The couple met and welcomed Kamber to their home. Hill mixed cocktails, but Rita declared she wasn't having any because she was tending to dinner. The men sat down with their drinks and the evening began amiably.

Rita chatted with them awhile, went into the kitchen to check on dinner, then came back and chatted a little while longer. During the course of the evening, her usually reserved demeanor subtly changed. At one point she turned to Kamber and said out of the blue, "You know, you look a lot like Ed Sullivan."

Kamber managed to reply, "Well . . . thank you."

Hill turned to Rita. "Oh, he looks nothing at all like Ed Sullivan!"

Rita's voice grew louder. "I tell you he's a carbon copy of Ed Sullivan!"

Hill rose from his chair. "And I tell you he looks no more like Ed Sullivan than . . ."

Rita screamed, "And I tell you . . ."

And Hill screamed, "You must be sneaking drinks out there!"

Kamber sat dazed while Rita and Hill stormed into the kitchen, where the argument continued. Soon there was a crash. The sounds issuing from the kitchen told Kamber that the elaborate dinner Rita was preparing had been thrown across the room.

Suddenly Hill dashed out of the kitchen, grabbed the arm of his guest, and hurried him out the door. The two men barely escaped the raging Rita. She followed them out of the house as they got into the car and raced away.

As was usually the case after such evenings, Rita did not remember much the next morning. Hill undoubtedly reminded her of her behavior, and as always, she regretted it. A few days later, Hill went to Kamber. "You know, Rita feels awful about what happened the other night. . . ."

There are many tales of people encountering Rita in situations such as this. Unfortunately, her dependence on alcohol, and the behavioral changes it brought about, would worsen. During this period of her life, however, these incidents occurred mostly in private circumstances.

Hill encouraged Rita to sort out her complicated legal entanglements. She began to part company with her longtime attorney Bartley Crum. In July 1959, after Rita and Hill returned to New York from a golfing tour of Scotland, Hill arranged for Rita and Aly (who was now Pakistan's delegate to the United Nations) to meet in New York. The latest bone of contention involved Yasmin's possible right to one fifth of the Aga's fabulous estate.

Both Rita and Aly agreed that all legal entanglements between them be canceled. "The only one hurt by all this is the child," Rita said. "She has her whole life ahead of her. Why should we complicate it? After all, I never wanted a dime for Yasmin, and that still stands."

Rita's split with Crum became final and she also announced she was definitely *not* suing Orson Welles for child support. "I never asked for a dime from him either, but what bothered me most was that the children and their friends in school might read these things in the papers about themselves." Most important in Rita's mind was that Yasmin and Aly should resume their visits to each other.

Several months later Aly came to Hollywood to visit Yasmin and see his circle of West Coast pals. His old friend Merle Oberon gave a dinner dance, and Rita and Jim Hill were invited. Rita and Aly danced together and had quite a long talk, and they agreed that Yasmin would spend the following summer with Aly at the Château l'Horizon.

Aly seemed, after many years, on the verge of another marriage—to Bettina, the woman who had modeled Rita's trousseau at the Fath salon. Bettina was with Aly in his Lancia on May 12, 1960, when the car was in a collision. Bettina, miraculously, survived. Aly Khan was killed.

Rita was on the golf course with Hill when Hill was called to the clubhouse and told the news. He relayed the tragic information to Rita. She was disbelieving—devastated. The death of one she had loved so deeply was a trauma for her—as the death of her mother had been. But Hill helped her momentarily pull herself together—there was someone more important than herself to consider: Yasmin.

Rita was determined to tell the child herself rather than allow her to hear it on the radio or from strangers. Hill had sent a chauffeured car to pick Yasmin up at her skating lesson and bring her directly home.

When Rita and Hill sat Yasmin down and broke the awful news, Yasmin was terribly upset. She had seen her father only three weeks previously, when he had flown out from New York before leaving for Europe. He had telephoned her from Paris only two days before.

Later in the day Hill helped a shaky Rita prepare a statement: "For both Yasmin and myself, I can only say at this time how deeply moved we are at the news of Aly's death. It will be a tremendous loss to Yasmin, who has always been most attached to her father."

Despite the hundreds, indeed thousands, of liaisons in his brief lifetime, Aly Khan had wed only two women, Joan Guinness and Rita Hayworth. They were the mothers of his children and the women he loved enough to marry.

With the death of forty-nine-year-old Aly Khan, an era truly came to a close.

TWELVE

Rita continued to work. In *The Story on Page One*, the ingredients of the production promised something unique. Renowned playwright Clifford Odets had always wanted to work with Rita. He wrote the script and would direct for the first time. Anthony Franciosa and Gig Young were Rita's costars, and legendary cinematographer James Wong Howe was in charge of photography.

This was the most dramatic role departure for Rita yet—not only was she a loveworn woman on trial for murder, but she was supposed to be lower middle class—never had Rita Hayworth been so deglamorized.

Rita's performance was excellent and the critics raved. But the film was a total disaster at the box office, and *They Came to Cordura* was also a disappointment financially.

The Hill-Hayworth marriage appeared to be faltering. Hill took up residence at the Château Marmont, and it was widely reported that he and Rita were living apart. Sheilah Graham stated outright, "Talk around town is that Rita and Hill are through."

The predictions of the doom-sayers were premature. Hill and Rita moved ahead with plans to do their own film. Hill left Hecht-Hill-Lancaster and formed a new company with Rita: Hillworth. Their first production would be a comedy about art swindlers, *The Happy Thieves*, and for the first—and only—time, Rita's name would appear on the credits (along with Hill's) as producer.

A first-class production was mounted. Rex Harrison was signed as costar. Veteran George Marshall was the director. John Gay wrote the script, based on a Richard Condon novel (*The Oldest Confession*). Others in the cast included Alida Valli (who had been heralded as "the new Garbo" at the time Rita was the industry's number one star), Joseph Wiseman, and a very beautiful young Scandinavian girl, Britt Ekland (who was still known at the time as Brita Ekman).

The Happy Thieves would be shot, in black-and-white, in Rita's favorite city, Madrid. On paper the production had the trappings of a winner.

However, even before the Hills left Hollywood, there was continued talk of discord in the Hill-Hayworth marriage. But all rumors were set aside when the couple left for Spain to begin shooting. Yasmin made her screen debut as an extra, in a group of young children trouping through the Prado while Rita and Rex are planning to steal a Goya. A natural for publicity, eleven-year-old Yasmin said, "I'm not allowed to talk to journalists."

Rex Harrison had known Rita socially but had never worked with her before. He was surprised at her shyness. "She was desperately shy and uncertain of herself, although she had worked for so many years. Rita was absolutely beautiful; the film was rubbish." He added that it had been "sloppy professional judgment" on his part to accept the role.

None of the ingredients of *The Happy Thieves* meshed. Rita's habit of never looking in a mirror was no asset at this point: her hairstyles and clothing were most unflattering.

Soon after returning to Hollywood, Rita and Hill proceeded with plans for a psychological thriller, *I Want My Mother!* Rita would play the mother of a psychopath. But *The Happy Thieves* turned out to be a fiasco and was only spottily released in the United States. The new project was dropped. United Artists was leery of another Hillworth venture.

Rita and Hill split.

The announcement was prepared by Henry C. Rogers—the same Henry C. Rogers who had arranged the famous *Look* interview back in Rita's early days with Columbia. He did it as a personal favor, at the request of Rita's agent, who invited him over to his office one afternoon: "There's an old friend of yours here, and I want to surprise you."

When Rogers arrived at the agent's office he was surprised—and pleased—to see Rita. "I hadn't seen her, except on the screen, for years."

After fifteen minutes of small talk—Rogers noted that Rita looked very good—the agent told him that Rita was divorcing Hill, and asked Henry, "As a favor, for old times' sake, would you prepare and issue a press release?"

"Of course," said Rogers. "But I'll need a little information." He turned to Rita. "When did you get married?"

"I don't remember."

"You don't remember?"

"I don't remember what year it was—I do remember it was Groundhog Day."

Rogers recalls that he was shocked that her memory was that faulty. But he assured her he would find the information and prepare the release.

On June 30, 1961, the press noted, "Rita Hayworth and her fifth husband, producer James Hill, have separated and a divorce is imminent."

In September she filed for divorce. About their "quiet evenings at home" she said, "He would come in the door, go straight to his room and wouldn't even talk to me all night." She added, "He said I was not a nice woman in too loud a voice."

Rita's modus operandi hadn't changed. After the split with Orson she had taken up with Glenn Ford and then Tony Martin; after the final split with Aly she had plunged into the disastrous relationship with Haymes; now, after her divorce from Hill, she embarked on a stormy new relationship. The actor who captured her attention was in her own age group, and had already been married, for ten years, to the tempestuous, fiery-tempered Bette Davis.

Davis and Gary Merrill had split in the spring of the previous year and were deeply involved in a bitter custody fight over their children. Bette had brought an action against Merrill to deny him visiting rights. She charged him with being "drunk and disorderly" and "incapable of behaving properly in front of his family." According to Davis, Merrill became violently drunk in the presence of the children and had been physically abusive to her. Merrill denied all charges, and eventually the court upheld his rights to visit the children.

"Security was always bad medicine for him," Davis said. "Once he had something, I'm afraid he didn't want it anymore." Gary Merrill and Rita Hayworth appeared to want each other very much in late 1961.

Rita had decided to flee Hollywood. Go back to Europe for a while. She even contemplated moving there. "That's what Ava has done," she noted. She headed for Madrid. There was talk that she and Merrill would make a film there, *On the Carousel,* but the project fizzled.

In Europe she threw caution to the winds as she and Gary traipsed through Spain and Italy, often barefoot and in jeans, appearing to be leading the bohemian life she loved. They drank heavily and brawled in public—not only with each other but with reporters, photographers, and even fans who intruded on their privacy.

Again, the pendulum of public opinion swung against her. The press began to censure her for her behavior. Some implied that she was carrying the torch for the dead Aly Khan: "It was said of Aly," wrote Louella Parsons, "that once a woman fell in love with him she never got over it."

These romantic interpretations of Rita's behavior collided with the realistic appraisals that she was just a drinker who had given herself over to hedonism. Or a woman who had taken to the bottle to escape the pressures of Hollywood.

Because of her reputation as a drinker, no one considered the possibility that her erratic behavior, her lapses of memory, her habit of "tuning out" could in fact be the early stages of another health problem.

Rita Hayworth and Gary Merrill returned to Hollywood, where they continued to generate unflattering gossip. Restaurateur Jean Leon has described a January night when Rita and Gary came to his restaurant with Yasmin, who was in California to spend her birthday and the Christmas holidays with her mother. The twelve-year-old princess was flying back to Switzerland to return to school. Rita and Gary were planning to drive her to the airport to catch a midnight plane. According to Leon, Rita and Gary "were charming as always when they came in the door. They waited fifteen minutes for a table. They had some appetizer and everything was fine. Then during the entrée there started a heated argument. Rita was saying things about Bette Davis.

"Everything else stopped. There was no eating being done; everyone was watching them. There were about one hundred and fifty people, all listening closely.

"I went over to their table. 'Rita, please lower your voice,' I asked.

"Then I said, 'Gary, please get up!'

" 'I'm not doing anything,' he said. 'Throw her out.'

"I couldn't throw Rita out. She is a good friend of mine. Besides, she's a woman. I couldn't use violence.

"I asked Gary again to leave. He asked for the check. I said, 'There is no check.' He went outside to get the car. Rita didn't follow immediately. She had another course. Then she left and I followed."

When Leon, accompanying Yasmin, got to the parking lot, the argument had flared up again. "They were hitting each other, and shouting." Leon finally calmed them down and Rita got into the car, but she leaped out when Merrill got in beside her. The actor stalked off, and Rita returned to the car. Because of the state Rita was in, the gallant restaurateur offered to drive her and Yasmin to the airport so that the girl could catch her plane.

"On the way to the airport Rita began criticizing me," Leon recalled. "She said I was taking Gary's part."

To top off the evening, when they arrived at Los Angeles International airport they discovered that Yasmin's flight was for noon the following day, not midnight as Rita and Gary had thought.

Leon drove Rita and the princess home.

A close associate of Rita's, who has known her for over forty years and knew her well during this period, points out that on the mornings after such outbursts, Rita would remember nothing.

Her affair with Merrill continued.

The actor was not only a successful film actor, but a stage actor as well. He was approached by producer Herbert Bayard Swope, Jr., and playwright Bernard Evslin about returning to Broadway in a play called *Step on a Crack*. Merrill read the script and passed it along to Rita, who said, "I love it and I'd like to play your wife."

Gary said, "You're kidding!"

Rita had been approached for many stage roles and had always turned them down. But this time she said, "No, I'm serious."

According to producer Swope, during a meeting with Merrill, "Gary said, 'You know, I know an ideal person for Ellen if she'd be interested.'

"I asked who, and he said, 'Rita Hayworth.'

"'That's a wonderful idea,' I replied, 'but now let's get on to other things.' I told Merrill he could show her the script if he wanted. The next day, I got a call that she was interested."

Although Rita Hayworth had never done stage plays, what producer wouldn't have been interested? Rita denied that Merrill had talked her into it. "It's my decision," she said.

Naturally, there were major, valid questions about whether she could cope with an eight-performance-a-week schedule—with no retakes. "The screen affords a lot of discipline that people aren't aware of," Rita protested soberly. "Getting up at five o'clock on a cold morning for location shots in Utah isn't luxury. And I've always worked out a character as a whole, not simply scene by scene."

Apparently it didn't occur to Rita to point out that she had received her initial training in "live" theater. As one of the dancing Cansinos, she had done twenty performances a week, week-in, week-out, as her father's partner in Caliente—had that not been the toughest training ground possible for a performer?

When asked, at this juncture, if she was a quick study, she replied, "That depends on the material. I should say I'm fairly quick. And I think I'll be able to fill a theater with my voice."

Although Rita had made the commitment in February, rehearsals didn't begin until August. Ample time to have prepared for the part, and yet . . .

Rita and Merrill spent the spring and summer back in California. For a while they were discreet about their relationship and restrained in their behavior, because that summer Merrill had custody of his son, Michael, for six weeks—over Bette Davis's objections. Bette had even hired private detectives to keep tabs on her former husband's activities while Michael was with him.

At the close of summer, Gary and Rita returned to New York to begin rehearsals. Rita was radiant with the press. "I'm not doing this simply to show I can," she said. "It's just that I have confidence. I feel I have changed. I feel more mature—I hope I am. I hadn't really ever thought of doing a play. There had been many scripts submitted, none that I wanted. I fell in love with this role."

Rehearsal started on August 14. Herbert Swope was directing, as well as coproducing with Roger Stevens. On the first day of rehearsals, Rita looked lovely in a simple, sleeveless black dress, hair casually but flatteringly coiffed, a pair of glasses hanging from a white cord around her neck. She and Merrill appeared very businesslike and friendly and visions of a new theatrical couple a la the Lunts must have loomed in the imaginations of many.

Swope introduced Rita and Merrill to the rest of the cast— Donald Madden, Margaret Hayes, Maggie McNamara, and Joey Heatherton. They did a read-through, looked at a model of the set, and discussed some early changes in the script. The Toronto opening was scheduled for September 8, 1962. But seven days after rehearsals began, Rita was hospitalized. Her physician, Dr. Harold Eiber, said, "I'm not letting her go back to the play. She's still anemic and needs three or four weeks of treatment." The show's press agent had said she was suffering from "nervous exhaustion." Someone connected with the production recalls, "She just couldn't do it." Nancy Kelly was brought in to do the part. Kelly was the "emergency star replacement" of the day. With almost no notice she had filled in for Margaret Sullavan in a TV drama when Sullavan had vanished a few hours before air time—it was the era of "live" TV.

Kelly had been bombarded with queries about Sullavan. "The phone was ringing all the time to ask what I knew about Margaret Sullavan—and I didn't know 'nothing.' I know nothing about Rita, either, except that if she's withdrawn because of illness I'm sure she's ill, and I hope they're kind."

Rita left the hospital on August 23 on the arm of her doctor. Omnipresent reporters and photographers assailed her with questions. "I just want to rest," she said to them all, very wearily.

"Where will you go? Are you going back to California?" They were unrelenting. "Where are you going to recuperate?"

"Probably . . . away."

She escaped back to Beverly Hills and became reclusive, but she pulled herself together and went back to New York in October, for the opening of *Crack*. She seemed relieved to be in the audience and not on the stage. Backstage after the show, she posed with Merrill for photographers. The familiar Hayworth smile clicked on when the flashbulbs popped, but she appeared nervous once the commotion abated.

Back in Hollywood she had spoken with veteran columnist Vernon Scott and tried to set the record straight: "Except for fatigue, there is nothing wrong with my health or my outlook. It's ridiculous for anyone to say I'm at the end of my rope. I'm looking for a good script."

Producers weren't offering her any.

She slipped into almost total seclusion for a while. "Rita Hayworth's moods confuse her intimates," wrote perceptive, longtime Rita-observer Dorothy Kilgallen. "One minute she's fearfully depressed, the next moment she seems to be floating on clouds . . ."

Hayworth was seen at local nightspots, on several occasions, dancing a lively version of the twist with handsome Jody McCrea, son of actor Joel McCrea. But she said she really wanted to work, not party, and let it be known she wanted very much to play the juicy role of Maxine, the hard-living hotel proprietress, in the upcoming film of Tennessee Williams's *The Night of the Iguana*. But director John Huston signed his pal Ava Gardner instead.

An offer came for Rita from Paramount Pictures to join the trouble-plagued production of *Circus World*. What had begun as a modest film had escalated to a superproduction. Frank Capra was set to direct John Wayne, Claudia Cardinale, and Lilli Palmer. But Capra had differences with the screenwriter Wayne had insisted on, James Edward Grant, and left the film.

Henry Hathaway was hired to direct. And when Lilli Palmer withdrew from the production, Rita was signed to replace her, portraying Claudia Cardinale's mother. She would get third billing, under Wayne (which was understandable) and Cardinale (which was an embarrassment). The producer was now Samuel Bronston. The film was shot in Madrid and in other locations in Europe.

Gary Merrill was with Rita constantly on the set—"never more than an inch away," wrote one reporter. Incredibly, the European press made a far greater fuss over Hayworth than Cardinale, who was the reigning sex symbol of the Continent. The publicity more than justified Rita's $100,000 salary, which many in the industry considered far too high for an actress whose best days were seemingly behind her.

Onscreen, Rita looked fine and subsequently garnered good reviews. But tough old pro Hathaway was vocal about Rita's heavy drinking and how she had caused many production delays.

When she returned to the States, Rita was invited to be a presenter on the 1964 Oscar broadcast. She was dubious—live television!—but she was persuaded to appear. Her *Fire Down Below* costar, Jack Lemmon, introduced her. She was very nervous as she read the list of those nominated for the "Best Director" award and mispronounced the name of the winner, Tony Richardson, calling him Tony Richards. (Richardson won for *Tom Jones*.)

"No one quite knows why Rita is so nervous," commented Sheilah Graham, echoing the thoughts of many.

At the lavish Academy party following the awards, Rita was the center of attention when Steve McQueen asked her to dance. Newsreel cameras whirred and photographers had a field day as McQueen twirled around the dance floor with the woman he called "one of my all-time favorites."

Rita made another TV appearance that year, but on film. To publicize *Circus World* she agreed to appear in a special, "The Odyssey of Rita Hayworth," to be presented as part of the NBC series *Hollywood and the Stars*, produced by Jack Haley, Jr., and David Wolper. She was shown at home, walking on the grounds of her house, lounging by the pool, playing with her dogs. Footage from *Circus World*, of course, was included. But what appealed most to viewers were clips from her old films—the love goddess in her prime.

But that Rita Hayworth no longer existed. After *Circus World* the producers of the hit TV series *Rawhide* offered her $25,000 (a huge fee at that time) to make her TV acting debut on their show. She accepted, and columns were filled with the news that Rita would bring her brand of magic to the tube at last. But, as the shooting date approached, she canceled out, and, for a while, was again inactive professionally.

The forty-five-year-old love goddess, along with Yasmin, attended Rebecca's graduation in June 1964. "It's a good thing Rita had those girls to keep her occupied," reflects a production executive who knew her from the days of her first marriage and through the 1960s. "Her eyes were always bright and alert when the girls were around—that wasn't always the case when she was with other people."

In 1965 Hayworth was on the big screen again when Columbia released *The Love Goddesses,* a feature documentary chronicling the careers of Rita and other sex symbols.

Producer Max Youngstein then offered her a character part in a film that would star her old flame Glenn Ford. Another old pal, Joseph Cotten, was in the cast. Elke Sommer had the female lead. Rita accepted, again receiving third billing (below Ford *and* Sommer). Her role was that of a worn-out waitress, an ex-girl friend of cop Ford.

Rita wanted her new friend, George Masters, the young cosmetics and hairdressing wizard, to do her makeup and hair for *The Money Trap,* but Masters wasn't a member of the necessary unions. It was arranged to set up a mobile home outside the studio, where Masters would work his magic on Rita.

One scene of the film called for Rita's character to be pushed off a roof and then to be photographed on the ground below, all bloodied and muddy. The day that particular shot was to be made there were many delays, which had nothing to do with Rita.

While they were waiting to be called, Rita and Masters drank a great deal of champagne as Masters improvised on her fall-from-the-roof makeup. Very late in the day an assistant director came to say they were finally ready for the shot. But it was too late—by that time Rita not only looked a sight but found it impossible to navigate her way across the street and to the studio.

In her few scenes in the picture, all with Ford, Rita was poignant and riveting. The rapport between them was once again evident, as it had been in *Gilda*. The dialogue came uncomfortably close to her own life.

"I was a lush," Rita's character says to Ford's at one point.

"Where've you been?" asks Ford.

"I've been around. What do you want from me?"

"What I've always wanted from you."

After they've spent the night together, Rita tells the corrupt cop portrayed by Ford, "You should have stayed with me. With me it wasn't the money, Joe."

Work was positive therapy for Rita, and she was happy being in front of the camera again. That was her craft, what she had been trained for, what she was good at.

Offscreen she palled around with George Masters. Masters was no novice at dealing with "star ladies." Since his discovery by Marion Davies a few years before she died, Masters had been in demand by such stars as Jennifer Jones, Marlene Dietrich, Arlene Dahl, and Cyd Charisse. He had been a close friend of Marilyn Monroe's. It was Masters who had created Marilyn's final, ravishing "look"—the white-blond hair, the angel-winged coiffure. But his favorite star lady was Rita Hayworth. "We were always together when we had any free time," he recalled, "and we are really friends. She's very generous to her friends and once posed nine hours for me when I needed some publicity pictures."

Masters found Rita to be an earthy woman who shunned artifice and the trappings of a star image. "I'll never forget the night she was going to a formal dinner without an escort. She had to meet the party at a restaurant in town, so I offered to take her there. When I arrived in my pickup truck, the only transportation I owned at the time, she burst out laughing and laughed all the way to the restaurant. The doorman, on the other hand, couldn't believe his eyes when he saw the famous and beautiful Rita Hayworth climb gracefully out of a pickup truck wearing a long evening gown and a fur around her shoulders."

However, Rita's social rounds were few. She was a "working

girl." Her manager, Curtis Roberts, showed her a script written by an unknown for an independent production. Although she hadn't heard of the writer, producer, or director, she signed for the role. In retrospect it seems unthinkable—Rita Hayworth, who had been one of the four most valuable properties in the industry, accepting a part in a "cheapie" production, financed by a car dealer. The property was called *The Grove,* and it was to be filmed in Fort Lauderdale, Florida.

An unknown actor, Dustin Hoffman, was originally mentioned for the key male role, but he picked another script—*The Graduate* —instead. (*The Grove* also dealt with the relationship of an older woman with a younger man.)

The original screenplay was said to have great potential, and many, including Rita, thought this could be her *Sunset Boulevard.* But the producer-director, a man named William Grefe, had rewritten the script. Rita's costar, Stephen Oliver, said, "What he had actually done was to make it over into a rather ludicrous sexploitation-type of film. Rita didn't say anything about the changes, but I knew she wasn't too happy with them."

Oliver reiterates what almost every one of Rita's costars has said, that she was a pleasure to work with and a true professional. "Only on one occasion did she say anything to Grefe, and she did attempt it with great tact and discretion. Instead of listening to her advice, which was very good, Grefe treated her very rudely in front of the entire company."

According to Oliver, Rita excused herself and left the set. Oliver followed her and found her crying quietly. She looked up at him: "I'm terribly sorry. I didn't mean to hold everybody up."

Oliver reassured her that she had forgotten more about making films than Grefe would ever learn. How right he was! *The Grove* was completed in 1966 but not released for five years, and even then with a new title, *The Naked Zoo.* Its commerciality was nil.

Meanwhile, *The Money Trap* had opened and Rita's reviews were the very best she had ever received. *Time* said, "Rita at forty-seven has never looked less like a beauty, or more like an actress." Kevin Thomas, in the *Los Angeles Times,* noted, "It is Rita Hayworth who is best of all. . . . She and Ford meet once again and make love and realize what might have been." He noted that Rita and Ford were "so sadly touching that for a moment you can see what *The Money Trap* might have been, too."

Producer Youngstein obviously saw possibilities as well. On the heels of *The Money Trap* he wanted to team Rita and Ford in *Welcome to Hard Times,* a western. All seemed set until Ford dropped out of the project and was replaced by Henry Fonda. Then Rita left, and the part went to Janice Rule.

While *The Money Trap* was neither a critical nor a box office hit, it successfully launched Rita into a new category: character actress. She followed with another great part. Hayworth went to Europe to offer her services for an international all-star motion picture filmed for television, *The Poppy Is Also a Flower,* which was produced with United Nations cooperation—the story was about drug smuggling and the evils of drugs.

Rita played the wife of the head of the syndicate which controlled drug traffic. The role of the husband was portrayed by Gilbert Roland, and Rita had one powerful scene with the man with whom she had made her *Ramona* screen tests some thirty years earlier.

One of the key moments of *Poppy* occurs when an investigator, played by E. G. Marshall, meets Rita and discovers that she has become a drug addict. Some of the dialogue from a subsequent scene might have applied to her personally. She is in the compartment of a train, talking in French to her poodle, Tu-Tu. Marshall, trying to find out where the drug dealer lives, asks, "Where does Tu-Tu live?" There's an extreme close-up of Rita as she answers, "In my mind. I also live in my mind."

In this film, Rita was back to looking like a woman of glamour. She was well photographed. Director Terence Young noted that many in the cast had paid their own expenses to be in the film, including Yul Brynner, Omar Sharif, and Rita.

Even before *Poppy,* Rita had signed to star in Young's upcoming Italian film, *The Rover,* to costar her old lover Anthony Quinn, Rosanna Schiaffino, and Richard Johnson. Rita went to Rome, where the film was shot at Cinecitta Studios. "My love for Quinn in the film was very tender—with none of the clichés I was known for in the old days," said Rita.

She enjoyed working in Italy. She stayed on. When Joan Crawford—fourteen years Rita's senior—dropped out of a film called *The Cats,* in which she was to portray an alcoholic mother of two grown sons, Rita replaced her.

"It's the story of a very human being who can't see her life as it really is," Rita noted. Once again, she might have been talking about herself. The film was eventually released in Europe as *I Bastardi* and in the States as *Sons of Satan.* It didn't have many playdates.

In May 1968 Rita was in London with Yasmin. A reporter asked her, "How have you maintained 'the look' all these years?"

"What look?"

"Your look—the Rita Hayworth look."

"By not fighting to keep it. There's nothing more aging to a woman's appearance than the awful strain of trying to look young. I'll never understand why so many of the new girls wear their hair long and stringy. There's nothing more youthful than a head of strong, well-brushed, healthy-looking hair."

That October Rita turned fifty. The love goddess was *fifty?* There were many ex-GIs and former bobby-soxers who suddenly realized time had passed swiftly by. As for Rita: "I don't sit and think about it. It's what's happening now—it's today—not yesterday."

The media took note of Rita reaching the half-century mark. NBC's Sander Vanocur interviewed her for *First Tuesday,* the network's news magazine show, in a special segment called "Rita Hayworth at Fifty." Dressed in a flowing caftan, Hayworth looked good but the interview proved bland. She didn't have much to say. After all these years, she was still not at ease at interviews. She did not want to discuss her private life—but, of course, that was what people wanted to know about. What was Rebecca doing now? And Yasmin? Not only did the girls share a famous mother, but each had a famous father. Interest in them was always high. But Rita always protected their privacy.

When Rita turned fifty, Rebecca Welles was a twenty-four-year-old graduate student at the University of Puget Sound in Washington State, and Yasmin was going to Bennington College in Vermont.

Rita was very proud that she had provided her daughters with their educations. And obviously, Rebecca was no longer interested in pursuing a career in show business. What both girls had seen of it from their very intimate vantage points apparently didn't engender any "roar of the crowd, smell of the greasepaint" fantasies. Quite the opposite.

Yasmin preferred to spend her time in Europe, where she was already moving in international circles with her two half-brothers. She was close to Karim, the new Aga Khan, and spent a great deal of time with him in Sardinia, where he was developing a new international resort. Rita, at Karim's request, occasionally visited Sardinia as well.

Referring to her daughters, Rita said, "My girls and I are everything to each other. Sometimes I would refuse work to make it possible for us to be together."

However, she was now free to accept all professional offers, and observed, "The world is wonderful for a performer today because you can travel easier and work in so many countries, different places with so many interesting people."

But there were still limits for Rita in this "Swinging Sixties" era of free-wheeling sexual liberation. "Everybody else does nude scenes, but I don't. I never made nude movies. I didn't have to do that. I danced. I was provocative, I guess, in some things. But I was not completely exposed."

Nor, it must be added, was Rita one of those women who would have gone along with "exposing" herself, had that been the acceptable order of her youth. Many of Hayworth's contemporaries would have been *Playboy* centerfolds had such "exposure" been commonplace.

Rita certainly liked the variety of characters she was playing now. "I've said no to all kinds of offers for the stage, musicals, and television to continue where my heart has always been—in films."

Hayworth remained active professionally, but at what cost? Physically, she was on a downward spiral. The years of alcohol were taking their toll, and this was compounded by the medication she now had to take to enable her to function.

She received a shock in December 1968, a few days before Yasmin's nineteenth birthday. Rita's father died. "Poor Rita—she was never any good at coping with personal disasters over which she had no control—especially the death of a loved one," observed Howard Newman, a publicist who knew the actress well. "She was like a child, so fragile, so emotional . . ."

Once again, flight was her solution. Rita went to the Canary Islands, to film *The Road to Salina,* yet another low-budget production in which she delivered a strong character performance. Georges Lautner was the director. Kevin Thomas, in the *Los Angeles Times,* summed up Rita's professional predicament: "The irony of Rita Hayworth's career is that she is making fewer (and increasingly obscure) pictures, but is giving better and better performances."

Again she returned to Beverly Hills. She described her home there as "my only shelter in the world." Around this time there was a big to-do in the press concerning Rita having a feud with her old pal and now neighbor, Glenn Ford, about a TV antenna on Ford's roof which spoiled the view from Rita's house.

As with many reports in the press, this was blown out of proportion. There was no feud at all. In fact, Rita and Glenn were close friends again during this period. He would often go up to her house in the evening and they would sit around reminiscing about the old days. Eventually it would get late and Ford would tell Rita he had to go because he had an early call in the morning. Then Rita, who had been drinking all evening, would become petulant, argumentative—and sometimes even throw things.

Of course, the next day she would remember nothing and Ford, being her friend, never brought it up. He would occasionally invite her to his house for dinner, and even though she only had to cross their back yards to get there, she would insist he call for her.

"As rightfully she should," Ford says. "She was always a lady."

Naturally, rumors sprang up that they were having a romance, and when actually confronted with this question, Rita bellowed a laugh: "Who said that? Me and Glenn? Oh, God, that's the funniest thing I've heard all week! A while ago, he took me to dinner at Dinah Shore's, if you call that romance."

In fact, the love goddess was again a semirecluse. The films she had made abroad had not received wide release in the United

States, and once again it seemed Rita would fall into the category of "What ever happened to . . ."

Peter Rogers, president and creative director of Peter Rogers Associates, the advertising agency that had masterminded the Blackglama mink "What Becomes A Legend Most" campaign, sought Rita Hayworth to pose for the ad. Lauren Bacall, Melina Mercouri, Bette Davis, Barbra Streisand, Judy Garland, Joan Crawford, Lena Horne, Marlene Dietrich, and Leontyne Price had already done it. Payment for the ad was the mink coat the lady chose to wear.

"I finally tracked down Rita's agent," Rogers has recalled, "and arranged it all through him."

The Blackglama people flew Rita to New York. Rogers wanted to escort Hayworth personally to photographer Richard Avedon's studio for the shooting. Rita was staying at the Plaza, and Rogers met Rita's agent in the lobby of the famed hotel.

"As we stood chatting, the elevators opened and a slightly chunky middle-aged woman with close-cropped hair approached me," recalled Rogers. Rogers thought the woman was the agent's wife. "Not until he introduced us did I realize it was Rita Hayworth."

For the shooting, the "Put the Blame on Mame" gown from *Gilda* had been duplicated.

"She danced like crazy through the whole shooting," Rogers has recalled, "and couldn't have been nicer or more cooperative. She's such a shy woman, it's hard to imagine her married to Orson Welles or Aly Khan."

Rogers confirmed what many people who worked with Rita have said: "Not until the music began to play and the camera clicked did she lose her reticence and become the Rita Hayworth I remembered."

When the ad appeared, however, it turned out to be the first one in which readers didn't recognize who the legend was. "A lot of people guessed Anne Baxter," said Rogers.

Rita wasn't seeing much of her daughters; Yasmin was in school and Rebecca had married a young sculptor named Perry Moede. An exploitation tabloid ran a story about Rebecca, proclaiming that she was "living in near poverty." Rita's incensed reaction: "Becky's gone to college. I did that. And she just moved into a two-story house with her sculptor husband, who is also working at a part-time job. If they want to call that 'poverty,' let them! Anyway, Rebecca is now twenty-five. I sent her to school and college, and she's married, and I think they should be on their own."

As for Yasmin, she and her mother occasionally traveled together. "She's twenty," observed Rita. "Yasmin wants to do what she wants to do. I'm all for it. Right now she's studying music. . . . Yassie is an interesting girl, not just 'pretty.'"

Basically, Rita now spent most of her time alone. One evening in September 1970 she was home watching the Carol Burnett show and saw "Golda," Carol's takeoff on *Gilda*. A movie buff herself, Burnett did parodies of classic movies as a regular feature of her program. Her Golda, complete with black strapless evening gown, long red wig, and platform shoes, was incredible satire, funny, loving—and unforgettable. Rita sent Carol a congratulatory telegram. Many phone calls ensued, and eventually Carol invited Rita to appear on the program.

Joe Hamilton, Burnett's husband and the producer of the show, called Joe Ritacco, the booking agent for the show, and said, "Rita Hayworth wants to do the show. Arrange it."

Ritacco called Rita and left a message. The following day her agent, Paul Kohner, returned the call. Yes, Rita wanted to do the show. She wanted to do three things: a comedy sketch, the charwoman routine, and a production number. Ritacco discussed it with Hamilton, who said, "Yes, anything she wants."

Kohner then called back and said that they would have to have the writers call Rita direct and explain exactly what she had to do, because she was very nervous about the appearance (although the show would be taped, it was performed before a live audience). Naturally, this was done.

Then Kohner called Ritacco again, to suggest that they have someone call Rita every day, "to keep her confidence up." Bob Wright, associate producer on the show, took over this chore.

Carol personally guided Rita through the week of rehearsals like a loving daughter. Rita couldn't do the production number and it had to be abandoned, but she appeared with Burnett and Vicki Lawrence in a comedy sketch.

At one point in the show Rita and Carol sat side by side on stools, watching and commenting on old Hayworth film clips. After "Put the Blame on Mame" flashed off the screen, Carol asked, "What held up that dress?"

"Two things," Rita answered, deadpan, with perfect timing.

Ritacco remembers, "All during rehearsals, Rita's smile was radiant. She was pleasant to work with, but very frightened, very nervous." He adds, however, that most of the film stars from the forties and fifties who did the Burnett show suffered from the same nervousness, working in front of live audiences.

A full-page ad featuring a photo of Rita and Burnett as the charwomen appeared in the trade papers, with the tag line, "Which one is the love goddess?" Rita obviously had a sense of humor about her old screen image.

The warmth and care the Burnett company lavished on the superstar were reflected in the finished show, which garnered tremendous publicity and high ratings. TV beckoned Rita Hayworth, ready to offer her top dollar.

She did Rowan and Martin's *Laugh-In,* appearing in several blackouts. She did a walk-on on the *Tonight* show. Johnny Carson was marvelous with her as she sat staring at him in a femme fatale fashion. "They told me I should flirt with you," she said, and his reaction was the perfect combination of lust and interest mixed with humor.

Rita was momentarily a hot property again, and Broadway beckoned. The Great White Way was the traditional rebirthing ground for former film stars. The most recent example was Lauren Bacall, who had done Broadway comedies—*Goodbye, Charlie,* a flop, and *Cactus Flower,* a smash—and was currently enjoying blockbuster success in *Applause,* the musical version of *All About Eve.*

It was a tremendously demanding musical role and that Rita Hayworth was sought as Bacall's summer replacement is incredible. Rita's debacle in *Step on a Crack* and her other publicized professional difficulties hardly made her the right choice for such an ultra-demanding vehicle. Yet there was magic in the Hayworth name; producers and directors felt that all obstacles might be worth the potential box office rewards.

After all, Rita Hayworth was more than a former "star." There were quite a few of those. But the Hayworth movie image conjured up the kind of glamour and wallop that was unique, a combination of magic and pizazz that simply didn't exist in most of the "new" breed of stars. The sole *genuine* young superstar of the sixties and seventies generation acknowledged the influence of the Hayworth mystique. When Barbra Streisand, in the first flush of her *Funny Girl* triumph on Broadway, was asked by Lee Strasberg, head of the highly respected Actors Studio, who her favorite actress was, she did not name Kim Stanley, Geraldine Page, or some other greatly admired thespian. Instead, the budding legend said, "Rita Hayworth."

Hayworth and Yasmin had been the guests of Streisand's agent ("It'll be a wonderful surprise for Barbra!") at the star's much-ballyhooed $250,000-a-week singing engagement at the new International Hotel in Las Vegas in the summer of 1969.

The deference shown to Hayworth by such current heavyweights as Burnett, Carson, and Streisand heightened the expectations of others in the business regarding a rebirth of Rita's box office popularity.

She accepted the invitation to star in *Applause*. "They kept calling me for a year to come to New York," she said, "and finally I went, paying my own air fare."

Her press agent announced, "The first thing she did was to buy herself an entirely new, complete summer wardrobe. Then she picked a voice coach and a dance teacher. She will now prove to the world that she can be as good as—if not better than—Lauren Bacall."

But there were problems from the start. Rita later explained, "I wasn't allowed to keep my three dachshunds. I had to send them to a country kennel to be cared for by a woman I know. I wasn't comfortable in my hotel and I'd forgotten that I hate elevators.

"Because the stage wasn't available, I had to take my vocal lessons at the hotel and rehearse my dancing at a studio. I couldn't get used to the New York weather. On one occasion I was laid up for a week because I caught a severe cold rushing from the dance studio—still soaked with perspiration—back to the hotel for voice lessons."

As with *Step on a Crack* nine years earlier, it became apparent, early on, that Rita was not capable of sustaining a live theater performance. Before long, headlines blared, "No Applause for Rita on Broadway."

The producers were kind in their explanations. Coproducer Larry Kasha: "Rita helped us to make the decision. She knew she needed more time. She is going back to California to work on the part. Then she will head a national company later.

"Rita was a terrific dame through the whole thing. She is singing marvelously. She just happens to work slowly. She is a slow learner like so many of those Hollywood actresses. They're not required to learn scripts fast. So it takes them five or six months.

"Lauren Bacall worked three months just getting into physical condition for the role," Kasha noted.

He also revealed that Rita had been watching the show and suddenly realized "that there was a lot more to it than she had expected."

Phil Silvers, however, sums up Hayworth's predicament in two words: "She panicked."

Rita vigorously denied that she was a slow study. "Bacall had a year to get ready for the part," she pointed out. "Rex Harrison took over a year preparing for *My Fair Lady*. Angela Lansbury had plenty of time for *Mame*."

"When I heard about Rita having trouble with lines," said Gretchen Wyler, Bacall's stand-by, "I thought maybe I'd finally get on." But Wyler was to be disappointed. Bacall never missed a performance, and when she left the show she was replaced as Margo by Anne Baxter (who had played Eve in *All About Eve*).

Needless to say, Rita did not head a national tour of *Applause*, or any other show. Back in Hollywood, to prove to the industry that she was still employable, she agreed to appear with Merv Griffin in a ninety-minute special announced as *An Evening With Rita Hayworth*.

Griffin is the most knowledgeable and sympathetic person imaginable with the great stars of the old studio days, but for Rita he came up with a concept that was too ambitious. Merv and Rita performed a song-and-dance number, which was clumsily executed. Since the show was taped, it could have been cut from the final show—but wasn't. Rita's hairdo and gown weren't flattering—when left to her own devices, without a Jean Louis or Edith Head or George Masters, Rita was sadly lacking in taste. Griffin placed too much emphasis on talking with Rita about the past. Rita was highly nervous to begin with, and after Griffin asked about Orson, she froze.

"Were you intimidated by Orson Welles?" he asked.

She paused. "No," she replied, "but I think *he* was intimidated by *me!*"

The audience roared its approval. But that was the high point of this show. She made a second appearance with Griffin, but unfortunately, trying to buoy her confidence, she had too much to drink. She had to be taken offstage during a break for a commercial, and she did not return.

Again Rita went into seclusion. She was despondent, but was rescued by a call from her old friend Robert Mitchum. He had suggested her for a major role in a film in which he was to star, *The Wrath of God.* It was an A picture, an offbeat film, and Rita didn't even ask to read the script before saying yes.

The picture, a tongue-in-cheek spoof in the tradition of *Beat the Devil,* was written and directed by Ralph Nelson and was shot in Durango, Mexico. Frank Langella was cast as an evil tyrant eventually gunned down by his own mother played by Rita Hayworth.

Liz Smith, in her review, described Rita as "the ever-fascinating Rita Hayworth," and said the movie was a "bang-up, fine, old-fashioned, totally incredible experience."

As far as the public was concerned, Rita was still a star making A movies. But *Wrath* was to be her last film, although she did attempt one more. In 1972, Rita was signed for a British picture, *Tales That Witness Madness,* and began work on it at Shepperton Studios in London. Peter McEnery, who was in the film, told friends that Rita was applauded by cast and crew her first day on the set. It helped build her confidence, but the roller coaster was racing to the abyss.

After only a few days of filming, she couldn't go on. A doctor confirmed she had the flu, but several days later Henry Thomas, director of World Film Services, stated, "Three doctors saw Miss Hayworth and declared her fit for work." Shortly thereafter, the film company phoned her and told her she had a 6:30 A.M. call the following Tuesday. But when the driver arrived to pick her up, he was informed that she "was not going to work that day." A few days later the film company learned that Rita had fled London altogether. World Films instituted suit against her for a million dollars, claiming breach of contract and stating she had behaved in an "unprofessional, undiligent and improper manner."

She was replaced by Kim Novak.

Back in Hollywood, Rita Hayworth's new companions were young men who reveled in her celebrity. As with all aging sex symbols, the men in her life now were men who wanted to *be* her, rather than bed her. Be her, that is, as she had been on screen. Some of these new friends kept her afloat, kept her amused, kept her involved.

Rita saw her ex-husband Dick Haymes on television. He was making a somewhat successful comeback. He said he was now a recovering alcoholic and had been dry since 1965. He was making guest appearances on TV dramas, doing musical specials with Betty Grable, and was even signed to sing in Vegas.

A close friend of Rita's says, "She was happy for him. She never said anything evil about anyone, including Dick Haymes."

But it mystified and angered her that Haymes could get work while she could not. There were people—Vincent Sherman was one—who wanted to use her in the TV shows they occasionally directed. But producers wouldn't take a chance. The industry knew the extent of her problems. The public, as yet, didn't.

She fell even deeper into her depressed state. Her seclusion became almost permanent. Then, once again, tragedy struck. Perhaps the greatest shock since the death of her mother occurred to Rita in March 1974. Within the span of one month, both of her brothers died. Eduardo Junior, only fifty-four, died of cancer. And Vernon, gravely ill himself, learning of Eddie's death, died shortly afterward.

Rita's melancholy was intensified, and she sought further escape —but then, at the urging of those close to her, she decided she *had* to pull herself together and get back to work. It was a long, slow process.

Her friends urged her to see people, and convinced her to give occasional interviews. She had to, they reasoned, in order to let the industry know she was seeking work. But she still loathed revealing anything of her private life and wouldn't discuss the past. "What do you want to know about me that hasn't already been written? I want to talk about working."

Projects were announced but never materialized. What press coverage there was was mostly unfavorable. Never had Hayworth been so adrift.

She dated a salesman, Bill Gilpin. An article appeared in the *National Enquirer* telling how he had seen her on the golf course, so he went over, introduced himself, and asked her for a date.

Her few public appearances were proving a trial. At a Golden Globe Awards ceremony, with Glenn Ford, she soddenly improvised a "Put the Blame on Mame" bump-and-grind, and Ford left the stage. One of her new friends later said, "The heel walked off, leaving her alone up there." But others defended Ford. "He's stuck by her longer than many others. But there were times even he couldn't cope with her behavior, and especially in public."

Reports were that she wasn't welcome in certain restaurants and nightclubs in Los Angeles. A few of her old friends, and some new friends, stuck by her through these troubled times. George Masters convinced her to have a facelift, despite her fears. With her great bone structure, the operation was much more of a success than it had been with many of her contemporaries.

Jim Watters, the entertainment editor of *Life,* eagerly looked forward to a luncheon date with the screen star. When she arrived at the restaurant, heads turned—she looked beautiful. "She looked like a forty-year-old Rita Hayworth," remembers Watters. Unfortunately, during lunch, Rita seemed to be in a world of her own. She had almost nothing to say, nor did she seem to remember much of her past. Watters found his encounter with her sad and disturbing.

During this period, Hayworth saw less and less of her children. Becky lived in Washington State, and Yasmin in New York. "I don't see Yassie much. I can't afford to fly back there all the time.

Yasmin can afford it, but she only visits once or twice a year. She calls me on the telephone sometimes."

By this time Yasmin was garnering her own press, and was frequently in the society gossip columns. Now in her midtwenties, she bore a striking resemblance to her mother (reporters always commented on the physical similarity) and was a leading member of the jet set. She possessed all the prerequisites: she was "The Princess Aga Khan"—photographed by leading photographers—lauded as one of *the* young beauties of the day. Her pals included Margaret Trudeau and Christina Onassis. There were several reported romances, including one with German Count Faber Castel, of the Faber pencil fortune.

Rita noted, "She'd like to be an opera singer, but her voice isn't developed yet. She'd better be more than beautiful-looking if she's going to make it. But she doesn't have to worry—she has money. Yassie graduated from Bennington and all that. Now she's got a New York apartment. I've told her if she wants to be an opera singer she shouldn't smoke, but she does. She's a happy girl and very nice, but she has to work if she really wants to make it. When I was sixteen, I was singing and dancing, so I can't excuse her at age twenty-four."

Rebecca had kept totally out of the spotlight, except for one instance: she posed with her father for a full-page ad advertising a brand of scotch.

Welles's old pal, Jackson Leighter, who was by then an executive with a liquor company, said that Welles gave Rebecca the entire $20,000 fee. Rebecca has had little contact with her father through the years, and the ad was at least a record of herself with her legendary parent.

Rita was still wildly protective of both her progeny. She wanted the girls to have the privacy they were entitled to, and she didn't like anyone gossiping about them. There is a story that Rita threw a glass of wine into the face of a woman she thought was insulting Yasmin—one of her many incidents indicating her seriously deteriorating mental health.

She continued to let the press know that she desired very much to go back to work. The woman who had never wanted to spend the rest of her life on a sound stage now sought desperately to return to one. Her intimates say it was vital to keep her busy. If left to herself, she would lapse into long periods of forgetfulness. "If you kept her active, she would remain lucid. But if not, she would just stare off into space."

Although she was not sought for roles, she was still in demand for film festivals, awards dinners, interviews. Some of these invitations she accepted.

Russell Harty, a British TV personality, invited her to London in 1976 for a special interview. Her health was precarious, but she said she'd go. The flight to London proved harrowing. Her old fear of flying resurfaced. When the plane finally landed at Heathrow Airport, she refused at first to disembark. A stewardess from the TWA flight was quoted: "Miss Hayworth had been drinking when she boarded the plane and had several free drinks on the flight. She made a bit of a nuisance of herself."

"She started shouting and waving her arms about," one of the officials at Heathrow said. "She did not want to leave the plane."

A French woman passenger, asked to substantiate, said, "There was a bit of shouting going on, and whether she was drunk we don't know. But she looked very ill."

The most devastating development was that photographers were there to record Rita's arrival, and within hours shocking photos of her as a disheveled, frightened, pathetic-looking woman with matted, stringy hair were flashed throughout the world. If there had been any producer, anywhere, who was thinking of hiring Rita Hayworth, these pictures had finally stamped her "unemployable." One of the longest-lasting and highest-flying motion picture careers of all time was clearly coming to an end.

Russell Harty later said that "someone warned the press at Heathrow that Miss Hayworth was 'unwell' on the flight," and noted, "it is ill-mannered to call somebody drunk." Harty censured both the press and those looking after Rita for having allowed the debacle to occur.

In the States there was no real followup to the awful incident. Producer Jennings Lang, formerly a top agent, now a successful producer, was saddened at Rita's condition, but he summed things up when he noted, "It's been coming for a long, long time."

Rita *did* manage to pull herself together long enough to appear on Harty's program only a few days later. She even allowed the army of photographers who had dogged her through the entire trip to photograph her on the golf course, where in Harty's words, the reporters "seemed surprised that she could walk and talk, sometimes simultaneously."

When she returned to Beverly Hills, those close to her tried desperately to persuade her to get help, but she refused. She was still functioning.

In October 1976 Rita went to Buenos Aires for a film festival and again was in the news, this time because of a bomb scare at her hotel. Soon afterward she returned to Beverly Hills and again did nothing for a while. But she was coming to the end of her rope.

In the winter of 1977 in Newport Beach, California, while Rita was at an art exhibition with Bill Gilpin, it became obvious to many that Rita was ill. This was not something she could sleep off. She was taken directly to Hoag Memorial Hospital. Unfortunately, reporters soon learned of her hospitalization.

Dr. James Miner admitted her to the hospital and later issued a statement that Rita was "gravely disabled as a result of mental disorder or impairment by chronic alcoholism."

Rita had lost total control. The court in Orange County, California, was about to put her in the hands of the public guardian's office, since Dr. Miner had stated that she was "now unable or unwilling to accept responsibility for her treatment." Yasmin was swiftly contacted and Rita's lawyer, Leonard Monroe, quickly spirited Rita out of the hospital and out of the state before any further action by the court could be taken.

Yasmin arranged for her mother to be admitted to Silver Hill, the famous, exclusive Connecticut retreat for people who are "trying to pull themselves together." Joan Kennedy and Truman Capote are only two of the dozens of famous people who have been there, at the cost of two to three thousand dollars a week.

It has been reliably reported that since Rita's treatment at Silver Hill she has completely given up alcohol—but unfortunately, her physical state was such that a certain amount of irreparable damage had been done.

Yasmin took over Rita's financial support and began spending more time with her. Rita checked out of Silver Hill as quietly as she had checked in. She returned to California and *looked* the picture of health, again on the golf course. Old friends called, and she inched back into a social life.

The Thalians, a group of celebrities who each year have a lavish affair for charity, were raising money for a mental health clinic at Cedars-Sinai Hospital. They decided to honor Rita and titled their twenty-second annual ball "You Were Never Lovelier."

Rita, accompanied by Yasmin, Leonard Monroe, and other friends, looked radiant. Her hair was beautifully cut and styled, her makeup was stunning, and she wore a dark green, flowing chiffon gown. The gala event was held at the Century Plaza Hotel, and in the lobby a brightly lit sign flashed a single word: *Rita*.

Inside the ballroom were blowups of Rita in her most famous roles, including Gilda, Salome, and Sadie Thompson. Film clips were shown. It was a star-studded event. Among those gathered to pay tribute were Glenn Ford, Robert Mitchum, Gene Kelly, Lana Turner, June Allyson, Janet Blair, Lloyd Nolan, Barry Sullivan, and Dame Judith Anderson.

Gene Kelly presented Rita with the "Ms. Wonderful Award," a statuette representing "Rita Hayworth's enduring contribution to the field of entertainment, spanning forty years."

Rita was applauded and cheered, and shouts of "We love you, Rita!" rang through the room. Ford was with her, onstage, with Gene Kelly, and Rita finally approached the microphone and said haltingly, "Glenn told me I should say thank you—and well, I guess I've said it—"

Debbie Reynolds, who was the president of the Thalians that year, rushed up to the microphone. "Our Rita is very shy and we promised her she wouldn't have to make a speech!"

A speech wasn't necessary.

Hayworth traveled to England, and later to Italy, where, in Bari, she accepted the Rudolph Valentino Award. Margo Hammond wrote in *Variety*, "After a dramatic entrance up the center aisle of the opera house amid flashing spotlights, strains of Richard Strauss's 'Thus Spake Zarathustra' and thunderous applause, a dazed Rita accepted her award telling the audience: 'This is the happiest moment of my life.' Perhaps it was."

Rita continued to be seen in public. She continued to *look* great. Top people worked with her—Way Bandy did her makeup. Francesco Scavullo took sensational photographs of her, which were published by major magazines throughout the world. She looked like her old self again. Peter Rogers said he wanted to rephotograph her for the Blackglama mink campaign.

Although she seemed to be functioning, she wasn't. People who had known her from the old days were always shocked when they went up to say hello to her in public. It was obvious she didn't remember them. Many assumed it was because she was drinking again, but they were later to learn this was not the case.

In the fall of 1979 Rita and Yasmin attended the opening of the Broadway show *Sugar Babies*. Mother and daughter inspired a near riot outside the theater. "You're looking very beautiful!" one of the autograph seekers shouted to Rita.

"I should be. I'm very happy!" replied the actress.

Yasmin was reportedly dating Bobby Shriver, son of Eunice Kennedy and Sargent Shriver. He was twenty-five at the time, Yasmin thirty. He had supposedly proposed to her. A friend of Yasmin's said, "It was almost love at first sight. But Yasmin is not that eager to get married. However, she hasn't said no either. They're a lovely couple and very happy together."

Yasmin's comment: "I really don't want to talk about it. I'm certainly not denying that we are together."

Yasmin's friend speculated that she seemed "most interested in her career right now, and I think that her singing really comes first in her life."

Yasmin's singing career hasn't to date materialized.

Rita returned to Hollywood, where in early 1980 she and a female publicist pal were spotted at premieres, parties, and restaurants. Her old friends the Leighters also saw her, but quietly and in private.

Although her friends tried to keep her lucid and in touch, Rita was fading fast. Yasmin finally had to take action. Leonard Monroe had filed a petition that he be put in charge of the actress's affairs because she was suffering from Alzheimer's disease, which meant she was in a state of presenility and was no longer able to care for herself. The court set a hearing date and appointed a lawyer for her—Robert Gary.

Yasmin engaged Mickey Rudin, a lawyer whose clients included Lucille Ball and Frank Sinatra. The princess petitioned the court to name her conservator of her mother's fiscal and physical well-being. She would move Rita to New York, where she could look after her more closely. Attorney Gary, after talking to Rita about the proposed move to the east coast, told the court that Rita "could not decide one way or the other."

The announcement that Rita Hayworth was suffering from Alzheimer's disease brought forth a flurry of public interest in this affliction that could make a woman of only sixty-two unable to care for herself.

Alzheimer's disease, named for the scientist who discovered it in 1907, is a fast-developing senile state affecting nerve cells of the brain. It is estimated that one out of every hundred adults in the U.S. is susceptible to it. Its origin is unknown, but it is believed to be a biochemical disorder, and it is thought that heredity plays a part. Alzheimer's disease first affects the memory, in its later stages it often reduces the victim to a perpetual childlike state.

As of this writing, alcoholism has not been directly linked to Alzheimer's disease, but alcoholics may be victims of other kinds of dementia leading to senility.

In July 1981 Los Angeles Superior Court Judge Ronald Swearinger appointed Yasmin her mother's conservator. Monroe had told the court, "I think it's in her best interests to be taken care of by her daughter. The move may be difficult but it can be accomplished."

Yasmin moved her mother from Beverly Hills and bought her a $600,000 condominium on Madison Avenue in New York City, near her own. She had already engaged a woman as Rita's full-time companion, and the woman moved from Los Angeles to New York with Rita. Nurses were later engaged.

In the last few years, Alzheimer's disease has received much publicity in the popular press, and almost always Rita's name is prominently mentioned. In late 1982, President Reagan declared

"National Alzheimer's Disease Week" and saluted those "working for an increased public awareness of this baffling disorder and the scientists whose research holds the promise of hope."

It was announced that Princess Yasmin had become a board member of the Alzheimer's Disease and Related Disorders Association, and that she was leading a nationwide campaign to publicize the fight against the disease.

Margarita's desires had been basic and simple but ultimately unachievable. The Cansinos were a show business family, and the girl's destiny had been laid out for her—but it was the plan for Margarita Cansino to work, to be successful, but ultimately to find love, marry, have children, retire. She might have danced for herself, even taught dancing, like the other women in the family. And like her aunt Elisa, she might have enjoyed a very long and fruitful life. But in the transformation of Margarita Cansino to Rita Hayworth, this plan went awry.

The pressures of maintaining a film career in the Hollywood of the forties and fifties took a drastic toll on Rita Hayworth. Even "tough" artists like Gene Kelly have stated that they couldn't cope with the megalomania and tactics of a man like Harry Cohn. Rita was subjected to Cohn's brand of sadism for twenty years.

Hayworth had tried to escape Hollywood. She had been willing to give up her career. But fate had prevented this. And she returned to the only business in which she knew how to earn a living—film. As a film star, Rita Hayworth reached the zenith.

Even today—eleven years after her last film—and thirty-five years after the peak of her popularity—her name instantly conjures up an image. Represents an era.

Hollywood created the star, but destroyed the woman. Only a few years ago, when asked what would she like to do the rest of her life, Rita had soberly replied, "Do what I'm doing. Be happy. Have health. And hope that I don't make anybody miserable." Alas, this was not to be. The woman will live out her days in a childlike state.

But the star will continue to flicker across theater and television screens—forever young, beautiful, totally carefree. Film lives on, and every year there are new additions to the love goddess's legion of followers.

Perhaps only another love goddess can give the most penetrating insight into the ultimately tragic life of Rita Hayworth. Brigitte Bardot says, "The only reason I am alive today is that I felt the need to escape the world of show business in time . . ."

Bardot explains: "On the outside, one is a star. But in reality, one is completely alone, doubting everything. To experience this loneliness of soul is the hardest thing in life."

Rita Hayworth
FILMOGRAPHY

Under the Pampas Moon. Fox, 1935. Produced by B. G. De Sylva. Directed by James Tinling. Screenplay by Ernest Pascal and Bradley King. CAST: Warner Baxter, Ketti Gallian, J. Carroll Naish, Jack LaRue, John Miljan, Rita Cansino.

Charlie Chan in Egypt. Fox, 1935. Produced by Edward T. Lowe. Directed by Louis King. Screenplay by Robert Ellis and Helen Logan. CAST: Warner Oland, Pat Paterson, Thomas Beck, Rita Cansino, Stepin Fetchit.

Dante's Inferno. Fox, 1935. Produced by Sol M. Wurtzel. Directed by Harry Lachman. Screenplay by Philip Klein and Robert Yost. Dance sequence choreographed by Eduardo Cansino. CAST: Spencer Tracy, Claire Trevor, Henry B. Walthall, Scotty Beckett, Alan Dinehart. (Rita Cansino was given eighteenth billing, as a specialty dancer.)

Paddy O'Day. Fox, 1935. Produced by Sol M. Wurtzel. Directed by Lewis Seiler. Screenplay by Lou Breslow and Edward Eliscu. CAST: Jane Withers, Pinky Tomlin, Rita Cansino, Jane Darwell, Francis Ford, Michael and Nina Visaroff.

Human Cargo. 20th Century-Fox, 1936. Produced by Sol M. Wurtzel. Directed by Allan Dwan. Screenplay by Jefferson Parker and Doris Malloy. CAST: Claire Trevor, Brian Donlevy, Alan Dinehart, Ralph Morgan, Scotty Beckett, Rita Cansino.

Meet Nero Wolfe. Columbia, 1936. Produced by B. P. Schulberg. Directed by Herbert Biberman. Screenplay by Howard J. Green, Bruce Manning, and Joseph Anthony. CAST: Edward Arnold, Joan Perry, Lionel Stander, Victor Jory, John Qualen, Dennie Moore. (Rita Cansino was given twelfth billing.)

Rebellion. Crescent, 1936. Produced by E. B. Derr. Directed by Lynn Shores. Screenplay by John T. Neville. CAST: Tom Keene, Rita Cansino, Duncan Renaldo, William Royle, Gino Corrado, Allan Cavan.

Trouble in Texas. Grand National, 1937. Produced by Edward F. Finney. Directed by R. N. Bradbury. Screenplay by Robert Emmett. CAST: Tex Ritter, Rita Cansino, Horace Murphy, Earl Dwire, Yakima Canutt, Glenn Strange.

Old Louisiana. Crescent, 1937. Produced by E. R. Derr. Directed by Irvin V. Willat. Screenplay by Mary Ireland. CAST: Tom Keene, Rita Cansino, Robert Fiske, Raphael Bennett, Allan Cavan, Will Morgan, Budd Buster, Carlos De Valdez.

Hit the Saddle. Republic, 1937. Produced by Nat Levine. Directed by Mack V. Wright. Screenplay by Oliver Drake. CAST: Robert Livingston, Ray Corrigan, Max Terhune, Rita Cansino, Yakima Canutt, J. P. McGowan.

AS RITA HAYWORTH

Criminals of the Air. Columbia, 1937. Produced by Wallace MacDonald. Directed by Charles C. Coleman, Jr. Screenplay by Owen Francis. CAST: Rosalind Keith, Charles Quigley, Rita Hayworth, Marc Lawrence, Patricia Farr, Ralph Byrd.

Girls Can Play. Columbia, 1937. Produced by Ralph Cohn. Directed by Lambert Hillyer, from his screenplay. CAST: Jacqueline Wells, Charles Quigley, Rita Hayworth, John Gallaudet, Patricia Farr, Guinn Williams, George McKay.

The Shadow. Columbia, 1937. Executive Producer, Irving Briskin. Directed by C. C. Coleman. Screenplay by Arthur T. Horman. CAST: Rita Hayworth, Charles Quigley, Marc Lawrence, Arthur Loft, Marjorie Main, Dick Curtis, Vernon Dent.

The Game That Kills. Columbia, 1937. Produced by Harry L. Decker. Directed by D. Ross Lederman. Screenplay by Grace Neville and Fred Niblo, Jr. CAST: Charles Quigley, Rita Hayworth, John Gallaudet, J. Farrell MacDonald, Arthur Loft, John Tyrell.

Paid to Dance. Columbia, 1937. Produced by Ralph Cohn. Directed by Charles C. Coleman, Jr. Screenplay by Robert E. Kent. CAST: Don Terry, Jacqueline Wells, Rita Hayworth, Arthur Loft, Paul Stanton, Paul Fix, Louise Stanley, Ralph Byrd.

Who Killed Gail Preston? Columbia, 1938. Produced by Ralph Cohn. Directed by Leon Barsha. Screenplay by Robert E. Kent and Henry Taylor. CAST: Don Terry, Rita Hayworth, Robert Paige, Wyn Cahoon, Marc Lawrence, Gene Morgan, Arthur Loft, John Gallaudet, Dwight Frye.

There's Always a Woman. Columbia, 1938. Produced by William Perlberg. Directed by Alexander Hall. Screenplay by Gladys Lehman (and, uncredited, Joel Sayre, Philip Rapp, and Morrie Ryskind). CAST: Joan Blondell, Melvyn Douglas, Mary Astor, Frances Drake. (Rita Hayworth received eleventh billing.)

Convicted. Columbia, 1938. Produced by Kenneth J. Bishop. Directed by Leon Barsha. Screenplay by Edgar Edwards. CAST: Charles Quigley, Rita Hayworth, Marc Lawrence, George McKay, Doreen MacGregor, Bill Irving, Edgar Edwards.

Juvenile Court. Columbia, 1938. Produced by Ralph Cohn. Directed by D. Ross Lederman. Screenplay by Michael L. Simmons, Robert E. Kent, and Henry Taylor. CAST: Paul Kelly, Rita Hayworth, Frankie Darro, Hally Chester, David Gorcey.

The Renegade Ranger. RKO, 1938. Produced by Bert Gilroy. Directed by David Howard. Screenplay by Oliver Drake. CAST: George O'Brien, Rita Hayworth, Tim Holt, Ray Whitley, Lucio Villegas, William Royle.

Homicide Bureau. Columbia, 1938. Produced by Jack Fier. Directed by Charles C. Coleman, Jr. Screenplay by Earle Snell. CAST: Bruce Cabot, Rita Hayworth, Robert Paige, Marc Lawrence, Moroni Olsen, Richard Fiske, Gene Morgan.

The Lone Wolf Spy Hunt. Columbia, 1939. Associate Producer: Joseph Sistrom. Directed by Peter Godfrey. CAST: Warren William, Ida Lupino, Rita Hayworth, Virginia Weidler, Ralph Morgan, Tom Dugan.

Special Inspector. Columbia, 1939. Produced by Kenneth J. Bishop. Directed by Leon Barsha. Screenplay by Edgar Edwards. CAST: Charles Quigley, Rita Hayworth, George McKay, Edgar Edwards, Eddie Laughton, John Spacey, Bob Rideout.

Only Angels Have Wings. Columbia, 1939. Produced and directed by Howard Hawks. Screenplay by Jules Furthman. (Uncredited contributors: William Rankin and Eleanore Griffin.) Based on an idea by Hawks. CAST: Cary Grant, Jean Arthur, Richard Barthelmess, Rita Hayworth, Thomas Mitchell, Allyn Joslyn, Sig Ruman, Victor Kilian, John Carroll, Donald Barry, Noah Beery, Jr.

Music in My Heart. Columbia, 1940. Produced by Irving Starr. Directed by Joseph Santley. Screenplay by James Edward Grant. CAST: Tony Martin, Rita Hayworth, Edith Fellows, Alan Mowbray, Eric Blore, George Tobias, Andre Kostelanetz, George Humbert.

Blondie on a Budget. Columbia, 1940. Produced by Robert Sparks. Directed by Frank R. Strayer. Screenplay by Richard

Flournoy. CAST: Penny Singleton, Arthur Lake, Rita Hayworth, Larry Simms, Danny Mummert, Don Beddoe, John Qualen, Fay Helm, Willie Best.

Susan and God. M-G-M, 1940. Produced by Hunt Stromberg. Directed by George Cukor. Screenplay by Anita Loos. CAST: Joan Crawford, Fredric March, Ruth Hussey, John Carroll, Rita Hayworth, Nigel Bruce, Bruce Cabot, Rita Quigley, Rose Hobart, Constance Collier, Gloria DeHaven, Marjorie Main, Dan Dailey.

The Lady in Question. Columbia, 1940. Produced by B. B. Kahane. Directed by Charles Vidor. Screenplay by Lewis Meltzer. CAST: Brian Aherne, Rita Hayworth, Glenn Ford, Irene Rich, George Coulouris, Evelyn Keyes, Lloyd Corrigan.

Angels Over Broadway. Columbia, 1940. Produced by Ben Hecht. Directed by Ben Hecht and Lee Garmes. Associate Producer, Douglas Fairbanks, Jr. Screenplay by Ben Hecht. CAST: Douglas Fairbanks, Jr., Rita Hayworth, Thomas Mitchell, John Qualen, George Watts, Ralph Theodore, Eddie Foster, Jack Roper, Constance Worth.

The Strawberry Blonde. Warner Bros., 1941. Produced by Hal B. Wallis. Directed by Raoul Walsh. Screenplay by Julius J. and Philip G. Epstein. CAST: James Cagney, Olivia de Havilland, Rita Hayworth, Jack Carson, George Tobias, Alan Hale, Una O'Connor, George Reeves, Lucille Fairbanks, Edward McNamara.

Affectionately Yours. Warner Bros., 1941. Produced by Hal B. Wallis. Directed by Lloyd Bacon. Screenplay by Edward Kaufman. CAST: Merle Oberon, Dennis Morgan, Rita Hayworth, Ralph Bellamy, George Tobias, James Gleason, Hattie McDaniel, Jerome Cowan, Butterfly McQueen.

Blood and Sand. 20th Century-Fox, 1941. Technicolor. Produced by Darryl F. Zanuck. Directed by Rouben Mamoulian. Screenplay by Jo Swerling. CAST: Tyrone Power, Linda Darnell, Rita Hayworth, Nazimova, Anthony Quinn, J. Carroll Naish,

John Carradine, Laird Cregar, Lynn Bari, Vicenté Gomez, Fortunio Bonanova, Rex Downing, Ann Todd, Pedro de Cordoba.

You'll Never Get Rich. Columbia, 1941. Produced by Samuel Bischoff. Directed by Sidney Lanfield. Screenplay by Michael Fessier and Ernest Pagano. CAST: Fred Astaire, Rita Hayworth, John Hubbard, Robert Benchley, Osa Massen, Frieda Inescort, Guinn Williams, Donald MacBride, Cliff Nazarro.

My Gal Sal. 20th Century-Fox, 1942. Technicolor. Produced by Robert Bassler. Executive Producer, Darryl F. Zanuck. Directed by Irving Cummings. Screenplay by Seton J. Miller, Darrell Ware, and Karl Tunberg. CAST: Rita Hayworth, Victor Mature, John Sutton, Carole Landis, James Gleason, Phil Silvers, Walter Catlett, Mona Maris, Hermes Pan.

Tales of Manhattan. 20th Century-Fox, 1942. Produced by Boris Morros and S. P. Eagle (later Sam Spiegel). Directed by Julien Duvivier. Screenplay by Ben Hecht, Ferenc Molnar, Donald Ogden Stewart, Alan Campbell, Ladislas Fodor, and Lamar Trotti. CAST (in sequence A): Charles Boyer, Rita Hayworth, Thomas Mitchell, Eugene Pallette, Helene Reynolds.

You Were Never Lovelier. Columbia, 1942. Produced by Louis F. Edelman. Directed by William A. Seiter. Screenplay by Michael Fessier, Ernest Pagano, and Delmer Daves. CAST: Fred Astaire, Rita Hayworth, Adolphe Menjou, Leslie Brooks, Adele Mara, Isobel Elsom, Larry Parks, Xavier Cugat and his Orchestra.

Cover Girl. Columbia, 1944. Technicolor. Produced by Arthur Schwartz. Directed by Charles Vidor. Screenplay by Virginia Van Upp, Marion Parsonnet, and Paul Gangelin. CAST: Rita Hayworth, Gene Kelly, Phil Silvers, Eve Arden, Lee Bowman, Jinx Falkenburg, Leslie Brooks, Otto Kruger, Jess Barker, Edward Brophy.

Tonight and Every Night. Columbia, 1945. Technicolor. Produced and directed by Victor Saville. Screenplay by Lesser Samuels and Abe Finkel. CAST: Rita Hayworth, Lee Bowman, Janet Blair, Marc Platt, Leslie Brooks, Florence Bates, Professor Lamberti, Dusty Anderson, Stephen Crane, Shelley Winters.

Gilda. Columbia, 1946. Produced by Virginia Van Upp. Directed by Charles Vidor. Screenplay by Marion Parsonnet. CAST: Rita Hayworth, Glenn Ford, George Macready, Joseph Calleia, Steven Geray, Joe Sawyer, Gerald Mohr, Robert Scott.

Down to Earth. Columbia, 1947. Technicolor. Produced by Don Hartman. Directed by Alexander Hall. Screenplay by Edward Blum and Don Hartman, based on characters created by Harry Segall in his play *Heaven Can Wait*. CAST: Rita Hayworth, Larry Parks, Marc Platt, Roland Culver, James Gleason, Edward Everett Horton, Adele Jergens, George Macready, William Frawley.

The Lady From Shanghai. Columbia, 1948. Produced, directed, and written for the screen by Orson Welles. CAST: Rita Hayworth, Orson Welles, Everett Sloane, Glenn Anders, Ted De Corsia, Erskine Sanford, Carl Frank.

The Loves of Carmen. Columbia, 1948. Technicolor. Produced and directed by Charles Vidor. Screenplay by Helen Deutsch. CAST: Rita Hayworth, Glenn Ford, Ron Randell, Victor Jory, Luther Adler, Arnold Moss, Joseph Buloff, Margaret Wycherly, Leona Roberts, Bernard Nedell.

Affair in Trinidad. Columbia, 1952. Produced and directed by Vincent Sherman. Screenplay by Oscar Saul and James Gunn. CAST: Rita Hayworth, Glenn Ford, Alexander Scourby, Valerie Bettis, Torin Thatcher, Howard Wendell, Steven Geray, George Voskovec.

Salome. Columbia, 1953. Technicolor. Produced by Buddy Adler. Directed by William Dieterle. Screenplay by Harry Kleiner and Jesse L. Lasky, Jr. CAST: Rita Hayworth, Stewart Granger, Charles Laughton, Judith Anderson, Sir Cedric Hardwicke, Alan

Badel, Basil Sydney, Maurice Schwartz, Rex Reason, Arnold Moss.

Miss Sadie Thompson. Columbia, 1953. Technicolor. Produced by Jerry Wald and Lewis Rachmil. Directed by Curtis Bernhardt. CAST: Rita Hayworth, José Ferrer, Aldo Ray, Russell Collins, Diosa Costello, Harry Bellaver, Wilton Graff, Peggy Converse, Charles Bronson.

Fire Down Below. Columbia, 1957. CinemaScope and Technicolor. Produced by Irving Allen and Albert R. Broccoli. Directed by Robert Parrish. Screenplay by Irwin Shaw. CAST: Rita Hayworth, Robert Mitchum, Jack Lemmon, Herbert Lom, Bonar Colleano, Bernard Lee, Anthony Newley, Peter Illing.

Pal Joey. Columbia, 1957. Technicolor. Produced by Fred Kohlmar. Directed by George Sidney. Screenplay by Dorothy Kingsley. CAST: Rita Hayworth, Frank Sinatra, Kim Novak, Barbara Nichols, Bobby Sherwood, Hank Henry, Elizabeth Patterson.

Separate Tables. United Artists, 1958. Produced by Harold Hecht, James Hill, and Burt Lancaster. Directed by Delbert Mann. Screenplay by Terence Rattigan and John Gay. CAST: Rita Hayworth, Deborah Kerr, David Niven, Burt Lancaster, Wendy Hiller, Gladys Cooper, Cathleen Nesbit, Felix Aylmer, Rod Taylor, Audrey Dalton.

They Came to Cordura. Columbia, 1959. CinemaScope and Technicolor. Produced by William Goetz. Directed by Robert Rossen. Screenplay by Ivan Moffat and Robert Rossen. CAST: Gary Cooper, Rita Hayworth, Van Heflin, Tab Hunter, Richard Conte, Michael Callan, Dick York, Robert Keith.

The Story on Page One. 20th Century-Fox, 1960. Produced by Jerry Wald. Directed and written by Clifford Odets. CAST: Rita Hayworth, Anthony Franciosa, Gig Young, Mildred Dunnock, Hugh Griffith, Sanford Meisner, Robert Burton, Alfred Ryder, Katherine Squire, Raymond Greenleaf.

The Happy Thieves. United Artists, 1962. Produced by Rita Hayworth and James Hill. Directed by George Marshall. Screenplay by John Gay. CAST: Rita Hayworth, Rex Harrison, Joseph Wiseman, Gregoire Aslan, Alida Valli, Virgilio Texera, Peter Illing, Brita Ekman (Britt Ekland).

Circus World. Paramount, 1964. Super Technirama 70, Technicolor. Produced by Samuel Bronston. Directed by Henry Hathaway. Screenplay by Ben Hecht, Julian Halevy, and James Edward Grant. CAST: John Wayne, Claudia Cardinale, Rita Hayworth, Lloyd Nolan, Richard Conte, John Smith, Henri Dantes, Wanda Rotha, Miles Malleson.

The Money Trap. M-G-M, 1966. Produced by Max E. Youngstein and David Karr. Directed by Burt Kennedy. Screenplay by Walter Bernstein. CAST: Glenn Ford, Elke Sommer, Rita Hayworth, Joseph Cotten, Ricardo Montalban, Tom Reese, James Mitchum, Ted De Corsia, Argentina Brunetti.

The Poppy Is Also a Flower. Comet Films, 1966. Technicolor. Produced by Evan Lloyd. Directed by Terence Young. Screenplay by Jo Eisinger. CAST: Senta Berger, Stephen Boyd, Yul Brynner, Angie Dickinson, Hugh Griffith, Jack Hawkins, Rita Hayworth, Trevor Howard, Jocelyn Lane, Trini Lopez, E. G. Marshall, Marcello Mastroianni, Anthony Quayle, Gilbert Roland, Omar Sharif, Barry Sullivan, Nadja Tiller, Eli Wallach (plus a number of guest stars playing themselves).

The Rover. Cinerama Releasing Corp., 1967. Eastman Color. Produced by Alfred Bini. Directed by Terence Young. Screenplay by Luciano Vincenzoni and Jo Eisinger. CAST: Anthony Quinn, Rosanna Schiaffino, Rita Hayworth, Richard Johnson, Ivo Garranti, Mino Duro, Luciano Rossi.

Sons of Satan (I Bastardi; The Cats). Warner Bros.–7 Arts, 1969. Technicolor. Produced by Turi Vasile. Directed by Duccio Tessardi. Screenplay by Ennio De Concini, Mario Di Nardo, and

Duccio Tessardi. CAST: Rita Hayworth, Giulano Gemma, Klaus Kinski, Margaret Lee, Serge Marquand, Claudine Auger.

Road to Salina. Avco-Embassy, 1971. DeLuxe Color. Presented by Joseph E. Levine. Produced by Robert Dorfmann and Yvon Guezel. Directed by Georges Lautner. Screenplay by Georges Lautner, Pascal Jardin, and Jack Miller. CAST: Mimsy Farmer, Robert Walker, Jr., Rita Hayworth, Ed Begley, Bruce Pecheur, David Sachs, Sophie Hardy.

The Naked Zoo. Film Artists International, 1971. Eastman Color. Produced and directed by William Grefe. Screenplay by Ray Preston and William Grefe. CAST: Rita Hayworth, Fay Spain, Stephen Oliver, Ford Rainey, Fleurette Carter, Willie Pastrano, Joe E. Ross.

The Wrath of God. M-G-M, 1972. MetroColor. Executive Producer, Peter Katz. Directed by Ralph Nelson. Screenplay by Ralph Nelson. CAST: Robert Mitchum, Frank Langella, Rita Hayworth, John Colicos, Victor Buono, Ken Hutchinson, Paula Pritchett.

SPECIAL APPEARANCES

Show Business at War. 20th Century-Fox, 1943. A *March of Time* episode, produced by the Editors of *Time*. Directed by Louis de Rochemont. Stars of stage, screen, and radio were billed alphabetically and shown contributing in some way to the war effort. Rita Hayworth was shown making a "Command Performance" broadcast with Phil Baker, Fred MacMurray, the Mills Brothers, Ginny Simms, and Don Wilson.

Champagne Safari. A Jackson Leighter Associates Production, released by Defense Films, 1952. Produced and directed by Jackson Leighter. A documentary starring Rita Hayworth and Prince Aly Khan.

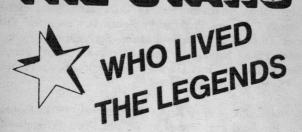

DAVID NIVEN

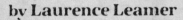

STARVING FOR ATTENTION

by Cherry Boone O'Neill

She was Pat Boone's daughter, oldest of four beautiful
talented teenaged sisters. An A student, at 13 she was
performing with her model Hollywood family before
audiences the world over. That was when it began—the diet
that escalated into days of rigorous fasting, and demanded
long hours of grueling exercise; that broke down in terrifying
secret binges and had to be resumed with a will of iron. It
began as a challenge. It became an obsession—a harrowing
battle between life and death.

A DELL BOOK   17620-4 $3.50